Contents

Preface

This book provides a practical guide to communication for all students, especially those preparing for business and secretarial examinations. Its range is comprehensive – from elementary level to Diploma – and the many worked examples and suggested answers make it suitable for individual or class use.

Chapters are devoted to the documents most commonly asked for in exams (and in the business world) and there are extensive follow-up exercises taken from recent English/Communication papers set for the examinations below:

	Code in text
Associated Examining Board	
English for Professional and Business Use	AEB EP&BU
English for Business Use	AEB EBU
Association of Accounting Technicians	
Certificate in Accounting	AAT C
Preliminary Examination	AAT P
Association of Medical Secretaries, Practice Administrators and Receptionists	
Certificate in Medical Reception	AMSPAR C
Diploma in Medical Secretarial Studies	AMSPAR D
The Institute of Chartered Secretaries and Administrators	ICSA
The London Chamber of Commerce and Industry	
English for Business	LCC EFB
Secretarial Studies Certificate / First Certificate in Office Technology	LCC SS
Private Secretary's Certificate / Second Certificate in Office Technology	LCC PSC
Private and Executive Secretary's Diploma	LCC PESD
Pitman Examining Institute	
English for Business Communication	PEI EBC
English for the Secretary	PEI EFS
English for Office Skills	PEI EOS
The Royal Society of Arts	
English Language	RSA EL
Communication in Business	RSA CIB
Diploma for Personal Assistants	RSA DPA
Southern Examining Group	
GCSE Communication Paper 1	SEG GCSE

The occasional longer assignment allows a realistic work situation to be explored more fully and a final chapter complements the written aspects by focusing on a variety of oral examinations.

Any answers or hints on answers are the sole responsibility of the author and have not been provided or approved by the examining bodies listed above.

William Cooke

Business English

William Cooke

Stanley Thornes (Publishers) Ltd

First published in 1990 by:
Stanley Thornes (Publishers) Ltd
Old Station Drive
Leckhampton
CHELTENHAM GL53 0DN
England

British Library Cataloguing in Publication Data
Cooks, William
Business English.
1. English language. Business English
I. Title
808.066651021

ISBN 0-7487-0425-6

Typeset by Tech-Set, Gateshead
Printed and bound in Great Britain at The Bath Press, Avon

Acknowledgements

Grateful acknowledgement is made to the following for permission to reprint material:

The Department of Trade for the statistics on 'Bankruptcy – Individual Analysis of Net Cases Administered ● *You*, the *Mail on Sunday* magazine, for 'Job ads – a guide to interpretation' ● Gareth David and NatWest *Moneycare* for the opening paragraphs of 'Just the Job' ● 'Forum, Council of Europe' for the passage 'European Music Year' and 'Young People and Rock' ● Gower Publishing Group for extracts from *Practical Security in Commerce and Industry* by Eric Oliver and John Wilson, and *The Security Survey* by Denis Hughes and Peter Bowler ● *The Economist* for a passage on electric vehicles ● Secker & Warburg Ltd and the estate of the late Sonia Bronwell Orwell for extracts from 'Politics and the English Language' and *1984* by George Orwell ● Myfanwy Thomas for a passage from *Feminine Influence on the Poets* by Edward Thomas ● the Nutmeg Press for two extracts from *The Funny Side of School* by Carlyn Webster and Roy Shipperbottom ● the *Wigan Evening Post* for 'Miners get TV Star for Opening' ● British Coal for the press release 'Jim "Fixes it" for Disabled Pitmen' ● BBC Enterprises Ltd for an extract from *Yes Prime Minister*, volume 1, by Jonathan Lynn and Antony Jay ● Patey Doyle (Publishing) Ltd for a passage on women in local government from *Public Services and Local Government* ● *The Geographical Magazine* for 'Transport Strategy for a World Without Oil' ● Pitman Publishing for 'Flexitime in the USA', 'Staging a Conference' by Leonie Grayeff from *2000* and an extract from *The Business of Transport* by Bell, Bowen and Fawcett ● the Post Office for an extract from the *Post Office Guide* on complaints procedures ● the *Guardian* for a passage on AIDS by Wendy Cooper ● the Consumers' Association for extracts from *Which?* and *Money Which?* ● ASH ● the European Parliament for an extract from *EP News* No. 11 ● Methuen & Co. for extracts from *Consumer Education* by Marion Giordan, *Residential Work with the Elderly* by C. Paul Brearley (Routledge & Kegan Paul) and *The Secret Diary of Adrian Mole Aged 13¾* by Sue Townsend (Methuen London) ● the *Financial Times* for 'Car Manufacturers May Liaise More', 'Seeking to Meet a Vital Need' by Ian Hamilton-Fazey and 'Giving Employees Something to Chew On' and 'A Little Extra Effort Eases the Pain of Redundancy' by Arnold Kransdorff ● Chronicle Communications Ltd and Longman Group UK for an extract from *The Chronicle of the 20th Century* ● JCB, Mencap and Rowan Advertising for their advertisements.

Grateful thanks are also due to the following examining boards that readily gave permission to reproduce past examination questions:

the Associated Examining Board; the Association of Medical Secretaries, Practice Administrators and Receptionists; the Association of Accounting Technicians; the Institute of Chartered Secretaries and Administrators; the London Chamber of Commerce and Industry; Pitman Examining Institute; the Royal Society of Arts; Southern Examining Group; and the validating body BTEC.

I wish to express my thanks to Lynn Jukes, Sara Sherwin and all the past students whose work is represented here. My thanks also to Brenda Coldham, Carole Hammersley, Anne McBratney and John Hawthorne for reading the book, in whole or in part, before publication. Finally I should like to thank Jenny Roberts and the students of LCC2 1988–9 for their help in typing sections of the manuscript.

Every effort has been made to trace copyright holders, but if any have been inadvertently omitted an appropriate acknowledgement will be made at the earliest opportunity.

1 _Communication: use of English_

... indicate precisely what you mean to say.
The Beatles, _When I'm Sixty-Four_

In 1988 Christy Nolan, paralysed and speechless from birth, won the Whitbread Literary Prize for his autobiography _Under the Eye of the Clock_. On average it takes him ten minutes to type out each word by means of a prong fitted to his forehead like a unicorn's horn.

His struggle to communicate should remind us of how carelessly we often use words. Take, for example, this extract from a police circular to members of a neighbourhood watch scheme:

> **At 3.00 p.m. Wednesday, 5 June, at the junction of Keelings Road and Brough Lane, a female was indecently exposed to by the following described person:**
>
> **Late teens, early 20's, slim build, with strawberry blonde hair (I ask you) cut short, having a spotty complextion wearing a grey and white 'T' shirt. He was also driving a peach coloured car (what ever is going on in the World).**
>
> **This fella seems so obvious that he has got to be known, or at least spotted by other people, other than those to whom he committs offences against.**

Hardly a flash of inspirational English! What should be a factual statement is interrupted by the writer's chatty asides and the reader is further distracted by the tortuous expression, not to mention the spelling and punctuation mistakes.

Mere correctness is not, however, a guarantee of good writing. Consider the following letter, written by a managing director in reply to a speculative job application:

> Dear Miss . . .
>
> I refer to your letter of 22 inst. In the state of the UK industrial scene, and I am sure it will be no surprise to you, we are looking for stability (if not contraction) of our employment scenario and with such general philosophy in mind there are no current vacancies.
>
> We have however retained your letter on file but it would be less than honest of me not to state that my current anticipations would indicate a lack of third party employment prospects for a number of years to come.
>
> Yours sincerely . . .

The letter is full of wordy jargon and what the writer is trying to say (that there will be no vacancies in the foreseeable future) could be expressed simply and less pompously. Perhaps both policeman and managing director should spend a week writing as Christy Nolan has to; they might then learn the virtues of clarity, precision and economy.

The above examples show how easily even routine messages can become blurred and imprecise. What should happen when communication takes place may be indicated by the following diagram:

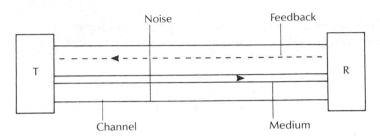

T (the transmitter) wishes to share an idea with R (the receiver). T decides on the medium of transmission (speech? the written word?) and then on the appropriate communication channel by which the message can be transmitted (telephone? post? telex?). This channel may be determined by the circumstances: a written record may be necessary; the message may be urgent; bad news may have to be broken as gently as possible. Feedback is any signal, verbal or non-verbal, conscious or unconscious, that tells T what R's response is to his message. It might be a question, a yawn, a letter of reply. Now the roles are reversed, with R becoming the transmitter and T the receiver. Noise is any interference outside their control.

Talking point

The following examples illustrate some of the ways in which communication can be affected – or even break down. Try to determine for each of them who is responsible – T, R, both or neither:

● The wrong language is used – which is beyond R's level of understanding. This might be a foreign language or language that is too technical or full of jargon. The DSS once wrote to a claimant:
  'The requirements of regulation 2 (1), 5, 14, 15 and 19 of the Supplementary Benefit (Requirement) Regulations as amended and where appropriate from 22.11.82, as further amended by regulation 1 (2), 2 (1), 2 (2), 2 (4), 2 (9), 2 (10) and 2 (12) of the Supplementary Benefit (Housing Benefits) (Requirements and Resources) Consequential Amendment Regulations 1982 (S1 1982/1126), and S1 1982/1124 of the Housing Benefits Regulations 1982, have been correctly applied.'
  The recipient commented: 'I can't understand it. The letter is utter rubbish.'[1]
● The right language is used but is distorted by accent. An immigrant in an Australian hospital heard the message 'You can go home today' as 'You can go home to die'.
● The message contains spelling, punctuation or grammatical errors that not only distract but may cause R to lose faith in T. An advertisement once offered special 'English as a Second Language' classes in which students would be able to 'improve their spoken and writted English'.
● The message is ambiguous. Another advertisement stated 'Dog for sale. Eats anything. Fond of children.'
● The wrong communication channel is chosen. An important announcement, made by a notice on a notice-board, may not be seen.

1 The *Oxford English Dictionary* gives the word 'bafflegab' as a synonym for jargon.

- The wrong attitude is shown or the wrong tone used. A superior may be condescending, a receptionist too casual.
- Personality conflicts undermine the message. A pupil who does not like a particular teacher sometimes finds it difficult to make progress in that subject.
- R is so preoccupied with his own thoughts that he cannot give his full attention to T. Here non-verbal signals may be misleading: a group of students staring in apparently rapt attentiveness may individually be thinking of boy/girlfriends, that evening's disco, etc.
- Noise affects the message – as when a train at a station blots out the announcer's voice on the public address system.

If messages have to be passed on, the possibilities for confusion increase. A chain of people may be involved:

$$A \longrightarrow B \longrightarrow C \longrightarrow D \longrightarrow E$$

with each recipient becoming a transmitter in turn. A useful class exercise is to transmit a telephone message through such a chain of students and compare their final version with the original. The outcome may not be very different from an apocryphal story from the First World War. It was said that the message 'Send reinforcements – we're going to advance' was whispered from soldier to soldier until it reached the reserve line. There the message was received as 'Send three-and-fourpence – we're going to dance'.

Effective communication clearly depends on numerous factors, but one of the most important is good English. For this reason this chapter is given precedence and not tucked away in an appendix. It should be read by GCSE student and graduate alike. It does not attempt to give a crash course in the proper use of the English Language; rather it focuses upon recurring problem areas in exams, loosely grouped under four main headings. Wherever possible, the examples are taken from students' own work.

Punctuation

The full-stop

A colleague once told me the story of one of his pupils who was having enormous trouble with punctuation. Then, at a parents' evening, her mother informed him that she had cured her daughter's problem: 'I told her to count ten words and then put a full-stop,' she said. Some examinees work on equally mysterious principles.

Punctuation marks are there to help you read effectively just as road signs are there to help you drive smoothly and safely. To prove this, try to read the following unpunctuated passage without 'crashing' from one sentence into another. Then copy it out, paragraphing it and adding all the necessary punctuation.

the beatles duly received their mbes today but the scenes outside buckingham palace were hardly as decorous as such occasions usually merit driven in a rolls royce the four beatles swept through the gates accompanied only by their manager brian epstein as they made their way to the royal investiture crowds of teenage girls struggled with hundreds of police specially imported to control the excitement as bemused tourists stared the youngsters screamed shouted waved banners and generally proved that nowhere is immune to beatlemania inside the palace far from the frenzy the beatles like everyone else attending the investiture enjoyed the pomp and circumstance of this great occasion the queen was reported to have asked them how long have you been together now quipped ringo forty years

How many full-stops did you insert? The original contained seven (see Appendix 1). If you used fewer than this, you are probably one of those students who commits the major punctuation error of exams – understopping.

Separate sentences cannot be joined with a comma. Consider the following:

Thank you for your letter of 9 July, I think we will be able to help you.

In respect of the first 50 days worked you will be paid a fee of £250, for each day worked in excess of 50 days you will be paid £8.

Both are wrong. A full-stop is needed in the first example, a semi-colon or joining word such as 'and' in the second.

At the other extreme are those students who use full-stops too freely – even after phrases that only masquerade as sentences:

In response to our discussion on 20 January.

With reference to your recent enquiry.

Neither contains a main verb and so neither is a sentence. A comma must replace the full-stop and the rest of the statement be completed:

In response to our discussion on 20 January, I am happy to tell you that a decision has now been reached.

With reference to your recent enquiry, I can confirm that the arrangements have been made.

If you consistently misuse the full-stop you are not in control of your writing and, like a poor driver, will leave a trail of confusion behind you.

The comma

Generally commas are scattered like confetti at a wedding – often missing their target and simply littering the sentence:

The half-day secretarial seminar, seems, to have a great deal of support, throughout the company.

It gives me great pleasure to inform you, that you were successful in your Part II examination, (Practical and Written), last summer.

Here all the commas should be swept away. As a general rule, if in doubt, omit.

Where then are commas necessary? In business they will be used principally to separate items in a list (chairs, tables, books . . .), after introductory word or phrases (furthermore, on the whole, for example,) and to separate anything that interrupts the main sentence:

Miss Anita Brookes, aged 28, has a pleasant personality.

Nigel Jay, the Sales Manager, offered her a job.

This office, recently decorated, is ideal for her.

Note that in this case two commas are necessary.

The apostrophe

Recently a cartoon in the *New Yorker* showed a traffic cop who had stopped a van driver. On the side of the van was painted 'ME AND WALLYS PRODUCE'. The caption reads: 'Sorry but I'm going to have to issue you with a summons for reckless grammar and driving without an apostrophe'.

Nowadays the apostrophe is either not used at all:

Lunch in the Directors Dining Room

or it adorns every *s* in sight:

Xma's card's for s'ale (Shop sign).

Sometimes its misuse can radically alter meaning. In the sentence:

The economic situation is still affected by the miner's strike

one might wonder who this miner was whose action could have such a dramatic impact! The Prudential may also have been concerned when a signwriter's attempt at their slogan ('Prudential – we're here to help you') consigned them to the unhelpful past ('Prudential – were here to help you').

The apostrophe is used:
1   to indicate missing letters (we're = we are)
2   to show possession.

First think of the longer version using 'of' or 'for'. If the noun that follows is singular or a plural that does not end in *s*, add *'s:*

the lamp of the miner	**the miner's lamp**
the canteen for the workmen	**the workmen's canteen**

If the noun following 'of' or 'for' is a plural ending in *s*, add only the apostrophe:

the strike of the miners	**the miners' strike**
the Dining Room for the Directors	**the Directors' Dining Room**

NB
- Never add an apostrophe to a verb.
- Do not use apostrophes in *yours, theirs, whose, ours, hers.*
- Do not confuse *it's* (it is) and *its* (belonging to it). If in doubt, substitute the full version of the former and see if the English still makes sense:

It's (it is)✔		it's (it is) ✗	
Its ✗	unusual for	its ✔	alarm to sound.

- Add either an apostrophe or *'s* to names ending in *s* to show possession. Thus *Charles Dickens' novels* and *Charles Dickens's novels* are both acceptable, but the Spanish inn sign:

THE CHARLES DICKEN'S PUB

is not.

The hyphen

One function of the hyphen is to join two words serving as a single adjective before a noun (all-out strike, well-known company) and its omission may lead to confusion or ambiguity. A church newsletter once announced:

> **The ladies of the church have cast off clothes of every kind and they can be seen in the church basement on Friday afternoon.**

Striptease or jumble sale?

Spelling

An examiner's report once commented:

> **One cause of failure was extremely poor spelling . . . a top executive who spells inacurrately may well be highly esteemed; a shorthand-typist, secretary or personal assistant – never!**

It is not only the more 'difficult' words that give trouble such as 'asterisk' (asterix, astrix, asterick, asperisk, astrith, asterous, astorist) but also such common words as 'wages' (wadges), 'whom' (whome) and 'possess' (pocess). What hope then for foreign names like Renault (Reno), Egon Ronay (Eager Ronny) or Chopin (Chaupin, Chopan, Chaupan, Chopain, Schauppan)? Below is a spelling test with a difference. What words do you think these students were trying to spell? (Answers in Appendix 1.)

1 aurniments
2 deadbury
3 kerizma
4 sexsess
5 cheak
6 glosterfobey
7 yernetin
8 sinucsm
9 crewe station
10 avid David

Homophones

These are words having different spellings but the same or almost the same sounds. They need special attention (especially in shorthand and audio-typing) or it becomes easy to refer to 'a sweet of offices', 'the bear essentials', 'waving our claws' (waiving our clause). Consider the unintentionally comic effect of these sentences:

> **She was wearing a bridle dress.**

> **The bride walked up the isle while the congregation sang a him.**

> **The wedding cake was in tears.**

Small wonder that one advertisement offered a good salary for someone with 'floorless English'.

Malapropisms

After a broadcast at the BBC TV Centre, Thor Heyerdahl, author of the *Kon Tiki Expedition*, was waiting for a taxi he had ordered. The driver came in but ignored him. The explorer approached and asked if his was the cab he had ordered. 'No mate,' replied the driver. 'I've come to pick up four Airedales.'

Mrs Malaprop, in Sheridan's play *The Rivals,* gave her name to a misuse of words that comes from their similarity of sound or spelling. Her spirit lives on – not only in the taxi-driver but in the mother who wrote to her son's teacher, 'Bobby will not be coming to school today on account of a billards attack' and in the candidates for a medical shorthand exam who referred to 'throat swaps', 'nasal guitar' and the fact that one woman had 'all her teeth extracted since she suffered from diarrhoea'!

A list of the most common spelling errors in business exams is given in Appendix 2. It includes the mistake made in the examiner's comment above – did you spot it?

Grammar

False concord

A verb must agree with its subject in number and person. This is called the concord of verb and subject. Mistakes occur when the real subject of the verb is not clearly identified:

1 **Rates and the cost of living is much lower.**

2 **The price of seats are too high.**

3 **There has been several complaints about working conditions.**

In **1** the writer is misled by the singular phrase 'cost of living' and forgets that the subject is plural ('Rates and . . .') requiring 'are'. In **2** the closeness of the plural 'seats' has affected the verb; the true subject however is 'price' which requires 'is'. In **3** 'have' is necessary as a plural follows.

Comparatives/superlatives

Quizmaster	**What 'B' is the superlative of the word 'good'?**
First contestant	**Brilliant.**
Second contestant	**Better.**

best superlative of good   good, best, better   comp. sup.

from Blockbusters

There are various problems with comparatives and superlatives. One is not being able to identify them correctly, as in the above exchange. What is the correct answer?

Remember that there are three degrees of comparison:

Positive	*Comparative*	*Superlative*
light	lighter	lightest
skilful	more skilful	most skilful

Note

- The comparative is usually formed by adding 'er' or 'r' to adjectives of one syllable or adding 'more' (or 'less') before longer words. A double comparative:

  It is *more* eas*ier* to work flexitime than conventional hours

  is always wrong.

- The superlative is normally formed by adding 'est' to adjectives of one syllable or by adding 'most' (or 'least') before longer words. Double superlatives are also always wrong:

  Of all the methods I would use the telephone as this is by far the *most* eas*iest*.

● The comparative is used of two, the superlative of three or more. So:

> **Of the two methods I would use the telephone as this is by far the easiest**

is also wrong.

● Some adjectives have irregular comparisons. Remember particularly:

bad	**worse**	**worst**
good	**better**	**best**

Like or as

Formal English does not accept *like* as a conjunction (a joining word).[1] So the sentence:

> **I passed the exam like you did**

is wrong, although:

> **I passed the exam as you did**

or:

> **I passed the exam like you**

are both correct. Remember that if a verb follows it is *as*. Shakespeare's play is called *As You Like It* not *Like You Like It*.

Misrelated participles

> **While wiping her eyes, the organ burst forth into the strains of the Wedding March.**

'Wiping' is a present participle (part of the verb ending in 'ing') and in a correct sentence the subject governing it needs to follow. However, this is often omitted, as in the above statement, thus creating a ludicrous effect. A second example shows the difference:

> **Using a pair of binoculars, a lighthouse could be seen.** X
> *Using* **a pair of binoculars**, *he* **could see the lighthouse.** ✔

Inconsistency

● Of agreement:

> **The board *has* decided that *their* offer should stand.**

Most collective nouns can be singular or plural as desired, but switching number halfway is best avoided.

● Of tense:

> **We *shall* be glad if you *would* arrange it.**

---

[1]A glossary of basic terms is given in Appendix 3.

Tenses must be consistent ('shall . . . will'/'should . . . would').

- Of listing. Many business documents require lists and care should be taken to prevent them from reading awkwardly. Often it is simply a matter of ensuring that each numbered point begins with the same part of speech:

✗	✔
Action	*Action*
1 Consult the workforce.	1 Consult the workforce.
2 Appoint a representative.	2 Appoint a representative.
3 Meetings should be held regularly.	3 Hold regular meetings.

Style

Correct English is important – but so too is the ability to adopt the most suitable style in a given situation (the 'register'). How would you react if you received a business letter written in the following manner?

```
Dear Sir

Re: Your Order No 076834

Thanks a bunch for your communication of 15 inst.

There's been a bit of a foul-up at this end since Mr Foot
kicked the bucket and at this moment in time we find ourselves
in a shortage of stock situation. But don't get uptight –
you're not being ripped off. We'll give you a bell in a week or
two when we've sorted ourselves out – OK?

Enclosed please find a copy of our latest brochure – it's fab!

Assuring you of our best attention at all times, we remain

Yours faithfully . . .
```

There are no spelling, punctuation or grammatical errors, but no organisation would send out this mishmash of slang and commercialese. The whole letter needs to be rewritten in an appropriate register.

For some writers this is difficult to achieve, but they must learn to adapt their style to differing circumstances just as they change their clothes according to where they are going. Imagine turning up at a football match in your best suit or going to an important interview in jeans and trainers. Similarly our thoughts should not be clothed too formally or too informally for the occasion. When asked to write to the clients of a travel agency telling them of a change in arrangements, one examinee wrote:

It is with deepest regret that I have to inform you that your holiday hotel has had to be changed.

Such a funereal tone (suitable for a letter of condolence) is just as misplaced as that adopted by another candidate who, asked to contact the dispatch manager about customer complaints, wrote:

Watch it pal, or you'll find yourself out of a job.

Besides using the wrong register, the above writer has given little thought to the person he is addressing or to the effect the message will have on him – prime considerations in any form of communication.

Talking point

Consider, in the light of the last statement, this real announcement by Captain Eric Moody to the 247 passengers in his aircraft:
'Good evening, ladies and gentlemen, this is your captain speaking. We have a small problem. All four engines have stopped. We are doing our damnedest to get them going again. I trust you are not in too much distress.'
Captain Moody eventually re-started the engines and made a safe landing to loud cheers.

To communicate well we need to avoid slovenliness of expression which usually follows slovenliness of thought.

George Orwell, in an essay called *Politics and the English Language*, stated:

A scrupulous writer, in every sentence that he writes, will ask himself at least four questions, thus: What am I trying to say? What words will express it? What image or idiom will make it clearer? Is this image fresh enough to have an effect? And he will probably ask himself two more: Could I put it more shortly? Have I said anything that is avoidably ugly?

The following guidelines will help any writer to achieve a more effective style:
- Avoid phrases or images that you are used to seeing in print – they are usually clichés ('the bottom line', 'taking [ideas] on board', 'tip of the iceberg'). Often, as Orwell comments, 'the writer knows what he wants to say, but an accumulation of stale phrases chokes him like tea leaves blocking a sink.'
- Never use a long word where a short one will do. Short words are easy to spell and understand – so instead of 'perception', 'initiate' and 'utilise' prefer 'view', 'start' and 'use'.

    Long words often lead to pretentiousness, vagueness and obscurity. For example, a New York psychologists' conference came up with this definition: 'the cognitive-effective state characterised by intrusive or obsessive fantasising concerning reciprocity of amorant and feeling by the object of amorance'. What do you think they were trying to define? (Answer in Appendix 1.)
- Do not use unnecessary words. 'At this moment in time' is 'now'; 'prior to' is 'before'; 'a free gift' is advertising jargon.

    Some students become addicted to the words 'very' and 'quite' which can usually be omitted without loss. Others think that the words 'so therefore' go together naturally like Siamese twins – but only one is needed. The word 'situation' should not be added to other nouns – 'a strike situation' is 'a strike'.

    The US Secretary for Health, Education and Welfare once advertised for 'an extremely confidential personal assistant . . . responsible for managing, performing and supervising work related to the operation of the Secretary's kitchen and eating area'.

Did he really mean 'Good cook wanted'?

- Never use a foreign phrase, commercialese or jargon if there is an everyday English alternative. So use 'a head' not 'per caput'; 'I enclose' not 'enclosed please find'; 'office' not 'individual work station'. 'I am available for interview at your convenience' should be used only if you are applying for the job of lavatory attendant.

- Avoid slang ('get the push', 'coming on heavy') and Americanisms. The UK and US have been described as two countries divided by a common language. Not only does American spelling sometimes differ from ours (catalog, thru) but so do many expressions (there you *meet with* people; here you just *meet* them). Some words can also have a completely different meaning: asking an American male if he felt like a fag might lead to a misunderstanding.

- Avoid euphemism. We are all familiar with the coded language of holiday brochures, estate agents' literature and school reports ('could do better' = idle; 'could do much better' = bone idle). But nowadays some American charwomen prefer the inflated status of 'floor beauticians' while a Wimbledon ticket tout described himself in court as a 'turnstile executive'. And whereas we once sent ambassadors to lie abroad for the good of their country, we now send the Cabinet Secretary to be 'economical with the truth'.

- Avoid ambiguity. After reading in the *Daily Express* that 'Fergie curtsied to King Olav in a blue silk tulip fronted dress', Spike Milligan wrote to the editor: 'Gad sir, I always thought that King Olav was straight. Do we have the first royal gay?'

A secretary recalled how she received the following dictation to a Member of Parliament:

Thank you very much for agreeing to address our afternoon conference in Stoke-on-Trent next week.

If you can get up in time, we would be delighted if you would join us for lunch.

She was astute enough to alter it before it was typed.

Ambiguous antecedents to 'it', 'them' and 'they' also entrap the unwary:

That night he got drunk and drove into a tree. His father, who was a scrap merchant, sold it.

Oxfam buy lorries, food, milk, etc. and make them up into parcels.

Hundreds of people come from the towns to help with the grape harvest. They are handpicked and carted away in lorries.

- Vary sentence length, but in general keep sentences short (no longer than 25 words). The following sentence (72 words) is reproduced exactly as it was printed on a life insurance policy. How many readers would find their way through this maze of words?

The Surrender Value of this Policy after ten full years' premiums have become due and paid shall be such a sum as bears the same proportion to the total amount payable under the policy, had the death of the Life Assured occurred immediately following the completion of the number of years' premiums actually due and paid, as the said number of premiums bears to the total number of years' premiums originally payable.

- Prefer the active to the passive voice, which is more concise and forceful:

  not **A receipt was issued by the manager (7 words)**
  but **The manager issued a receipt (5 words)**

- Be careful to never split an infinitive (*sic*). In Orwell's terms, this is 'avoidably ugly'. There are occasions, however, when a split infinitive will be necessary – either for emphasis or, as in the following example, to avoid ambiguity and to convey the exact shade of meaning:

  He failed to completely understand the question.

  If, when you split an infinitive, you know what you are doing and why, the chances are that it will be correct.
- Avoid unintended humorous effects. A recent news item stated that 'both Bishop Muzorewa and Mr Banana have denied any split', while a similarly comic effect emerges unwanted from the earlier pastiche letter ('since Mr Foot kicked the bucket').
- Avoid the non-sequitur – which occurs when what follows has no relation to what has gone before. In exams it is often the result of trying to combine notes given in the question:

  Our freezing factory is well known for its high standards of hygiene and so we request that our visitors wear warm clothes.

- Avoid all naivety of expression:

  The Clarendon Hotel is rather posh so a dinner jacket will be necessary . . .

  and all naivety of thought:

  There may be vegetarians so make sure there is plenty of lettuce.

- Avoid self-contradiction, apparent or real, to which people are especially prone when on the defensive, as these genuine extracts from motor insurance claim forms show:

  I collided with a stationary tramcar coming in the opposite direction.

  To avoid collision I ran into the other car.

  There were plenty of lookers-on but no witnesses.

Clarity of expression is encouraged by clarity of thought. So think what you want to say, then say it as simply and precisely as you can in the best format. The rest of this book considers the main forms of communication available in the business world.

Further reading

George Orwell, *Politics and the English Language,* 1946
The Economist Pocket Style Book, Economist Publications, 1987

P. A. CLOW

Exercises

1 Students should in turn speak to the group on a problem in communication that they have experienced – at college, at work or in their social lives. They should explain the nature of the problem and say how this relates to communication theories. They should state what in their opinion caused the difficulties and what advice they would give to the parties concerned.

2 Case study

Alan White is head of the Accounts Department of APT Ltd, a large industrial company on the outskirts of London. For some time consideration has been given to the possibility of moving the computer section of the Accounts Department to the new works situated in a new town in County Durham. No definite decision has been taken but if the relocation is to take place no one would be forced to move and no one would be laid off. Those who did not wish to go would be offered suitable alternative employment.

Jimmy Cooper, an office junior in the Accounts Department, is a keen member of the firm's table tennis club which plays in a local league. One morning Jimmy was in Mr White's office when the telephone rang. Mr White answered the telephone and after listening for a few minutes was heard to say, 'Yes – the move to Durham. I'll be up there soon to look around.' Jimmy did not take much notice of this but when he was walking home that evening with some of the girls from the typing pool, he heard some of them talking about the Accounts Department's move to Durham.

Jimmy was worried about this so he took the matter up with Mike Galloway, his section head, who was also the captain of the table tennis team. Mike knew nothing of the move and asked Jimmy where he got the information. 'It's all round the typing pool,' Jimmy said, 'and I even heard Mr White confirming the move on the telephone.'

Mike was perturbed. Not only was his team doing well but he had just bought a new house and his wife was expecting a baby. He decided to talk it over with the other section heads. None of them knew anything official but several had heard rumours of a proposed move. After two days Mike decided to approach Mr White, but when he went to his office to make an appointment he was told that Mr White had just left for a week's visit to Durham. During the week of Mr White's return Mike twice attempted to see him but was rebuffed as Mr White said he had 'a great backlog of work to catch up on'.

After this morale deteriorated and work suffered, so much so that Alan White was called in front of the General Manager and asked what was wrong with his department. Shortly after this, Mike Galloway handed in his resignation.

The situation shows what problems can be caused in an organisation by poor communication. Discuss the parts played in the episode by

a) Alan White

b) Jimmy Cooper

c) Mike Galloway

paying special attention to any mistakes they made.

RSA CIB Stage II Summer 1982

3 Comment on the English in the following:

A a) (*Shop sign*) Sweet's, ice cream's, gateaux's, can's of coke.

   b) (*Shop sign*) Would customer's please. Be careful by this counter incase they. Knock their legs. Thankyou.

   c) (*Prescription*) Use 2 drops 4 times a day, discard after one month into the left ear.

   d) (*Wimbledon commentator*) 'Everyone in the crowd are willing him to a first-round victory.'

   e) (*Football commentator*) 'The manager is in the happy position of having a fresh pair of legs up his sleeve.'

f) (*BBC Radio*) 'Once again Lloyd Honeyghan is World Welterweight Champion of the World.'

g) (*Instructions in Morocco hotel bedroom*) To make the English tea – put bag in cup and stir until dark.

h) (*From an examining board's instructions*) Candidates should clean the capillary tubes by passing water through them.

i) (*Church magazine*) The preacher for Sunday next will be found hanging on the notice-board.

j) The vicar announced that he would be having an additional font in the church so that babies could be baptised at both ends.

B **a)** (*Estate agent's leaflet*) Occupying a prime position in a much sought-after road, we are delighted to offer this property.

b) (*Estate agent's leaflet*) A noble stone-built farmhouse of unprecedented proportions requiring a donation of both innovation and investment to crystallise the internal static metamorphosis . . .

c) (*From a property valuation*) We recommend the mortgage company to only lend £10 000.

d) (*BBC Radio*) 'After inspecting a guard of honour, the President's motorcade moved into the centre of Moscow.'

e) (*Afghan spokesman on Soviet withdrawal*) 'There will be spontaneous demonstrations, but we haven't planned them yet.'

f) (*From 'Airport'*) You can often see Concorde taking off through the restaurant window.

g) (*Police circular*) Any schoolchildren been bullied into parting with any money by other schoolkids, we would like to know about please.

h) (*News reports*) A policeman stopped a Brighouse man from committing suicide by jumping off a railway viaduct for the second time in 18 months.

i) A hayrick which has recently been burned down is being hunted by detectives at Horsham police station.

j) Police found drunk in shop window.

C **a)** (*Advertisement*) Slim and Trim muscle toning machine, exercise the easy way in a smart briefcase.

b) (*Sales letter*) If you are looking for a way to clear up all those overdue bills laying on your desk or kitchen table, then this may be the solution to your problems.

c) (*News item*) A £250 000 giant water chute may be installed at Long Eaton swimming baths to stop the slide in attendances.

d) (*For sale*) Wheelchair with installed belt, curtains, chandelier, guitar, other useful items.

e) (*From motor insurance claim forms*) I collided with a stationary tree.

f) A lamp post bumped into my car, damaging it in two places.

g) One wheel went into the ditch. My foot jumped from break to accelerator pedal, leaped across the road to the other side and jumped into the trunk of a tree.

h) Coming home a tree damaged my car and I was somewhat concussed.

i) (*Headline*) Mortuary will be built despite stiff opposition.

j) (*Advertisement*) Wedding Dress and Bridesmaids for sale from £40.

a) Wanted: Nightwatchman, 11 a.m. to 6 p.m.

b) For sale: 1938 black hearse with original body.

c) (*GCSE question*) Using the statistics provided about a girl's scout pack, work out how many are in the club.

d) (*Poll tax leaflet*) Persons refusing to supply, or who knowingly supply, false information may be liable to a £50 fine.

e) (*Overheard*) 'I've got a lovely bunch of Friesians on my window-sill.'

    f) (*Bookshop notice*) *The Satanic Verses* – singed copies available.
    g) (*School report*) He must pay grater atention to his werk.
    h) (*Headlines*) Subsidence fears prove groundless.
    i) Mild fertility drug produces quadruplets in 3 minutes.
    j) 'Help, help!' shrieks unconscious landlady from window.

4 Below are some of the most commonly confused words. Write out the correct word for each sentence.
    a) I may have to give instructions on (who's/whose) job it is.
    b) We should be delighted to (except/accept) Miss Snaith's offer.
    c) It was debatable (wether/whether) there would be enough room.
    d) If you wish to apply for the post of (Personnel/Personal) Secretary, apply to the (Personal/Personnel) Manager.
    e) In (principle/principal) she had no objection to redeployment; her (principle/principal) concern was to keep her job.
    f) As a result of the strike we shall (loose/lose) orders.
    g) If (your/you're) between the ages of 15 and 20, this is for you.
    h) They will continue to campaign until (there/their) goal is achieved.
    i) He asked for a (new/knew) (draft/draught) of the report.
    j) The television (program/programme) had a profound (affect/effect) on him.
    k) Our (advise/advice) was to send a (check/cheque) at once.
    l) (Practise/Practice) makes perfect, so (practice/practise) your spelling.
    m) (Formerly/Formally) Mr Downing was in charge of the (stationery/stationary).
    n) (Now/Know) it has (it's/its) own bar and dining-room.
    o) By discussing areas (where/were) there is room for improvement, (moral/morale) will be raised.

5 **Spelling test**
Write down what you think are the 25 correct words in the sentences below, then check your answers against the spelling list in Appendix 2:
    a) Furnished (accommodation/accomodation) will be provided.
    b) The accident (occurred/occured) in the print room.
    c) There was a (definate/definite) (commitment/committment) to buy.
    d) He asked for an (independant/independent) survey to be carried out; his (colleagues/colleges) disagreed.
    e) They (recieved/received) the results of the (questionnaire/questionaire).
    f) There will be a (seperate/separate) (enrolment/enrollment) list for evening classes.
    g) There are (occasions/occassions) when (correspondance/correspondence) is delayed.
    h) He sends his (apologise/apologies), but owing to (unforseen/unforeseen) circumstances he can no longer attend.
    i) He (refered/referred) to the fact that so many of the workforce had been (transferred/transfered).
    j) It was a (priviledge/privilege) to meet the distinguished guest.
    k) The report (recomended/recommended) that the branch be closed down (immediatley/immediately).
    l) He thought he was (indispensable/indispensible) but he was still made redundant.
    m) He was allowed to pay by (instalments/installments) to save any further (embarassment/embarrassment).
    n) He (sucessfully/successfully) applied for the post of (maintenance/maintainance) man.
    o) He was most (greatful/grateful) for the opportunity.

Score: *25–23 Excellent*
            22–20 Good
            19–15 Could be better
            14–0 Learn the spelling list!

6   Vocabulary test

The letter total for each word is shown beside it as a number. (Some of the words have been used in this chapter or appear elsewhere in the book. The answers are given in Appendix 1.)

a)	V . . .	(8)	word for word
b)	S . . . M	(7)	a word having the same or similar meaning
c)	G . . . NE	(9)	unofficial source of information
d)	PR . . . T	(9)	widespread
e)	C . . . Y	(12)	belonging to the same time
f)	M . . . O	(9)	declaration of policy
g)	IN . . . LE	(11)	easily set on fire
h)	CR . . . N	(9)	standard
i)	D . . . TE	(8)	entrust or commit
j)	I . . . Y	(9)	plan of a journey
k)	F . . . Y	(7)	a wrong but prevalent idea
l)	AF . . . T	(9)	written declaration on oath
m)	I . . . Y	(9)	detailed list of goods, etc.
n)	E . . . O	(7)	ban
o)	P . . . HE	(8)	a composition made up from various sources
p)	R . . .	(4)	list of persons or duties
q)	C . . . ESE	(13)	business jargon
r)	A . . . X	(8)	an addition to a book
s)	C . . . S	(9)	agreement (of opinion)
t)	R . . . R	(8)	the style and vocabulary appropriate to particular circumstances
u)	P . . . AL	(10)	having narrow views
v)	H . . . Y	(8)	unpaid
w)	A . . . A	(6)	list of items for a meeting
x)	A . . . S	(9)	of double or doubtful meaning

Score: 24–20 Excellent
             19–15 Very good
             14–10 Not bad
              9—0 Read more!

7   The following extracts are taken from examinees' work. What changes would you make?

A   a) The Beatles eara finally put the dampers on rock and roll.
   b) Many of the rock stars were idles to the youngsters.
   c) The town has a railway station which runs regularly to London.
   d) I would travel by the supersonic Concorde which travels faster than the speed of sound.
   e) The rest of my garden is in bad shape having only just moved here.
   f) The citrus trees look beautiful when walking down the street.
   g) By 9.30 all visitors shall be washed, dressed and eaten.
   h) The first thing that hits you as you walk into the room is the smoke from the frying pan, half of which is escaping through the window.
   i) Food handlers should keep their fingers cut short.
   j) Higher purchase is out of my reach.

B   a) The Bill was submitted for Royal Ascent.
   b) Terrorists threaten to kill politicians and normal people.
   c) When Dick looses his temper he becomes quite viscous.
   d) James Bond would of shot him.
   e) Due to cut backs the football and rugby teams are in jeopardy.
   f) In one corner there was a fish tank. The ideal thing to calm the nerves, which are so often strategically placed in dentists' waiting rooms.
   g) The animal became extinct for a long time.

h) An archaeologist is a person whose life is in ruins.
i) The rainbow contains all the colours of the rectum.
j) To mend a puncha stick a plasta on the in a choobe.

C a) Sedimentary office workers should take some form of exercise.
b) Mail is a vital source of information to most managers, soon to be electronically dealt with.
c) A partnership is considered dissolute when a partner dies.
d) When using electrical equipment with long hair always tie it back.
e) The company will be held reliable if accidents occur.
f) A memo and ballet slips were sent to all the secretaries.
g) As a momentum of your visit, you will receive discount shopping vouchers.
h) Do not fill the top draw of the filling cabinat.
i) The prophet of a company is very important.
j) (Open-plan offices) Offices built without walls.

D a) Recently there has been conflicting views about office development.
b) The new offices are more lighter and spacious.
c) Junction 12 of the M5 is only ten minutes drive away.
d) If you need to employ additional tempory help, please let me know so that I can contact the employment agency?
e) Failure to fulfill duties is a criminal offence not only the employer but the employee will be liable for persecution.
f) A decreasing amount of persons are paying their bills.
g) This amount, together with all associated expenses, are rechargable.
h) The decline in attendance figures have been mainly due to poor publicity.
i) We will do our up-most to help.
j) If you have any comments or proposals please write to us, they will receive the most careful consideration.

8 Insert/delete apostrophes as necessary in the following passage:

Its the first time Ive really understood how to use the apostrophe. Once Id put apostrophes everywhere – even on simple plurals and verbs (eg Im taking the dogs out before he arrives). But now I can see how silly that was (cant you?) and in future I shall use them chiefly to show possession – e.g. Miss Rothery's hat, Miss Davies pen, the secretaries lunch-break, the workmens sandwiches.
   Ill never go wrong again!

9 Punctuate the following:
a) *Syme, a specialist in Newspeak, addresses Winston Smith:*

its a beautiful thing the destruction of words of course the great wastage is in the verbs and adjectives but there are hundreds of nouns that can be got rid of as well it isnt only the synonyms there are also the antonyms after all what justification is there for a word which is simply the opposite of some other word a word contains its opposite in itself take good for instance if you have a word like good what need is there for a word like bad ungood will do just as well better because its an exact opposite which the other is not or again if you want a stronger version of good what sense is there in having a whole string of vague useless words like excellent and splendid and all the rest of them plusgood covers the meaning or doubleplusgood if you want something stronger still . . . you dont grasp the beauty of the destruction of words do you know that newspeak is the only language in the world whose vocabulary gets smaller every year

George Orwell, *1984*

b) *Edward Thomas on John Clare:*

he reminds us that words are alive and not only alive but still half wild and imperfectly domesticated they are quiet and gentle in their ways but are like cats to whom night overthrows our civilisation and servitude who seem to love us but will starve in the house that we have left and thought to have emptied of all worth words never consent to correspond exactly to any object unless like scientific terms they are first killed hence the curious life of words in the hands of those who love all life so well that they do not kill even the slender words but let them play on and such are poets the magic of words is due to their living freely among things and no man knows how they came together in just that order when a beautiful thing is made like full fathom five . . . grown men with dictionaries are as murderous of words as entomologists of butterflies

Edward Thomas, *Feminine Influence on the Poets*

10 Reference books. The best way to learn about reference books is to handle them. Discuss, in class, the books that might be consulted on the following topics (some questions involve more than one book) and then go to your library and look up the answers.

a) In the course of reading several articles you come across some details that puzzle you. Discover:
  i)   the meaning of:
       Chinese walls (business context)
       guillotine (Parliamentary context)
       dump (computer context)
  ii) what the following stand for:
       ABTA, CBI, ACAS
  iii) the reason why (*sic*) appears in the sentence below:
       Their claim that 'an advanced computer was indispensible (*sic*) to the operation' proved untrue.
  iv) the meaning of these abbreviations, found in a footnote:
       pp, ibid, cf

b) Your boss is preparing an important talk.
  i)   He is lost for a word but knows it is close to 'prohibit'. Write down five synonyms for him.
  ii) He is not sure whether to use 'compare to' or 'compare with'. Look up the difference for him.
  iii) He wishes to use the quotation 'Tomorrow to fresh fields and pastures new' but first wants you to check its accuracy and origin.

c) A number of VIPs will be flying into Manchester for an important meeting at your office there. Some of them will be staying overnight. Find the name and telephone number of i) a five-star hotel and ii) a theatre in the area.

d) Prince Charles is to visit your new factory and you are to be introduced to him. How will you address your royal guest?

e) Your employer is a recording executive who is preparing a programme note for a pop spectacular. You need to find out for her:
  i)   the name of the most successful group in the world in terms of record sales
  ii) which individual has been awarded the most golden discs
  iii) the names of three songs that have each been recorded over a thousand times
  iv) an address to which she can send an invitation to Paul McCartney
  v)   the name and address of a printer in your area who can prepare the programmes and invitations.

f) You are to travel to London for a conference at the Barbican. You do not know where this is. Find out, draw a sketch map of the area, and discover how to get there by the underground from Euston station.

g) Your principal wishes to contact the following and asks you to discover an address at which they can be reached:
  i)   your local MP
  ii) your local chamber of commerce
  iii) the Ombudsman
  iv) the Department of Trade.

h) Your employer is to travel to the People's Republic of China on a trade mission. He asks you to compile a simple factsheet for him, using the following headings and giving the required information:

Name of President	Religion
Name of Chairman	National Day
Area and Population	Important Magazines/Newspapers
Capital	Visa Requirements
Language(s)	Name of Chinese Ambassador
Currency	Address of Chinese Embassy
Principal Exports	Name of British Ambassador
Principal Imports	Address of British Embassy

i) You are helping to set up a training agency for secretarial students. A 'model office' is to be an integral part of the agency and you are asked to recommend a list of books that every office should have. Compile a list of your 'top ten' reference books.

j) Before correcting an important set of proofs, you decide to refresh your memory of some of the standard signs used in such checking. Make a copy of the following and complete the third section.

Marginal mark	Mark in text	Meaning
NP	[	
⊂/	beeu	
9 9	/ vital /	
stet/	necessary	
not/	which is/necessary	
⊙	which is not necessary /	
⅃	←[which is not necessary. ⅃	
∂	w/here	
⌒	re move	
i/	definate	
uc	yours faithfully	
lc	Yours Sincerely	
caps	exercises	
#	alot	
trs	(is/it)essential	
ital	essential	
∿	essential	
run on	⌒	

11 The following have all appeared in print. Copy them out and, using relevant signs from the previous exercise, indicate what corrections you would make.

A a) (*Seventeenth-century Bible*) Thou shalt commit adultery.
   b) (*Theatre advertisement*) OKLAHOMO!
   c) The show is now considered suitable for children or people who are easily offended.

d) Part-time assistant cashier for treasurer's department. 20 hours per week – current range of pay £1950 to £3606 per hour. Pay award pending.

e) Lendl is reported to be worth £30, but he dismisses thoughts that he might be embarrassed by his wealth.

f) Mr Ronald Irving gave birth to triplets, all boys.

g) He pleaded guilty to threatening behaviour. The bench ruled that he should not use, possess or carry a fireman for twelve months.

h) What Mrs Thatcher's closest friends are wondering is whether, as the signs suggest, she is beginning to suffer from metal fatigue.

i) (*Armand Hammer of the Prince of Wales*) 'In my opinion he will make a great king. He is a young man wise beyond his ears.'

j) (*Film guide*) A French window and an American vet meet and fall in love. Starring James Caan . . .

B **a)** (*Sticker on bananas*) Sell by Jan. 6, 1691.

b) (*From menus*) Bean on toast
Pissoles and chips
Coq au van
Ham, eggs and baked bears

c) TUXEDO, suit tall man, 34″ wrist, 38″ chest.

d) Something new which no motorist should do without – the self-grip wench.

e) Sincere caring gentleman, aged 509, no ties, wishes to meet smart lady in her thirties with view to permanent relationship.

f) (*From a communication manual on spelling rules*) i before e exept after c.

g) (*From an examiner's report*) There were three very serious faults:
(1) very bad errors in grammer . . .

h) (*TV guide*) 7.30 THE EDUCATION PROGRAMME
– Workbase. A new trade union
and employer iniative to give
workers a second chance at such
basic skills as spelling . . .

i) (*Advertisement*) Car Boob Sale

j) Solicitors seek poof-reader for their Word-Processing Department.

2 Business letters

Is there a letter in your bag for me?
The Beatles, *Please Mr Postman*

Good letters are concise and to the point, as demonstrated by this real suicide letter: 'Dear Coroner, I am going to kill myself. Your verdict should be suicide. I hope this will save everyone's time. Kindest regards . . ' The coroner described it as 'remarkable in its consideration towards me' and duly recorded a suicide verdict.

Even briefer (though less considerate) was the letter written by a tenant to his landlord after many attempts to evict him: 'Dear Sir, I remain, Yours faithfully.'

However, the shortest letter on record is undoubtedly that of Victor Hugo who, enquiring about the sales of his latest book, wrote to his publisher '?'. He received the reply '!'.

Examiners regard letter writing as a basic test of secretarial/administrative competence and they are looking for 'mailable' copy – letters that are correctly displayed and well organised, concise yet complete, accurate and free from jargon. Such letters help promote the right image of a company.

Display

The display is the first thing to create an impression. There are various formats in use in the business world, but for exam purposes it is best to choose one that is acceptable to the examining board and use it thereafter. Although different displays will be seen in the questions in this section, the suggested answers will all feature the most modern format – fully blocked with open punctuation – as illustrated in the following outline:

Name and address of company	**RUBBER SOUL COMPANY** **126 Abbey Road** **London**　　　**SW2 3LR**
Telephone/ Telex numbers	**Tel:　071–73928** **Telex: 236719**
Reference	REF JK/WTB
Date	20 November 19..
Name/position and address of recipient	Mrs Rita Henderson Office Manager Apex Limited 35 Penny Lane Liverpool　　　LS2 8TY
Salutation	Dear Mrs Henderson
Subject heading	STATE THE THEME
First section	Introduce the subject or acknowledge any previous letter.

Second section	Give or ask for the required information in a logical sequence. Sub-headings and numbered points may be used for complex material.
Third section	Conclude the letter suitably, perhaps by referring to who will take the next action and what that will be (a reply, telephone call, visit, meeting, etc.).
Complimentary close	Yours sincerely
Space for signature	(Signature)
Writer's name *Designation*	Jonathan Kite Sales Director
Enclosure(s)	Enc(s)
Copy/copies to	Copy to Miss Claire Bridgett

Note

- The above outline is appropriate when an organisation writes to another company or to an individual. When an individual writes to an organisation (a letter of enquiry, complaint, application), the letter begins with the individual's address (but not his name) and there will be no reference in the first letter although in subsequent correspondence the individual may quote a reference he has been given.
- Everything is aligned with the left margin.
- Everything above the salutation and below the complimentary close is unpunctuated; the body of the letter is punctuated normally.
- The reference number often consists of the initials of the person who dictated the letter (in capitals) followed by the initials of the typist (sometimes in lower case).
- The date dispenses with the 'th' after the numeral and the comma after the month.
- It is always preferable to use the name if you know it – but ensure that it is correct. Sacha Distel is tired of being addressed 'Dear Mr Dettol' or even 'Dear Slasher'.
- If you do not know the name/designation of someone to write to and simply address the company, the appropriate salutation is 'Dear Sirs'.
- A subject heading is to be recommended in most business letters. Ask yourself 'What is this letter all about?' to concentrate the theme in a few words.
- It is best to avoid old-fashioned openings such as 'With reference to . . .', 'Refering to . . .' or 'In response to . . .' which often lead to grammatical errors. A letter of reply should naturally begin 'Thank you for your letter of (date)'. Do not repeat the words of the subject heading if you have used one.
- As paragraphs are not indented, it is important to leave a suitable space before beginning a new paragraph – especially in exams that are handwritten.
- The final paragraph should avoid outdated commercialese such as 'Assuring you of our best attention at all times' and other non-sentences such as 'Looking forward to hearing from you'.
- The salutation affects the complimentary close, thus:

Dear Sir/Madam		**Yours faithfully**
Dear Mr/Miss Mrs/Ms	**(+ name)**	**Yours sincerely**

● Appropriate space should be left for a signature. Sometimes you will be asked to prepare a letter for your employer's signature and should therefore leave the space blank; at other times *you* will be expected to sign the letter – either because you are the letter writer or because you employer is absent. In the latter case the easiest formula to follow is:

<table>
<tr><td>Yours sincerely</td><td>*or*</td><td>Yours sincerely</td></tr>
<tr><td>(Your signature)</td><td></td><td>(Your signature)</td></tr>
<tr><td>for Jonathan Kite
Sales Director</td><td></td><td>Secretary to Jonathan Kite
Sales Director</td></tr>
</table>

NB The typed name that follows the signature does not normally include any courtesy title for a man.

The rest of this chapter will illustrate some of the main types of business letter and show how to plan them, adopt the correct style and avoid some common pitfalls.

Example Letter of enquiry/reply

You work as assistant to Mr Peter Phillips, Branch Manager of Radiorama Limited, 22 High Street, Greystone, Midshire GS3 9GT, a retail store specialising in radio and hi-fi products.

This morning the following letter arrived in Mr Phillips' post:

```
                                            146 Parkside Road,
                                            Millchester,
                                            Midshire.
                                            GS9 4BS

                                            21st June, 19..

The Manager,
Radiorama Limited,
22 High Street,
Greystone,
Midshire.       GS3 9GT

Dear Sir,

     I was interested to read your advertisement in last week's Greystone
Gazette concerning your current 'special low price offer' on portable
radios.
     My daughter has her sixteenth birthday next month and has been dropping
broad hints that she would very much like a portable radio to play in her
room, listen to with her friends, take on outings and so on.
     As you must serve a number of customers like my daughter, I thought I
should write to you for further details about the three portable radios you
advertised and ask your advice on what you think might be most suitable.
     I look forward to hearing from you.
                         Yours faithfully,

                         James Richards
```

The sales details of the advertised radios are as follows:

---

1 GLOBEMASTER
   For the enthusiast! High-powered portable with 'dial-the-
   world' highly accurate tuner. Long Wave, Medium Wave,
   Short Wave and VHF frequencies. Suit language/current
   affairs students. Mains and Battery Power Operated. All
   metal construction. Very robust. Leather carrying case.
   Weight: 9 kg.
   Price: Normally £99.99. Now: £79.99 inc VAT

2 STROLLER
   For all occasions! Go-anywhere portable radio. Pre-set
   positions for Radios 1, 2, 3 and 4 for instant push-button
   tuning. Long, Medium and Short Wave frequencies. Battery
   Powered. Moulded Plastic Construction. Vinyl Simulated
   Leather Carrying Case. Weight: 5 kg.
   Price: Normally £49.99. Now: £35.00 inc VAT

3 REKORDA
   Record your favourite programmes! Combined radio and
   cassette recorder with play-back. Records all Radio 1, 2,
   3 and 4 programmes for instant play-back. Mains and
   Battery Powered. Metal and Plastic Construction. Elegant
   as Table-Top Model. Ideal for Picnics. Plastic Shoulder-
   Strap Attachment. Weight: 6 kg.
   Price: Normally £69.99. Now: £49.00 inc VAT

Mr Phillips showed you the letter and briefed you as follows:

'I'd like you to compose a letter in my name to send to Mr Richards. You'd better check over the sales details carefully of the three portables on offer. I think you need only concentrate on the two which you think are the most likely to interest Mr Richards and meet his daughter's needs. Recommend the one you think more suitable. You can send him the relevant brochures to help him make up his mind.'

Assignment

Compose a suitable letter (but *not* brochures) as requested by Mr Phillips. Use a letter layout with which you are familiar.

RSA CIB Stage 1 June 1979 (*25 marks*)

Commentary

1 In the above letter the semi-blocked layout is used with closed punctuation (i.e. the addresses, salutation, and complimentary close are fully punctuated).
2 It is a straightforward example of a letter of enquiry and if Mr Richards had made brief notes before writing it, his plan would have looked something like this:

```
                                                    Own address

                                                    Date

  ┌─  The Manager
  │   Radiorama
  │   Address

  └▸ Dear Sir

        Para 1   Introduce subject by referring to recent ad. about portable
                 radios.
        Para 2   Focus on reason for writing: teenage daughter's birthday –
                 hints – brief details of kind of radio sought.
        Para 3   Request further information and seek advice.
        Para 4   Conclude suitably (action?).

  └▸ Yours faithfully
```

3   All the information needed for the reply is given in the question, but care must be taken with the spelling of 'Phillips', 'Greystone' and 'Millchester'. The sales details from which candidates may select information are not yet in a style suitable for a letter and should not simply be copied.

4   The instructions must be followed: you are asked to concentrate on only two radios (which two?) and recommend the one that you think is the *more* suitable. (Remember that the comparative is used of two – see page 8.)

5   Before you can begin to write any letter you need to outline it, however briefly. The following is the plan on which the suggested answer is based:

```
      Radiorama
      Address

      Ref

      Date

   ┌─ Mr James Richards
   │  Address

   └▸ Dear Mr Richards

      HEADING?

      Para 1   Acknowledge: 'Thank you for . . .'
      Para 2   Name the two suitable radios – describe the first.
      Para 3   Focus on second.
      Para 4   Make a recommendation.
      Para 5   Refer to enclosures and conclude suitably.

   └▸ Yours sincerely


      Peter Phillips
      Manager

      Encs ◂
```

Assignment

Plan and then write your own reply before reading the suggested answer below.

Suggested answer

Radiorama Limited
22 High Street Greystone
Midshire GS3 9GT

Tel: 093 4782

Ref PP/AB

23 June 19..

Mr James Richards
146 Parkside Road
Millchester
Midshire   GS9 4BS

Dear Mr Richards

PORTABLE RADIOS - SPECIAL OFFER

Thank you for your letter of 21 June in response to our recent advertisement.

Two of our radios are particularly suitable for your daughter: the Stroller and the Rekorda. The first is a battery powered, lightweight radio that can be used anywhere. It offers long, medium and short wave frequencies with pre-set positions for Radios 1, 2, 3 and 4 for instant push-button tuning. It is a moulded plastic construction and comes in a vinyl, simulated-leather carrying case. Our offer price is £35.00 including VAT, a saving of £14.99.

The Rekorda is a combined radio and cassette recorder, making it easy to tape favourite programmes from all the main radio stations for immediate playback. It is made of metal and plastic and powered by mains or battery. This makes it both stylish in the home and, with its shoulder-strap attachment, ideal for picnics. It weighs only 6 kg and costs £49.00 inclusive of VAT instead of its normal price of £69.99.

The Stroller would perfectly suit your daughter's requirements, but I would recommend the Rekorda which offers an exciting extra.

I enclose brochures giving full details and hope to be of further service.

Yours sincerely

Peter Phillips
Manager

Encs

Example **Letter of complaint/adjustment**

27, Lindamere Drive,
Orpington,
Kent.   KT5 7TL

1st June, 19 . .

Mr J.R. Hallam,
Instant Publishing Co., Ltd.,
12 Greychurch Lane,
London.   EC2

Dear Sir,

Early last year I joined your company's national book club scheme and undertook to purchase monthly one volume from the advertised selection. At the time I was told that I could terminate membership whenever I chose, upon giving one month's notice in writing.

In January 19 . ., I decided to end the arrangement and notified your accounts department of my decision, enclosing payment for the book due in February. Since then I have received three further unsolicited books at monthly intervals, a letter from your circulation manager regretting my decision to withdraw from membership, and various bills for payment. I have telephoned your main office twice and each time have been assured that the matter would be dealt with promptly.

Today I received yet another book together with a most objectionable demand for settlement of my alleged debts.

I should be most obliged if you would give this matter your immediate attention since the whole affair has caused me considerable annoyance.

Yours faithfully,

M.A. Stevens (Mrs)

Write a reply for Mr Hallam's signature.   RSA DPA June 1973

Commentary

1   The above is a good example of a letter of complaint. It is restrained in tone and gives all the necessary information, the first paragraph sketching in the background, the two middle paragraphs providing full details of the complaint, and the final paragraph indicating the desired action. In writing such a letter you should be rude only as a last resort.

2   When a company receives such a letter it must consider whether the complaint is justified. When it is, as in the above case, a reply (called a letter of adjustment) is sent, which may offer some form of compensation, replacement of faulty goods or reimbursement of money spent. When the complaint is not justified, the reply must tactfully point this out. This letter is often more difficult to write.

3   The opening paragraph of a letter of adjustment needs some thought as it is one of the few letters where the standard acknowledgement is less appropriate. Indeed, 'Thank you for your letter of 1 June expressing your annoyance with our company' sounds a trifle masochistic! Mr Hallam could, of course, thank Mrs Stevens for bringing the matter to his attention.[1]

[1] When a customer complained to a store about out-of-date sweets she had been sold, she received a reply which began: 'Thank you for your complaint about the out-of-date product and may I say how totally apathetic we are about it, ie we couldn't give a toss . . .' The store was last reported to be holding an urgent investigation to identify the employee allegedly responsible.

4   Good replies would apologise, briefly explain how the situation arose and assure Mrs
    Stevens that it would not happen again. She would also wish to know what to do with
    the unsolicited books (how many?) that she had received. Would Mr Hallam ask her to
    return them or send someone to collect them? Is there a better solution? A suitable
    close is to restate the apology (but using different words from the earlier apology to
    stop it from sounding mechanical).

Assignment

Plan and draft a reply of your own before comparing it with the suggested answer
(which was written by a student).

Suggested answer

```
Instant Publishing Co Ltd
12 Greychurch Lane
London EC2

Tel: 071-79854   Telex: 17963

Ref JRH/LW

5 June 19..

Mrs M A Stevens
27 Lindamere Drive
Orpington
Kent          KT5 7TL


Dear Mrs Stevens

I was most concerned to receive your letter of 1 June informing me of your
attempts to terminate membership with our national book club. I am very
sorry indeed that you have been put to so much trouble.

I have personally looked into the matter and have discovered that another
member with the same name and initials as yours was deleted in error from
our main computer.

However, I can assure you that the matter has now been dealt with and you
will not receive any further communications from us. As a small token of
our apology, I should like to offer you the four books in your possession
with our compliments.

Once more may I say how I regret the inconvenience you have suffered and
hope that this incident will not affect any dealings you may have with our
company in the future.

Yours sincerely



J R Hallam
Sales Director
```

Extracts from real letters

Letter from student on school trip

> Dear Mother,
>   Please write soon if it is only two or three pounds,
>   Love,
>   Clint

Letters to teacher

> Dear Miss
>   Veronica was absent with permission because her sister had a baby. Please thank the Headmaster very much.

> Dear Sir,
>   please excuse John from school today as his father is ill and the pig has to be fed.

Letter of reference

> If you can get him to work for you, you will be most fortunate.

Sales letter

> If you have not yet ordered a copy of this unvaluable book, we suggest you do so without delay.

Letter to DSS

> My mother suffers from a fallen stomach and I am her only means of support.

Example   Circular sales letter

You work for the Sales Manager of Qualbest Confections Limited, a company which manufactures chocolates. To encourage the public to buy its products, the company is planning a nationwide competition. Members of the public will be able to obtain entry forms from retail stockists or, if they wish, by writing to the company for a form. Completed entry forms will have to be posted to Qualbest before a closing date in about three months.

The competition will entail answering various questions and solving simple puzzles. A panel of celebrities will judge all entries. There will be no entry fee; however, every entry will have to be accompanied by a wrapper from a box of the company's chocolates (so that the competition will stimulate sales).

There will be no limit to the number of entries a person may send in. The winner of the competition will be offered a choice of several attractive prizes, each worth over £2 000 (including at least one prize of special appeal to men, one of special appeal to women and one of special appeal to children).

The competition will be widely advertised and retailers will probably need to obtain large additional stocks in order to meet the anticipated demand.

On behalf of your Sales Manager, draft *one* of the following. Select the information you require from the data given (you may invent any appropriate extra details where necessary):

Either

a) Draft a circular letter to all the company's retail stockists, setting out clear and concise details of the forthcoming competition and encouraging retailers to place extra orders for chocolates. Include a brief tear-off slip to allow them to send in their immediate orders.

Or

b) Draft a circular letter to be distributed to thousands of households, setting out clear and concise details of the forthcoming competition and encouraging the public to enter the competition without delay. Include a brief tear-off slip to allow members of the public to apply to Qualbest Confections Limited for an entry form.

LCC PSC June 1979 (30 marks)

Commentary

1   There are occasions when the same letter is sent to a number of people. In this type of letter the name and address of the recipient can be omitted and a generalised term such as 'Dear Customer' or 'Dear Householder' used as the salutation. However, with the advent of the word processor even this letter is being personalised more and more – sometimes with surprising results. Prince Charles recently received a 'mail-shot' special offer letter from a London store where he has an account. It was addressed to 'H R H Prince, Charles' Buckingham Palace, The Mall, London SW1' and began: 'Dear Mr Prince, What would your neighbours think if you pulled up outside Charles' Buckingham Palace in a brand new red Ford Fiesta, complete with sunroof and alloy wheels . . . ?'

2   The retail stockists in (a) will probably be sufficiently interested to read through the letter to the end and respond; the thousands of ordinary people in (b) may need to be stimulated to read on as unsolicited mail is often thrown away after a cursory glance.

3   It is therefore vital in (b) to catch the reader's attention in the first few words – either by a striking heading or a striking opening. Brief paragraphs are then appropriate to create the impression of quick, undemanding reading and the whole letter needs to be lively and engaging.

4   It is necessary to invent incidental details (as the question suggests) in order to generate interest and desire. At the very least the panel of celebrities should be named, the prizes specified and the closing date stated.

5   The tear-off slip should be self-contained and give the firm's name and address in case the original letter is discarded before the slip is returned. It should also be as easy as possible to complete in order to maximise the response. This means space for the name and address of the person returning the slip and a simple statement with space for requesting forms.

Talking point

The suggested answer to (b) that follows was written by a student. Analyse its merits (paying regard to style, organisation, accuracy, invention, use of capitals, etc.) and then write a letter of your own to the retailers.

Suggested answer

Qualbest Confections Limited
103 Bounty Street
Southampton   SO4 3PT

Date as postmark

Dear Customer

LET YOUR SWEET TOOTH GET YOU TO DALLAS!

Would you like the chance to win a super prize worth over £2000? Yes? Well read on!

We are launching a nationwide competition for the whole family. All you have to do is answer a few questions and solve some simple puzzles. What could be easier?

A panel of celebrities consisting of FAITH BROWN, LENNY HENRY and BOB HOLNESS will judge all entries and you could be one of the lucky winners.

And what prizes are in store! Gentlemen, how would you like to wine and dine with the vivacious VICTORIA PRINCIPAL, and ladies, with hunky PATRICK DUFFY? After that you can retire to Southfork, yes SOUTHFORK - because that's where you will be spending two fabulous weeks with your family!

And for the children we've arranged an unforgettable trip to DISNEYLAND! What a prize! And there are plenty more!!

All you need is an entry form which you can get from your local shop or supermarket or from us by returning the slip below. What's more, entries are FREE - all you need is a wrapper from a box of our delicious chocolates with each entry and you can enter as often as you like.

But don't delay. Remember that entry forms have to arrive at our offices no later than 1 October 19.. - so send for one TODAY.

Yours sincerely

Robert Roundtree
Sales Manager
- ✂- - - - -

To: Qualbest Confections Ltd, 103 Bounty Street, Southampton SO4 3PT

Please send me ...... form(s) for the Dallas Competition.

NAME   ....

ADDRESS   ....

          ....

Example **Circular to staff/clients**

You are the secretary to the manager of Comlon Advertising Agency, a London-based company which is planning to open one or two branches in Europe. There will be opportunities for some of the junior staff to transfer to a European branch for a year or two, provided that they fulfil certain conditions. For example, they must either speak French or German reasonably well or be prepared to attend an intensive three-week refresher course at the firm's expense. Furnished accommodation can be provided in apartments at a subsidised rent which is comparable to rents in London.

Your manager asks you to draft the body of a circular letter which will be personalised on a word processor and sent to about 80 junior staff, telling them about the opportunity in Europe and inviting applications for a transfer. Those who successfully complete one or two years in Europe will be well placed for promotion. However, the manager expects there will be reluctance to go.

Be sure to include the basic details necessary, such as the locations of the European branches, the approximate dates when transfers will take effect, any financial concessions, etc. You should also aim to encourage staff to apply. Let them know of any restrictions regarding age, family commitments, health, etc.

To show how your letter would look when actually sent out, include the name and address of a junior member of staff with appropriate salutation, etc.

LCC PSC Dec 1982 (*30 marks*)

Commentary

1   Some circulars aim primarily to inform rather than to sell. For example, a company may write to its clients notifying them of a removal to new premises or a travel agency may write to inform a number of its clients of changes in their travel or hotel arrangements. In such cases there is no need to adopt the 'selling' register of the previous letter; indeed, the sales or persuasive elements are likely to be subdued or non-existent. In the answer to the above question this element will be present only to counter the expected reluctance of the junior staff.

2   The letter that follows was written by a student. Read it and then, before reading the rest of the commentary, make a list of possible improvements. You should consider the display, the order and accuracy of the information, the style, the quality of the English and finally whether the letter is 'mailable'.

```
Manager
Comlon Advertising Agency
London

TA/DE                                    Date as Postmark

Danielle Jackson
43 St. John's Close,
Whitehall,
London.

Dear Danielle,

Our company is gradually expanding in business throughout Europe, which
has now given us the opportunity to open one or two branches in France and
Germany.

        I have decided to give 80 of our junior staff the opportunity to be
transferred over to one of these branches. You will be transferring
during the month of July, 19..
```

Those who are interested in applying for the trip must be able to speak French or German, or attend an intensive three-week refresher course; at the firm's expense. Also may I confess that when I say junior staff, I mean those who are aged 18-25. I would more like those who are single and have no marriage prospects within the next couple of years. Health has also got to be considered, if you have no health problems then you have nothing to worry about.

If you match all the above then you could well be on the way. You are provided with transport, accomodation and facilities all at the firms expense, but your nеɡcessities will have to be encountered on you.

May I also point out that those who successfully complete one or two years in Europe will be well placed for promotion.

Further enquiries please telephone my secretary.

Yours sincerely

Tom Adams
Manager

---

3   The letter is not 'mailable' copy. Some of the more obvious faults are as follows:
   ● The display is poor and it never succeeds in becoming the fully-blocked format with open punctuation that it presumably intends to be.
   ● 'Manager' should not precede the letterhead but a courtesy title should go before the recipient's name. Is the salutation too informal?
   ● The opening paragraph would be improved by the substitution of the more familiar 'we are' for the distant 'our company is' (the writer is after all addressing his employees). Note that the locations of the branches are not given here or elsewhere in the letter – a basic omission. The English is already uncertain – to what does 'which' relate?
   ● The second paragraph seems to suggest that there is the chance for eighty of the staff to transfer. (What is wrong with 'transferred over'?) Danielle might be startled to read that she is apparently being ordered to go.
   ● In the third paragraph is 'trip' the right word? Could the information concerning linguistic fluency be clearer? The style deteriorates at this point, especially with the unnecessary embarrassment over the age restrictions, and basic spelling and punctuation errors are evident.
   ● The fourth paragraph contains more spelling and punctuation mistakes and it ends with a nonsensical statement.
   ● Paragraph five provides the encouragement – but it has been copied word for word from the given information.
   ● The letter fizzles out with an awkwardly expressed 'paragraph' which should contain an extension number and a deadline.

Assignment

Plan and write the letter. A suggested answer is given in Appendix 1.

Example **Letters arranging visits, conferences**

You are secretary to Mrs Phyllis Jack, Customer and Public Relations Director of Comlon International plc (a frozen food company). She has received the following letter:

```
                                        Primrose Cottage
                                        Larkhill
                                        Steepleford
                                        SR1 2LK

                                        1 June 19..

Dear Mrs Jack

I understand that you welcome visitors at your fish-processing factory at
Sandthorp, near Grimsby.

Members of the Larkhill Women's Institute have expressed an interest in an
outing to your factory at some time during the next 3 or 4 months.

We meet weekly on Wednesday afternoons, and we are hoping that a visit can
be arranged during October.

I look forward to receiving your reply.


Jennifer Hughes (Mrs)
Secretary, Larkhill Women's Institute
```

Using the notes below, write a reply for Mrs Jack's signature:

Notes

Maximum group size 30
Facilities for disabled, but regret no guide dogs (food factory)
Tour takes up to 3 hours
Visiting hours 1000–1600
Either Wednesday 21 October or 28 October suitable
Warm clothing advisable
No children please
Guided tour covers whole operation – fresh fish to frozen product
Light refreshments provided (on arrival and departure)
Introductory talk by Production Director (Vernon Lambert) on arrival
Visitors receive discount shopping vouchers and recipe book
Quick reply please – many requests for visit
Estimated number of visitors (approx) and date chosen. Please inform.

LCC SS June 1987

Commentary

1 The notes cover most of the basic data for this type of letter: the date(s), time of arrival and expected time of departure, where the group should assemble, an outline of the programme, the upper limit on numbers (if any) and other restrictions (children/ disabled), the cost (if any), eating and parking arrangements, advice on clothing, etc.

2 In the case of conferences, details of accommodation, conference rooms, private bars and dining rooms, audio-visual aids, exhibition space, special menus, maps, information on travel and the area's facilities may also be required.

3 The given notes are not yet in the correct sequence and a fairly detailed plan is necessary to ensure that the letter reads fluently. Draft a plan of your own before reading the version below.

Dear Mrs Hughes

HEADING?

Para 1   Acknowledge: 'Thank you for your letter . . .'

Para 2   Accept visit: offer alternative dates – give visiting hours – indicate how long tour lasts.

Para 3   Outline programme: introd. talk – guided tour of whole operation ∴ need for warm clothing – light refreshments – gifts on departure.

Para 4   Mention restrictions: maximum group size – facilities for disabled but no guide dogs/children.

Para 5   Request action: quick reply with preferred date, time and approx. number.

Para 6   Close suitably.

Yours sincerely

---

4 Once the outline is clear, an appropriate tone should be considered. Obviously such visits serve a useful PR function and the company would be glad to organise them in order to promote its image and its products. The letter writer should therefore sound genuinely pleased to have received the request. The restrictions should also be mentioned tactfully and not in the manner of these candidates, quoted in the examiner's report:

Children are not allowed.

Dogs are not welcome.

Our food is kept clean – we do not need mucky hands or paws.

Assignment

a) Write the reply to Mrs Hughes for Mrs Jack's signature.   *(40 marks)*

b) Write Mrs Hughes' reply to Mrs Jack, giving her the information requested.
                                                                    (10 marks)

Suggested answers are given in Appendix 1.

Example **Letter of invitation/tactful letter**

Imagine that you are the secretary of a club which is about to hold its annual dinner. You are responsible for the arrangements, including the invitations to speakers. You had persuaded a member to make the speech proposing the health of the guests, but he or she has had to withdraw at a late stage. You must now approach another member of the club, who may possibly know that he or she is not your first choice. Write a letter of about 150–200 words to this member in such persuasive terms that will lead him or her to do as you wish.

RSA EL Stage I May 1980 (*20 marks*)

Talking point

This is obviously a more delicate letter to write than the usual letter of invitation and, like a number of other letters, calls for considerable tact. At the same time basic details need to be conveyed or confirmed – the day, date, time and place of the dinner, and exactly what is expected of the speaker.

The following are three extracts from students' letters. Comment on their persuasiveness, use of English, display and any other points of interest before planning and writing your own letter. A suggested answer follows.

1

```
Dear Member,

Due to the annual dinner I feel that it would be of great dignity for a
member of our club, to make a speech proposing the health of our guest.

This was already arranged by a former member of our club but due to personal
circumstances I regret that we now have nobody to make a speech.

In looking through our members records I came across your name, who I
believe to be very intelligent confident and capable of making a speech.

If you would so like to do so, I would be most grateful to you.

Yours faithfully
```

2

```
Dear Mr. K. Tildesley,

On the 2nd June it will be our clubs annual Dinner and as usual I have been
responsible for invitations to speakers. What I usually do is work my way
down a list from the longest member to the newest so that everyone gets a
turn and this way it makes it fare.

    You may already know that I had chosen Mrs. Chesters to make the speech
this year. Unfortunately she has been taken seriously ill and will be
unable to make it, so as you are next in line I wondered if you would be able
to make that speech by bringing your turn forward a year then Mrs. Chesters
would read next year.
```

3

> Dear Mr. T. F. Timmis,
>
> The National Farmers Union are holding their annual Dinner Dance at the Wayfarer, Leek, on the 2nd June. Our members would be honoured if you would be the Guest Speaker, proposing the health of the guests. Being a most successful Farmer in Staffordshire winning many prizes for beef competitions at the Agricultural shows we could not wish for any one else.
>
> I am sorry I did not contact you sooner but as you probably know Mr. A. Palmer was asked to be our speaker. Unfortunately he is unable to except he was unexpectedly rushed into hospital for tests and it is unknown how long he will be there.
>
> The Farmers Union did not ask you first of all because we did not know you were back from your trip to Canada until last week.
>
> Hoping you will understand the position we are in, and being a respected member of our union we hope you will be able to oblige.
>
>   Yours faithfully...

Suggested answer

> Pickwick Literary Society
> 4 Milton Rise
> Howarth
> Yorks   YO2 1AB
>
> 12 June 19..
>
> Mr Robert Browning
> 11 Scott Place
> Milk Wood
> Yorks   YO2 6MW
>
> Dear Mr Browning
>
> As you know, we are holding our annual dinner at the White Hart on Friday, 20 June at 7.30 pm and we are delighted that you have already accepted our invitation to attend. Most of our members have indicated that they will be present and everyone is looking forward to the occasion.
>
> Unfortunately, at this late stage, we have been faced with a problem that threatens the success of the evening. Mr Pope, who was to have spoken briefly, has been taken ill and will not be able to come.
>
> Several members immediately urged me to invite you to speak in his place. We well remember the evening when you gave a reading of your poems to the Society - certainly the most memorable event of this year's programme - and we feel sure that everyone would enjoy listening to you again.

```
Mr Pope intended to speak for about five minutes and then to propose a toast
to the health of the guests. I do hope that you will be able to accept our
invitation to replace him and I look forward to hearing from you.

Yours sincerely


Virginia Woolf (Mrs)
Secretary
```

Example   **Letter of application**

The following advertisement appeared in a newspaper on 6 June 19… Write a letter in reply to it.

Leaving college? Are you leaving college this summer and wondering what to do? If you have a good educational background with shorthand and typing qualifications, we may be able to help you.

We have many different clients in Publishing, Banking, Advertising, Insurance, Property, Television, Films, Travel Agencies, etc with vacancies both at home and abroad.

For an interview, write telling us about yourself, mentioning any holiday work you have undertaken and the kind of career in which you would be interested.

Address your letter to Jane Johnson at Job Opportunities, 17 Short Street, London W1A 4EB

LCC SS June 1979 (*30 marks*)

Commentary

1   This kind of letter is one of the most important you will ever write. If it impresses the recipient you may get an interview – and perhaps a job. Impeccable presentation, correct English and sound structure are therefore vital.

2   Letters of application may be written in response to a job advertisement or they may be speculative. In the latter case, the letter should indicate clearly the type of work you are seeking, your qualifications and suitability.

3   Some letters are covering letters accompanying an application form or a *curriculum vitae* (a biographical sketch). Their purpose is to introduce the application, mentioning the job title and where it was advertised, and to direct attention to those areas of experience and qualifications that make you a suitable candidate. You should add further details to reinforce your suitability without duplicating what is on the enclosure.

4   A *curriculum vitae* will usually include:
   ● full name, address, telephone number
   ● date of birth, age, nationality, marital status
   ● details of education and qualifications (with dates)
   ● employment record (with dates)
   ● other relevant information (health, courses attended, publications, etc.)
   ● interests
   ● referees (with full title and status).
   An example is given in Figure 1.

CURRICULUM VITAE

NAME	**Erika Joanne STEELE**
ADDRESS	45 Beacon Close Shrewsbury Salop SA7 9TL
TELEPHONE NUMBER	(0743) 928
NATIONALITY	British
DATE OF BIRTH	3 June 1965 AGE 25 years
MARITAL STATUS	Married
EDUCATION	Redland College of Further Education (1983-84) Brierley Sixth Form College (1981-83) Arnold Orme High School (1976-81)
QUALIFICATIONS	Diploma for Personal Assistants RSA Stage III Typing RSA Shorthand (80 wpm) } 1984 RSA Stage II Word Processing GCE 'A' levels in English Literature (B) French (D) } 1983 German (D) 6 GCE 'O' levels 1981
EXPERIENCE	Personal Assistant to General Manager (1987 to date) Walter Wall Carpets Halton Estate Salop Secretary (1984-87) Easy-Does-It Office Equipment Barnes Road Salop
INTERESTS	Horse riding Ballroom dancing Travelling
REFEREES	Ms C Hammersley BA Dip RSA General Manager Walter Wall Carpets Halton Estate Salop Mr E White Sales Manager Easy-Does-It Office Equipment Barnes Road Salop

Figure 1

5   A personnel manager spends about 30 seconds on a *curriculum vitae* before deciding whether or not to reject it. Information must therefore be concise and easy to read. Space, at-a-glance headings and the judicious use of underlining will add impact. Start your career history with your most recent employment and highlight your achievements. It is a good idea to type your CV but handwrite the accompanying letter on matching paper.

6   The full application letter (with no enclosure) is more detailed and will tell the potential employer a lot about you – especially how you select and order information about yourself and make it relevant to the advertised post – in short, how you 'sell yourself' on paper. You may be instructed to 'apply in writing' so that a sample of your handwriting can be seen (and for some jobs analysed by experts – up to 500 British companies are known to employ graphologists to vet job applications).

7   The letter asked for above is to an agency. The advertisement is aimed at college leavers who will probably be looking for their first full-time job. Such applicants need to make the most of their qualifications (without producing long rambling lists) and of any work experience, either as part of the course or of a temporary nature. Convincing reasons rather than vague generalities should also be given for choosing the specified area of work. As a person's interests can be very revealing, they should not be neglected here – but beware of trivia: 'I have a pet rabbit, won at a fair', wrote one exam candidate. As this is not a real letter it would be permissible to invent some of the information to make it as interesting as possible.

Assignment

Write your own letter before reading the suggested answer which is an adapted version of a student's letter.

Suggested answer

```
    'High Green'
    14 Banbury Road
    Oxford      OX2 7DN

    6 June 19..

    Ms Jane Johnson
    Job Opportunities
    17 Short Street
    London      W1A 4EB


    Dear Ms Johnson

    I was very interested to read your advertisement in today's edition of the
    Evening News and I should like to be considered for an interview leading
    towards a position in banking.

    I am seventeen years old. After attending Newman's High School where I
    obtained 6 GCSEs (including English Language and Mathematics), I took a
    secretarial course at Oxford College of Further Education. I shall be
    taking the LCC Secretarial Studies Certificate later this month along with
    RSA Shorthand (80 wpm) and Typing (Stage III).
```

I have recently completed two weeks' work experience at one of the High Street banks. I found the work fascinating, especially as I was allowed to work in different departments within the organisation.

This experience has given me an insight into banking and I believe that it would be the ideal career for me, since I thoroughly enjoy meeting people and have had experience of doing so by working every Saturday (and during the holidays) in a Fruiterer's and Florist's for the past two years. This work has been of great benefit to me. The opportunity of serving the public has given me confidence as well as self-discipline and the chance to work on my own initiative.

My interests also being me into contact with members of the general public. I am a member of the college drama society and have appeared in two plays staged by our local Repertory Theatre. Each month I help to record a 'talking newspaper' for the blind and I occasionally help with the Oxford General Hospital radio service. I enjoy most sports and have recently taken part in a sponsored squash event to raise money for heart research.

My course ends on 20 June and I shall be available to start work from 23 June. If you wish to call me for an interview, I shall be pleased to attend at any time.

Yours sincerely

Karen Holland (Miss)

Exercises

1   Using the list of words given below, fill in the blank spaces in this passage:

semi-blocked	punctuation	name	Sirs
fully-blocked	recipient's	Madam	day
post-code	year	code	month
capitals	space	Street	counties
month	reference	Co.	Road

There are two main forms of letter layout – the _____ and the fully-blocked. The _____ form of layout is often without _____. When you write a personal letter you do not put your _____ at the top of the letter. In a personal letter the _____ address does not have to be included. When letters are addressed to a company the abbreviation _____ may be used. When you are addressing a company you use the salutation Dear _____. If you are writing to a woman who is married or unmarried use Dear _____. When replying to a letter you should quote the correspondent's _____ if one has been used. The best order for writing the date is _____, _____, _____. Never abbreviate the _____ when writing the date. The _____ should be the last item in an address. It should be written in _____ without punctuation, with a _____ between the two halves of the _____. When writing an address the abbreviation for names of _____ may be used but words like _____ and _____ must be written in full.

2 Comment on these extracts from letters composed by students, some of which contain grammatical, (audio) typing or shorthand transcription errors:

A **a)** (*To Lost Property*) I am writing on behalf of a pair of gloves.

b) (*A tactful refusal*) I will be delighted not to attend your exhibition.

c) (*An acknowledgement*) We shall be replying to your letter in the next year or two.

d) (*Letter of confirmation*) Mr Dennis Ford will be your hostess throughout the day.

e) (*From 'Gourmet Enterprises' – a home-catering service*) Although most people enjoy cooking themselves . . . we can provide erotic delicacies. We will discuss your menu with you, then forget it.

f) (*Asking for a reference*) The above-named has applied to us for employment with our subsiding company.

g) (*Staff outing*) We shall see the sights of London floating down the Thames.

h) (*From a travel agent*) Unfortunately, we are not responsible for your spoilt holiday.

i) (*Sales letter*) Our cars come in all the latest styles with manuel or automatic pilot.

j) (*Letter or adjustment*) I therefore apologies for any inconvenience which this has caused and I can assure you that it will happen again.

B **Arranging a conference**

a) We should like to book your Conference Suit.

b) The conference to commence on 22 July opening at 10.00 a.m. to 5.00 p.m.

c) Adequate seating should be provided in the conference room to seat everyone comfortably.

d) Lechers will begin at 10.30 a.m.

e) Audio-visual aids should include an automatic head projector.

f) We should be grateful if you would prepare 80 people for lunch.

g) The menu should cater for all pallets.

h) Main course: roast duke with mussel sprouts or lamb with mink sauce.

i) We would be pleased if you could send us a map and available space for car parking.

j) Hopping to hear from you in the near future.

3 The following letter is composed of fragments of students' work. How many errors can you find? What other improvements would you make?

```
BLOGGS AND BLOGGS LTD
THE PITS BACK OF BEYOND

RU/18

31 September 19..

Messers Carter & Sin
Nowhere in Partic


For the attention of Mr Brian Cartwright

Dear Brain

With reference to the letter recieved off you today.

We are very sorry if you have been mislaid by any action on our part.

As a long-stanking customer, our firm will send you suggestive
designs.

We are able to offer delivery to your whorehouse and your consignment
of cut grass will be despatched immediately. Packaging will be
provided by means of invisible packing cases.

Payment may be made by any major credit card - Access, Bupa, etc.
```

You will find dull details in the enclosed brochure.

Our next Bored Meeting will be holding a revue of our supply network to the Home Countries and we expect to exterminate some contracts.

In the meantime to make an appointment, would your representative please my secretary any afternoon next week.

Assuring you of our inert attention at all times.

Yours for ever

Mr S T Evans
Manger

4 a) Punctuate, paragraph and display the following letter of enquiry:

alderman blackstone comprehensive school dale road durnley near hockton snowshire ho6 4cd 13 june 19.. the manager select sports 47 lower bridge street hockton snowshire ho1 7be dear sir i am interested in finding new suppliers of sports equipment for our school and i saw your advertisement in the hocton bugle as you may know we are a large school with almost 1500 pupils so we use a great deal of sports equipment would you be able to supply this for us and what are your terms at the same time may i ask you to help me in an urgent matter our equipment bag for the first eleven cricket team has been stolen we urgently need six good cricket bats three mens size three harrow size six sets of cricket pads three mens three youths one pair of mens wicket keeping gloves six pairs of batting gloves three mens three youths a scorebook a cricket bag and two sets of stumps and bails we need these by the end of next week we would like good equipment but nothing unnecessarily expensive could you let me know quickly how much these things will cost and when you could deliver them i look forward to hearing from you yours faithfully j p crowe headmaster

b) Assume that you are working as general assistant to Mr Michael Fry, Manager of Select Sports. He says to you:

'We must reply to this letter at once, because this could be very good business for us, and we would welcome regular orders from the school.
'Tell Mr Crowe that he can order at any time, either by letter or by telephone. We will open an account at once, and send a bill at the end of every month. We will give a special discount of 10 per cent on all prices, and will sometimes make special offers. Also, if pupils or staff from the school come to our shop, with identification, we will give them a 10 per cent discount on anything they buy. 'As for the cricket equipment they want, we can supply it. If the school lets us know if the prices are acceptable, by telephone, our delivery van will deliver on any day next week. Look at our price-list and select suitably priced equipment. Do not quote anything which is very expensive. You might add that there will be a special introductory discount, for this order only, of 15 per cent.'

You examine the price list. You find the following:

	Maker	Size	Price
Cricket Bats	Trethowan	Men's	£75 (each)
	Trethowan		
	Test Match	Men's	£85 (each)
	Randall	Men's	£35 (each)
	Randall	Harrow	£30 (each)

Cricket Pads	Ladybird	Men's	£15 (per pair)
	Ladybird	Youths'	£13 (per pair)
Batting Gloves	Bouncerproof	Men's	£35 (per pair)
	Ladybird	Men's	£12 (per pair)
	Ladybird	Youths'	£10 (per pair)
Wicket-keeping Gloves	Ladybird	Men's	£20 (per pair)
Scorebooks	Keepscore	—	£7 (each)
Cricket Bags	Carriwate	Large	£20 (each)
Stumps and Bails	Shatterprufe	—	£15 (per set)

Compose a suitable letter to Mr Crowe, for Mr Fry to sign, using an acceptable format, including Select Sports' name and address, and any other necessary details. Do not attempt any mathematical calculations: just give prices where relevant.

RSA CIB Stage 1 June 1985 (*25 marks*)

5   Your doctor–employer says to you, 'That wall switch is flashing again when you turn it on and off. We really must get the surgery re-wired. Do a letter to Domestic Electrics Ltd – they're at 12 High Street, Stoneford – tell them roughly what the job is. We would want an early inspection, an estimate and, if this is OK, we would want the work completed before the end of the year.'

AMSPAR D Dec 1987 (*20 marks*)

6   Your work for the secretary to the Headmaster, Mr R. Carter, Elmpark Comprehensive School, Highwood Chase, Brighton, BR8 54U. Draft a letter to Mrs Janet Blackwood, a former pupil of the school, who has recently returned from three years' working in schools in Nigeria. She has written a book about her experiences and has become a local celebrity. Mr Carter would like her to talk about her work at the Senior Prizegiving on Friday, 11 December at 2.30 p.m. and to present the prizes to the senior pupils. After the Prizegiving there will be an opportunity for informal chat and refreshments. Mrs Blackwood lives at Flat 32, Grove Court, Brighton, BR9 76T. The letter is for Mr Carter's signature. His reference is RC/HJ.

PEI EB Elementary (*23 marks*)

7   Mr and Mrs R. Sutton, 'Wyngate', King's Lane, Braintree, Essex BR8 76F recently went on a holiday to Jersey organised by Sunway Holidays, 29 The Precinct, Southend-on-Sea, Essex SN8 76T. They were very unhappy with this holiday. Although they went in late September they were given no indication that inferior service would be provided. Much of the menu was out of date and the selection of wines was almost non-existent. Many of the shows and holiday attractions had closed down. The hotel staff were not at all helpful and any query met with the same reply 'It is the end of the season'. Write a letter from Mr and Mrs Sutton to Sunway Holidays expressing their annoyance and asking for some form of compensation.

PEI EBC Elementary (*20 marks*)

8   You work for the Albert Ross Travel Agency of 12 Kingston Highway, Blackburn, Lancashire BN6 4LA. A customer, Mrs Hartley, telephoned to complain about the holiday she recently booked through Albert Ross. In your absence a colleague took the message, notes of which are below:

Mrs A. Hartley rang at 10.15 today. She was wild. She went to Ibiza and the airline sent her bags to Malta. The hotel was full of teenagers who played transistor radios all the time. On their way back there was a strike at the airport and they were sitting on the plane for 12 hours.
As you know, we are not responsible for much of this. We can register a complaint at the hotel. If Mrs H. had paid a supplement for our Three Star Holiday Insurance Scheme, she would have been entitled to compensation for the inconvenience caused by the strike – we have an insurance clause for such events. This does not apply to our ordinary package-holidays scheme. But it may

be that Mrs H. has taken out her own insurance and she should check this. Mrs H. did not tell me which holiday she had taken. The address is 28 Pendle Road, Harwood, Lancs BN9 6LV.

You consult the file and find that Mrs Hartley is not covered by the Three Star Scheme.

Write a suitable letter to Mrs Hartley. Express sympathy but explain the situation and say what action the Albert Ross Travel Agency can take. A suitable answer will probably use between 120 and 180 words exclusive of addresses.

RSA CIB Stage 1 June 1982 (20 marks)

9 You work in the Personnel Department of a firm which, although basically in the food wholesale trade, also owns two medium-sized supermarket retail outlets. The Managing Director comes to you in the absence of the Personnel Manager and asks you to investigate an allegation he has received and to draft a suitable reply for him to send. The situation is as follows:

John Duffy is a well-known local businessman, a prominent councillor and one of the biggest customers on the wholesale side of the business. He also lives near one of the supermarkets where he is known as an arrogant, argumentative, rude and generally unpopular customer. However, staff have been given instructions to be especially tolerant to him. The letter he has sent states that he has never really trusted the firm and that his worst fears were confirmed on a recent visit to the supermarket where he claims to have seen an assistant blatantly pocketing his money after he had paid her. He says that he was so astonished that he could not bring himself to say anything at the time and then launches into an attack on the efficiency of all levels of management for allowing this to happen. He finishes by demanding that everyone involved be prosecuted or his business will be taken elsewhere.

You investigate and find that he had arrived at a checkout just before the assistant was due to leave for lunch. Because of his reputation, she had served him where she would have turned other customers away. In addition, when he arrived, she had been in the middle of a personal transaction, changing a £10 note for ten £1 coins and had put the £10 note into the till but not taken her ten £1 coins out. As his bill had come to £9.05, she had given him 95p from the till and pocketed the ten £1 coins given by him. You are satisfied that no offence has been committed.

Draft your Managing Director's reply to Mr Duffy.

AEB EP&BU June 1983 (20 marks)

10

A Comment on the effectiveness of the following openings to real sales letters:
   a) Congratulations! You have been selected to receive one of the valuable gifts listed below. Provided that you claim the gift in person, subject to the conditions listed below, you will receive one of the following . . .

Timeshare

   b) As you read this someone, somewhere, is being injured in an accident.

   Have you ever stopped to consider how your family would cope financially if *you* were seriously injured? It isn't a subject that most people like to dwell on, but facts must be faced.

Accident Insurance

   c) Wouldn't it be marvellous if someone handed you a Treasure Chest containing £10 000 worth of glittering Gold Sovereigns? Or simply gave you a cheque for £10 000 to spend exactly as you wished?

(A prize draw accompanying a fashion brochure)

   d) The time is right to ring the changes in your home. And our bright new Phones for the Home Catalogue will show you how to do it in style.

British Telecom

   e) Everybody likes a new baby.
   So why not be our guests on the 12 and 13 of September and come and wet its head? The new Mercedes 190.

B   Write the opening paragraph(s) to circular sales letters promoting:
a) a burglar alarm
b) a DIY car manual
c) a local garden centre
d) a life insurance policy
e) a monthly magazine for investors in the stock market

11 You work for Mr Stuart Gardner, Sales Manager (UK) of Regency International. Regency is shortly to launch a Business Class car rental service intended to appeal to executives.

Mr Gardner asks you to compose a sales letter to inform all existing clients of this new service and highlight its main 'selling' points. In conversation with you he says:

- remind them we are the largest car rental company in the UK and one of the largest in the world: we offer a professional and reliable service in contract hire
- announce the new service for the busy executive (don't forget a 'catchy' heading – something like PRESTIGE CARS FOR THE UPWARDLY MOBILE)
- highlight special features
  * all the latest models (manual or automatic)
  * all cars less than 6 months old
  * modified vehicles available for the disabled executive
  * all cars cleaned and safety checked before hire
  * car telephone, electric tinted windows, sunroof, radio
- tell them we offer 24–hour service, unlimited mileage, full insurance, a round-the-clock emergency service from the AA, all at highly competitive rates (daily/weekly/monthly)
- remind them we're so easy to contact: 150 locations nationwide; rail drive at more than 70 InterCity BR stations
- and for the executive abroad don't forget we have 2500 locations in over 100 countries and offices at more than 500 airports
- no deposit, instant credit, all major credit cards accepted or pay by cash, cheque or company account. No hidden extras. The price we quote is the price you pay
- end by urging them to use us – something like 'Rent a car locally and let an international name look after you. Written details on request. 10 per cent off all tariff rates for a limited period.'
- make it readable but don't go 'over the top' – I don't want a lot of words like 'fabulous' scattered all over the place.

12 On 4 February Far & Wide Travel, a firm which arranges package holidays, was informed that the Seaside Hotel at Montego Bay, which was to be used during the forthcoming season, had been badly damaged by a hurricane and would not therefore be available to accommodate their clients.

As secretary to the Sales Manager, prepare a circular letter to be sent to clients who have reserved holidays at this hotel. Explain that a limited number of vacancies are available at other hotels; holiday price unchanged; same amenities and standards, etc; some hotels away from beach; 5 kms from Montego Bay; have swimming pools etc; free transport provided from hotel to coast during holiday; 20 per cent discount given if booked immediately; money refunded; deposits returned.

PEI EBC Advanced (20 marks)

13 You work as an administrative assistant for Amethyst Books Ltd whose head office is at New Century Buildings, Vine Lane, Bristol, Avon BR16 7AJ. The Managing Director is Ms Elizabeth Sibbald.

At a recent monthly meeting of the Forward Planning Committee, concern was expressed about the number of customers who do not pay their bills on time. Customers are sent an invoice when the books are despatched and if payment is not made within a month a further invoice is sent. A further notice is sent after three months' non-payment. It was decided at the meeting that for a trial period personalised letters produced by a word processor would be sent to accompany the one-month and three-month notices.

The idea is that the first letter is a gentle reminder and the second is more of a threat that further action might be taken for the recovery of the debt. You have been asked to produce these letters for Ms Sibbald's signature.

Write two letters to be duplicated using a word processor. One will be sent to those who have not settled their account one month after the despatch of the books purchased and one will be sent if the bill has not been paid after three months. Both will accompany the appropriate invoice.

(**Note:** You can assume the company's headed notepaper will be used, but you should prepare complete letters using an appropriate format.)

RSA CIB Stage II June 1985 (*20 marks*)

14 You are Joan Graves, private secretary to Mr Robert Cammish, Managing Director of Comlon Video, a firm specialising in the manufacture of cine- and video-display equipment. The firm places great emphasis on cordial staff relations, and operates through 36 Area Sales Managers. Mr Cammish is at present on holiday in New Zealand. This morning you found the following recorded message on the telephone answering machine:

'Joan, I've been mixed up in a car crash here – broken both legs and one arm – looks as if I'll be in hospital for at least six weeks.

'I'd like you to arrange the annual conference and training session we planned for the Area Sales Managers during early December. Try the Clifton Hotel on Queen's Parade. Mr Clarence is usually very helpful and his charges are right. Most of them will want overnight accommodation – if they have travelled long distances they'll probably need two nights in town. Make provisional bedroom bookings (to be confirmed later, when you've had their replies) but make a firm booking now for the Queen's Suite and a private dining room and bar. Stress that we shall need exhibition space with plenty of lighting and power points. He has a good 16 mm sound projector (made by Comlon, would you believe it?) that we can use for the training films. We really want to combine the conference with the launch of the new model, the MG 694. Have the models on display on the Tuesday morning.

'We'll give the press a chance to look in. Lay on a sherry reception before lunch – better make it a buffet lunch, it gets them to mix better. The Chairman's promised to take the opening session – "Whither Comlon Video?" – and then said he'll put his head on the block and answer questions. Peter Sawyer (Development Manager) will give them a demonstration and talk about the new model. The new Regional Manager of British Telecom (Forshaw – Bill, I think, but you can make sure) has promised to speak at the Dinner. I expect the Directors will turn out in force for the evening reception and the Dinner. On the Wednesday fit in a sales training session and then we'll show some films and cassettes before lunch. Let them have an Open Forum before they go – find out, will you, if they've particular topics they want to discuss. Don't forget their coffee and tea breaks – we'll settle the menus nearer the date.

'When you've made all these arrangements I'd like you to write a letter to each of the managers – invite them to the conference and enclose a copy of the detailed programme, if you will. Sign these and any other letters on my behalf. By the way I'd like you to be at the conference. Sort out my diary, will you, cancel engagements up to the end of August. I'm sure I can leave it all to you, Joan. Many thanks.'

Write a letter to the hotel, outlining the required arrangements.

LCC PSC June 1982 (*30 marks*)

15 You work in the West Country office of an insurance company. One of your clients, Qualbest Carpet Mill, has inadvertently failed to pay a premium by the due date and now faces a heavy fire loss. Your principal, Mr Trethowan, is at present in Glasgow. He has telephoned you to say that he will visit the client next week. He asks you to write to Qualbest to let them know. They are one of your firm's most important and reputable clients and he will do his best to see that the fire claim is met. You are to mention this in your letter without actually committing your firm to any legal obligation.

Meanwhile, it is essential that the outstanding premium is paid immediately so that the mill is covered against any further fire losses. A loss adjuster from your office will need to visit the mill at the earliest opportunity to make a detailed preliminary inspection (he may also wish to question staff, examine documents and have on-site consultations with senior management) and you should make suitable tentative proposals in your letter.

Using as much of the foregoing data as you need, and inventing any additional minor details as appropriate, write the letter as if ready for posting. No technical knowledge of underwriting, carpet manufacture, etc. is required.

LCC PESD June 1981 (*30 marks*)

16 Brackwith Industries as part of their expansion programme will in the New Year be opening premises on the industrial estate serving Brent Mill, a thriving 'new town' 60 miles from the firm's main factory at Falkington. However, there is at Brent Mill a severe shortage of the various engineering skills vital to the successful running of the new plant. The management of Brackwith are therefore anxious to persuade suitable skilled men, preferably those with families, to remove from the company's employment at Falkington and to settle in Brent Mill. Generous inducements are being offered to those willing to transfer, but the initial response to the firm's overtures has been disappointing.

In order to strengthen their appeal and to counter the natural reluctance of employees and wives to move into strange surroundings the Brackwith management have approached individual skilled men directly and have proposed an organised trip for a party of wives so that the women can see for themselves what the new environment of Brent Mill has to offer.

As his PA, prepare for the personnel manager a first draft of a letter of invitation to be sent individually to wives of selected employees. You should assume that the reader will in general be aware of the circumstances which have given rise to the letter, but should nevertheless underline the financial benefits which will arise from the new job. By careful choice of language and information you should maximise the appeal of Brent Mill without either producing a guidebook or misleading the reader. Only the body of the letter is required. (A suggested answer is given in Appendix 1.)

RSA DPA June 1975 (*15 marks*)

17 Assignment: 'Just the Job'

Learning outcomes
This assignment enables the student to:
a) draft a series of letters relating to a job application
b) compose a CV
c) prepare for and take part in a job interview.

Resources
This can be purely a classroom assignment but it would be immeasurably more valuable if Task 4(e) could be videotaped for later analysis and comment.

Situation
Salamander are a large media and communications group. Among their activities they publish novels, textbooks and music, as well as a number of specialist magazines and journals. They also produce and distribute records, tapes, compact discs and television programmes which are sold to corporations for broadcast in England and overseas.

This enterprising and successful organisation has recently opened a new office in Dryden House, Newtown NT1 5SM, and is now advertising vacancies for Receptionists, Shorthand Typists, Secretaries/PAs, Accounting Staff and Administrative Assistants.

Task 1

You decide to apply for one of the posts. Write to Iris Pemberton, Personnel Manager, at the above address. State why you are applying and why you believe you are a suitable applicant. In addition compose a CV to go with your application.

Task 2

You would like a former course tutor/employer to support your application. Write to that person, giving details of the job and asking if (s)he would act as a referee on your behalf.

Task 3

You expect to be called for an interview.

a) Write a list of the things you would do to prepare yourself for this interview.
b) Formulate five important questions which you think the interviewer might ask you.
c) Formulate three important questions which you might ask the interviewer.

Task 4 Group activity

a) Draw up a shortlist based on the work predicted for Task 1.
b) Write a letter inviting the selected candidates for interview.
c) Write to the referees of the shortlisted candidates, asking how long they have known them and requesting comments on their character, trustworthiness, reliability and punctuality, etc. Give brief details of the job and ask whether they think the candidates are suitable. Assure them that you will treat the matter as confidential and thank them for their co-operation.
d) As the former tutor/employer, write a reference for one of the selected candidates.
e) Interview the shortlisted candidates.
f) Write a letter to the successful candidate, offering the job and confirming such details as starting date, salary and method of payment, etc.
g) Write to the other interviewees, telling them that the post has been filled.

Task 5

As the successful candidate, write a letter of resignation to your present employer.

From a real interview

Interviewer:	Do you have a clean driving licence?
Interviewee:	Yes, I always keep it in a plastic cover.

3 *Memoranda and reports*

From me to you . . .
The Beatles

Memos are used for communication within an organisation. They come in all shapes and sizes – from the brief note to the memo which is several pages long.

The former are straightforward as they consist of only one or two short paragraphs. They are multi-purpose and might, for example, be used for reminding, requesting, briefing or confirming. (*See* pp. 55, 130, 133, 172.)

However, a more substantial memorandum might be required, in which case considerations about how to organise and display the information are important. A useful outline is given below:

MEMORANDUM

To: Mr[1] John Doe   Date: 5 June 19 . .

From: Jane Asher   Ref: JA/MS

Subject: How to compose a memorandum[2]

FIRST SECTION[3]

The opening paragraph is a brief introduction to what the memo is about and why it is being written (with references to any phone-calls, meetings, earlier discussions, etc. that are relevant).

SECOND SECTION

The middle paragraph(s) give(s) the information. Suitable methods of presentation (as illustrated in Figure 2) might include:

1   using headings
2   numbering or listing points for clarity
3   underlining key words for emphasis
4   indenting and spacing to carry impact.

FINAL SECTION (if required)

This last paragraph rounds off the memo, perhaps by pointing to any action that needs to be taken (with deadline as appropriate).[4]

Enc(s)

Copy/Copies to

Notes

1   Some examining boards (such as the RSA and LCC) prefer the courtesy title to be used before the recipient's name.
2   The heading should be brief and precise.
3   There is no need for addresses or salutation.
4   No complimentary close is required and the inclusion of the sender's signature or initials is optional.

MEMORANDUM

TO: ALL STAFF

EXCESSIVE ABSENCE

Due to the excessive number of absences during the past year, it has become necessary to put the following new rules and procedures into operation immediately:

1 **Sickness**

   This is no excuse and the company will no longer accept your doctor's certificate as proof. We believe that if you are able to get to your doctor you are able to attend for work.

2 **Leave of absence for an operation**

   We wish to discourage any thoughts you may have of needing an operation and henceforth no leave of absence will be granted for hospital visits. The company believes that as long as you are an employee here you will need all of whatever you already have and should not consider having any of it removed. We engaged you for your particular job with all your parts and anything removed would mean that we would be getting less than we bargained for.

3 **Visits to the toilets**

   Far too much time is spent in this particular practice. In future the procedure will be that all personnel should go in alphabetical order.

   For example: Those with surnames beginning with the letter A will go from 9.30 to 9.45. B will go from 9.45 to 10.00 etc...

   Note: Those of you who are unable to attend at your appropriate time will have to wait until the next day when your turn comes.

4 **Death (other than your own)**

   This is no excuse. There is nothing you can do for them and henceforth no time off will be allowed for funerals. However, in case this should cause hardship to some of our employees, there are those who might care to note that on your behalf the company has a special scheme in conjunction with the local council for lunch-time burials, thus ensuring that no time is lost from work.

5 **Death (your own)**

   This will be accepted as an excuse. We should like two weeks' notice, however, since we feel that it is your duty to train someone else for your job.

Figure 2 Found on an office notice board

Example

It is 22 June. You work in the Sales Office of Supreme Sewing Machines Limited for Mr Gordon Baxter, Senior Clerical Officer. Your company buys sewing machines from a range of manufacturers and sells them to a variety of retail shops and stores. All the senior staff in your office, including Mr Baxter, are away today at a conference and are due back at about 4.00 p.m.

You are alone at present in the office, 'holding the fort' during the lunch-hour. The telephone has just rung and you have received the following message:

'... I see, well, perhaps you can help me! My name is Jack Simpson, proprietor of Simpson's Sewing Machines, High Street, Kirkford – telephone Kirkford 86742. I've had an order outstanding with you for the past five weeks – my order number SSM 3654. It's for 10 Sew-Rite Junior, 8 Sew-Rite De Luxe and 12 Sew-Rite Stitchmaster sewing machines. I *know* there's a strike or something at Sew-Rite – your representative here keeps telling me so, but I must have the De Luxe and Stitchmaster part of the order within seven days or my customer will go elsewhere. Haven't you got any of these machines in one of your warehouses or somewhere? I may say I spend *thousands* with your firm each year! Look, I've got to go – a customer – now, you won't let me down, will you? Let me know by 4.30. Goodbye now!'

Earlier today the following telex message was received on your office teleprinter:

8965342 SUPREME SEWING MACHINES LIMITED 22-6-79 1045 INDUSTRIAL DISPUTE SETTLED 0930 TODAY DELIVERIES TO YOUR CENTRAL STORES GUARANTEED AS FOLLOWS

JUNIOR   25 JUNE
DE LUXE   26 JUNE
STITCHMASTER   30 JUNE

ALL ORDERS DEALT WITH IN STRICT SEQUENCE OF RECEIPT AT OUR MOORBRIDGE ORDERS DEPARTMENT

SEW-RITE SEWING-MACHINES LIMITED
MOORBRIDGE WORKS BIRMINGHAM 4

The daily computer print-out of your Central Stores stock position included the following information:

SEWING MACHINES IN STOCK		22 JUNE
TYPE	QUANTITY	CODE
PRINCESS MANUAL	246	PM/124
PRINCESS ELECTRIC	142	PE/125
REGAL MODERNE	53	RM/237
REGAL ULTIMA	26	RU/238
SEW-RITE JUNIOR	NIL	SRJ/146
SEW-RITE DE LUXE	NIL	SRDL/147
SEW-RITE STITCHMASTER	15	SRST/148

You are due to leave the Sales Office at 3.30 p.m. to deliver some urgent documents. Compose a memorandum to Mr Baxter in not more than 160 words informing him of Mr Simpson's problem and stating clearly the information you think Mr Baxter needs.

RSA CIB Stage I June 1979 (*25 marks*)

Commentary

1   The memo needs to be self-explanatory as you will not be there to answer any queries when Mr Baxter returns. A word limit is imposed to stop examinees from simply

copying out the telex message and computer print-out – intelligent interpretation of them is called for.

2   Following the outline given above, the rough plan of an answer would look something like this:

Subject Order No

FIRST SECTION

Refer to Mr Simpson's phone call, giving details of his order and problem.

SECOND SECTION

Solution

1   to Stitchmasters – refer to stock position
2   to other machines – refer to telex

THIRD SECTION

Action required: Ask Mr B to ring Mr S – give number and mention deadline.

Assignment

Write the memo before reading the suggested answer below.

Suggested answer

MEMORANDUM

To: Mr G Baxter   Date: 22 June 19..
From: Hilda Bourne   Ref: HB/SSM

URGENT: ORDER NUMBER SSM 3654

Mr Simpson (Simpson's Sewing Machines, High Street, Kirkford) rang for information about the above order, placed five weeks ago, for 10 Junior, 8 De Luxe and 12 Stitchmaster machines. He must receive delivery of the De Luxe and Stitchmaster models by 29 June or lose his customer.

Solution

1   Today's computer print-out shows that although there are no Junior or De Luxe in stock, there is a sufficient number of Stitchmasters (code SRST/ 148) which could be despatched immediately.

2   A telex from Sew-Rite received today told us that the strike is over and that deliveries of Junior and De Luxe models will definitely reach our Central Stores by 25 and 26 June respectively. Therefore the rest of the order can be sent out before Mr Simpson's deadline.

Action

Mr Simpson has to be informed of the position by 4.30 pm today. Would you please ring him on Kirkford 86742.

Reports

Reports vary in length and status from simple printed forms (such as accident reports – *see* p. 89) to the major investigative reports commissioned by governments. A notable example of the latter was the report of the Warren Commission, whose terms of reference were 'to ascertain, evaluate, and report upon the facts relating to the assassination of the late President John F Kennedy' (Executive Order 11130). When the report was published in 1964 it was 888 pages long and was accompanied by 26 volumes of supplementary evidence. Despite such apparent thoroughness, there have been critics of the report and its method of investigation ever since and many of its principal conclusions have been challenged.

Thankfully, exam candidates have nothing so momentous or extensive to deal with; nevertheless, they still regard a question asking for a short report as 'difficult'. Part of the problem lies in their fear of choosing the wrong format – is it a *formal* or *informal* report? Their error is in trying to impose a rigid (and often inappropriate) framework on the material instead of letting the material dictate the best pattern for that particular report. There is no fixed structure – although most reports benefit by having a beginning, a middle and an end. The more flexible the approach, the easier this question should become. At the end of the day (or exam), if the report follows the given instructions and conveys the information effectively, it is a good report, irrespective of the format chosen.

The remainder of this chapter will discuss some of the short report formats at your disposal.

Short informal report

This is basically a two- or three-section report and the following outline can be adapted to the material or situation with which you are dealing. Alternative headings are suggested, but these can be omitted or replaced by any that you feel are more appropriate for your particular report.

CONFIDENTIAL[1]

To:[2]

TITLE

INTRODUCTION/BACKGROUND/SITUATION

This section briefly outlines the reason for the report, perhaps by referring to what the writer was asked to do and by whom, and sometimes indicating how the material was obtained.

INFORMATION/FINDINGS/OUTLINE OF PROBLEM

Unless the material can be conveyed in a simple paragraph or two, one of the following methods of presentation should be considered:

1   Heading
    This method details all the information that has been gathered under suitably headed paragraphs.[3]

2   Heading
    2.1   This alternative method may be used.
    2.2   Each headed section consists of separate numbered sentences.
    2.3   It is most useful when the report is simply to bring someone up to date by providing the latest information.[4]

CONCLUSIONS/RECOMMENDATIONS/ACTION
If the writer was asked for conclusions/recommendations, (s)he now
lists them. Alternatively, (s)he may point to any further action that is
thought necessary.

Name
Position

Date

Notes
1 Delicate or sensitive material may require a suitable classification.
2 Some exam questions ask for a memorandum report in which case the memo headings (To, From, Date, Ref) should be used. Any short internal report may be presented in memorandum form.
3 Refer to any supplementary material such as maps, plans, price lists, at the appropriate point in the body of the report – e.g. (see Appendix A).
4 An information report of this kind may well end after this section.

Example

You are employed as Senior Accounts Clerk in the Accounts Department of the Brunswick Trading Company plc which supplies office equipment.

Your superior, Mr Blunt, the Accounts Office Manager, receives a complaint from one of your firm's regular customers, UK Carriers plc, Timperley Street, Manchester M12 7SL. They inform him that they have received a statement indicating that payment of their account is overdue and that settlement must be made immediately. The amount stated to be outstanding is £1300.60. According to the customer a cheque for this amount was paid on 23 February but acknowledgement of receipt was not received.

You receive the following memorandum from Mr Blunt:

BTC

MEMORANDUM

```
To:      YOU, Senior Accounts Clerk          Date:   21 March
From:    I M Blunt, Accounts Office Manager   Ref:    IMB/85/19

Customer Complaint
UK Carriers plc, Timperley Street, Manchester M12 7SL have written to me
complaining that they have received a statement indicating that payment of
the sum of £1300.60 is overdue. They assure me that this account was
settled on 23 February but they did not receive acknowledgement of payment.
Please thoroughly investigate the above complaint and
    1  Write a short informal report
    2  Write an appropriate letter to UK Carriers based upon the results of
       your investigations

Thank you    IB
```

Your investigations reveal that an incorrect ledger entry was made on 26 February. Payment of £1300.60 was actually credited to the account of UK Airways plc. February was a month in which there was staff turnover in the office.

Write your report to Mr Blunt.

AAT P Pilot 1985 (20 marks)

Assignment

Write the report before reading the suggested answer below.

Suggested answer

To: Mr I M Blunt, Accounts Office Manager

REPORT ON CUSTOMER COMPLAINT: UK CARRIERS PLC

BACKGROUND

I have thoroughly investigated the above complaint as you requested in your memo of 21 March. I spoke to all the accounts clerks and checked the ledgers relevant to this account. I also checked the accounts of companies with a similar name.

FINDINGS

A cheque for £1300.60 was received on 23 February from UK Carriers plc. However, on 26 February this was wrongly credited to the account of UK Airways plc and a receipt issued to them. The error almost certainly arose as a result of the increase in staff turnover during February which placed all employees under considerable pressure.

ACTION TAKEN

1   I have amended the accounts of the two companies concerned and written a letter of apology to UK Carriers plc (copy attached).
2   I have notified UK Airways of the wrongly issued receipt which I have cancelled.
3   I have sent a memo to all our accounts clerks bringing this type of error to their attention to avoid any future repetition.

Your Name
Senior Accounts Clerk

22 March 19..

Enc

Example

Prepare for the Sales Director a brief report on each of *two* contrasting short-listed candidates for the post of Personal Assistant, summarising their business experience, personal qualities and qualifications.

RSA DPA June 1973

Commentary

1 A memorandum report is perfectly suitable for this situation.
2 The report should have ease of reference for a busy executive with the information given under headings (which can be drawn from the question).
3 The 'two contrasting short-listed candidates' should be named and their particular strengths and weaknesses outlined. Obviously, to depict one as a model of excellence and the other as Dopey Alice would be unrealistic: to be on the short-list either would be potentially suitable.
4 Two approaches are acceptable: the writer can imagine either that the report precedes the interviews (when it will be based on the candidates' applications and the opinions of their referees) or that it follows the interviews (in which case it will also include impressions gained of the applicants during the interview). In the latter case, a final paragraph offering some guidance as to the more suitable candidate would be helpful and expected.

Assignment

Prepare a report of your own before reading the suggested answer in Appendix 1.

Short formal report

This is basically a five-section report which is suitable for more complex and important investigations that are to be reported to senior management. Unless it is specifically requested or obviously required, it is perhaps best avoided in exams because of its rigid structure and the pretentiously formal impression it can create.

The following outline should show that this format would have been far less appropriate for the two previous reports:

To:

TITLE

1 **TERMS OF REFERENCE/INTRODUCTION**
This section outlines what the writer was asked to do, by whom and by what date.

2 **PROCEDURE/ACTION TAKEN**
The steps taken to carry out the instructions are listed. They may include interviewing people, visiting places or sites, watching machinery in operation, etc.

3 **FINDINGS**
This is the core of the report where all the information is suitably presented (e.g. by using sub-headings and numbered points).

4 **CONCLUSIONS**
The main deductions from the above information are made.

5 **RECOMMENDATIONS (if required)**
If the writer was asked for 'suggestions' will (s)he now make them.

Name
Position

Date

Note
The style of a formal report is less relaxed than that of the informal. Familiar, colloquial language should be avoided and impersonal constructions are preferred – so instead of 'I spoke to all the accounts clerks' (informal) use the passive construction 'All the accounts clerks were consulted' (formal).

Example

You are a member of the Qualbest Music Society, a large amateur group which gives about three public concerts each year, usually in a local school or church hall. It used to enjoy strong local support. During the last eighteen months the attendance figures for its four concerts have been:

300 (full house)   240   190   130

It has been suggested that there are several possible reasons for these declining attendance figures. For example, the type of music performed may not appeal to popular taste; the standard of playing may have fallen; rehearsal time may be inadequate; the arrangement whereby each member of the Society tries to sell a small number of tickets may not be working well; publicity may be at fault; seat prices may be too high.

The Chairman of the Society, to which you have recently been appointed secretary, has asked you, together with two other members, to look into the problem carefully and to let her have a formal report, incorporating any helpful suggestions you may wish to put forward.

Prepare a suitable report ready for submission. You should use any of the data given above which you think suitable and may invent any other minor details as required. No special knowledge of amateur music-making is expected.

LCC PSC Dec 1980 (30 marks)

Commentary

1   A formal report is explicitly asked for as an investigation needs to be carried out on which the very existence of the Society could depend. Recommendations are also required.
2   It is obvious from the given information concerning rehearsals and ticket sales that members of the Society will have to be interviewed; equally the opinion of members of the general public will have to be sought on the question of the music's appeal, seat prices and publicity (through a survey or questionnaire?).
3   The brief set of statistics given in the question is an important finding and should not be omitted. A tabular array of the attendance figures might be considered with dates and some indication of the type of music performed on those occasions.
4   Recommendations should follow logically from the findings and conclusions – for example, if seat prices are too high you could suggest that special discounts (for senior citizens, students, the unemployed) should be introduced.

Assignment

Write the report before reading the suggested answer that follows.

Suggested answer

QUALBEST MUSIC SOCIETY

To: Mrs Eleanor Rigby, Chairman

REPORT ON DECLINING ATTENDANCES

1 TERMS OF REFERENCE

On 11 November you asked us to investigate the causes of declining support for the Society's concerts and to submit a report with recommendations by 1 December.

2 PROCEDURE

2.1 The attendance figures for the last 18 months were obtained.
2.2 Members of the Society were interviewed.
2.3 A survey was conducted in Qualbest on Saturday, 25 November.
2.4 A questionnaire was sent to 150 local residents who were known to have supported the Society in the past (*see* Appendix).

3 FINDINGS

3.1 Attendance Figures

The figures for the last four concerts were as follows:

May	19..	Music in Maytime	300*
Dec	19..	Christmas Concert	240
June	19..	Summer Extravaganza	190
Nov	19..	Electronic Sound	130

*Full house

3.2 Performances

3.2.1 Members of the Society feel that rehearsal times are inadequate and that consequently the quality of their playing has suffered - a view echoed by local opinion.
3.2.2 The type of music performed recently has been too experimental for general taste.

3.3 Ticket Sales/Publicity

3.3.1 The system for selling tickets is not working: tickets reach members so late that it is proving difficult to dispose of them.
3.3.2 Members of the public have been deterred by the increases in seat prices in June and November.
3.3.3 Advance publicity has been neglected.

4 CONCLUSIONS

Attendance figures show a serious and rapid decline as a result of high seat prices, poor publicity and concern at the type and quality of the music performed. Failure to rectify the situation may lead to the end of the Society.

5   RECOMMENDATIONS

5.1   More rehearsal time should be allotted so that the former high
      standard of performance is restored.

5.2   A more balanced programme should be introduced.

5.3   Tickets should be made available to members at least one month
      before each concert; sales outlets in Qualbest should also be
      explored.

5.4   Special discounts should be introduced for students, senior
      citizens, the unemployed and those who buy a ticket for all three
      concerts.

5.5   Concerts should be well publicised in the local press and on local
      radio; car-stickers, posters in public places (libraries,
      theatres) and circulars to householders should also be
      considered.

Margaret Barnett
Brenda Coldham
Ian Wright

30 November 19..

Appendix: Questionnaire

Exercises

1   Using the words supplied at the bottom of the question fill in the blank spaces:
Within a business _____ are the equivalent of _____ sent to people outside.
They are in fact _____ correspondence. They are usually written or _____ on
specially _____ forms which are often of _____ size. Memoranda should be as
short as possible. There are many variations in the _____ of a memorandum but
there are some _____ items that must appear. The word _____ sometimes
abbreviated _____ always appears at the top of the form. The space where the
names and titles of the _____ and _____ are to be written are indicated by the
words _____ and _____. The word _____ is followed by the space in which
the date is written. If a _____ is included it is written in the space indicated by the
abbreviation _____. The word _____ indicates that a title or heading is needed.
As memoranda are used for internal correspondence there is no need for a _____ or
_____.

Memoranda	Letters	Salutation	Reference	To
From	Memo	Typed	Printed	A5
Internal	Subject	Ref	Recipient	Complimentary close
Sender	Important	Memorandum	Date	Layout

PEI EBC Elementary (*20 marks*)

2   Write a memorandum from the Personnel Officer, Mr I Grant, of the Smartweave Basket
Company to all Accounts Department Staff telling them that on Monday, 1 September
Miss Susan Hull, a disabled young lady, will be joining them. She is confined to a
wheelchair, but has been educated at an ordinary school and has left with very good
academic qualifications. Suggest that their help might be needed from time to time, but
tact will be necessary as Susan likes to be as independent as possible.

PEI EBC Elementary (*20 marks*)

3   As secretary to a Hospital Administrator, compose a memorandum for distribution to Heads of Department, reminding them of safety regulations in general and that fire doors must be kept closed, but never locked.

AMSPAR D December 1983 (*10 marks*)

4   Assume that you are private secretary to Mrs D Lambourne, personnel manager of Reliable Insurance Company Limited. The company has recently decided to introduce an anti-influenza vaccination service for its staff and is keen to see the scheme accepted as a means of combating staff absences during winter months. Today's date is 12 June 19...

Mrs Lambourne has asked you to compose a memorandum for her to send to all staff informing them of the new scheme and what they should do if they wish to take advantage of it. She has passed you her rough notes to assist you:

> anyone wishing to have an 'anti-flu jab' – see me by 23rd Aug.
> scheme to be introduced on 1st Sept.
> staff unable to see doctor at company – must make own arrangements with his receptionist.
> company reckons over 2,000 working hours lost in last year's flu epidemic.
> Dr Jenkins visiting company offices each Wednesday in Sept – 11·30 to 12·30.
> staff don't have to join scheme.
> vaccination not foolproof – too many different types of influenza – but does cut down risk.
> scheme free to all staff.
> further info from me including checking procedures in case of allergy to vaccine.

Write the memorandum for Mrs Lambourne, using a layout with which you are familiar. The memorandum's message should not exceed 120 words.

RSA CIB Stage I June 1978 (*20 marks*)

5   It has been established practice for all staff within your company to be granted use of the company switchboard to make personal telephone calls. The procedure laid down by the company has been:

- identify name and extension number
- state personal nature of call
- state number they wish to call.

This information is recorded in a notebook by the switchboard operator, and this record is forwarded daily to the Accounts Office. It is *your* responsibility as Senior Accounts Clerk to make out monthly Personal Telephone Accounts for staff which are then forwarded to those staff concerned by internal mail.

Recently you have made the following observations:

- The switchboard operator maintains that some Stores staff do not state the personal nature of their calls despite the fact that the same numbers are regularly called by the same persons. As the calls have not been identified as 'personal' staff are not liable to be charged.
- Despite bills being repeatedly presented an increasing number of staff are not paying them.
- The overall volume of personal calls is increasing.

You approach your superior, Mr Blunt, about these matters and tell him of your observations. He tells you to:

- immediately circulate staff with an appropriate memorandum to try to resolve the problems
- suggest, in memorandum form, what action could be taken (with reasons clearly stated) if the situation does not improve by the end of the next month.

a) Write the circular to all staff. *(15 marks)*

b) Write the memorandum to Mr Blunt outlining what action could be taken. *(15 marks)*

AAT P Pilot 1985

6   Using the notes below write a report to the Export Sales Manager outlining the ways in which the installation of telex could help to overcome the problems in his Department:

Telex messages typed – carbon copy kept for filing – conformation unecessary;

no difficulties hearing as with some telephone calls;

increasing number of firms now using telex machine – can be left unattended, but switched on to receive messages 24 hours; messages can be sent at any time, often by direct dialling;

present typists could be trained to operate machine;

costs of installation and annual rental probably less than wages of any additional staff; cost of calls probably offset by increased efficiency and additional business; suggest detailed investigation.

PEI EBC Intermediate *(26 marks)*

7   Assume that you work in the office of Sundale Office Supplies Co. Ltd of Southampton. You have been there for two years and have recently been promoted to the post of assistant to Mr Raymond Kelsey who is Sales Director and, as such, in charge of the administration.

In the past the office has been virtually in one large open-plan room but, with the expansion of the company, it will now be possible for an area of up to twice the present size to be used, perhaps divided by partitions of some kind. It will be Mr Kelsey's task to make the final decisions but, knowing that you have worked in the office for some time and will have seen both the advantages and disadvantages of the present system 'from the inside', he thinks you may have some helpful ideas.

'Obviously we don't want to waste money on unnecessary work,' he says to you one morning, 'but the advantages of some privacy and of being able to interview clients and more junior staff are clear. Nevertheless I can see difficulties. I can imagine young Dawn Nokes in the typing-pool doing only half the work if she isn't under someone's eye, and, more seriously, real problems of communication arising. After all we have four supervisors, nine typists and eight general clerks. The clerks, as you know, do everything from operating the switchboard to selling on the trade counter. Now, you are familiar with the situation here. I expect you can see it from the aspect of the general efficiency of the office. Would you please let me have an informal report detailing some points that I should consider when making my decision on how to partition the office – if at all?'

Write the report requested by Mr Kelsey using a format with which you are familiar. It should not exceed 150 words.

RSA CIB Stage II June 1980 *(20 marks)*

8 You work as Private Secretary to Mrs V. Chalmers, the Personnel Director of Comlon International plc. Over the past three months she has become concerned at increasing evidence of petty pilfering and what appear to be small but deliberate acts of vandalism in the company. During a long meeting with her this morning you took the following notes:

Things taken: staplers, stationery (whole reams!), filing wallets, 2 pocket cassette dictation machines (£40 each), several purses, leather coat from cloakroom, etc. Mainly small items. Staff too careless?

Building very open: easy access to and from production and office areas. Too easy for public to enter building? A lot of new (mainly young) staff on work experience programmes. Difficult to recognise all new faces. No evidence of intruders breaking into building. Check personal files for evidence of criminal record? Unlikely to reveal anything (all staff checked on appointment).

Damage done: nothing major, but worrying and annoying. Graffiti in cloakrooms and lifts. Machinery/equipment suddenly discovered not working. No apparent reason. Unlikely to be accidental – happening too often. Staff carelessness?

Staff morale: difficult to assess. Recent compulsory redeployment upset many. Little union opposition – staff resented this. Staff clearly more tense than last year. Noticeable increase in absenteeism and complaints about working conditions, etc.

Action: dangerous to over-react at this stage. MD wants matter discussed at next Directors' meeting*. FAIRLY HIGH PRIORITY. Prepare brief report *to be issued only at meeting* (except advance copy to MD). Explain situation so far. Need for senior staff to be more alert in noting misbehaviour, anything suspicious, increase in complaints, etc. Tighter checks on locking removables away. Notices in all working areas warning staff of risk of personal accidents from damaged equipment, need to report all damage immediately etc. Ask for advice/information from all senior staff.

*18 July

a) Prepare the report mentioned at the end of your notes for Mrs Chalmers to submit to the next Directors' meeting.   *(30 marks)*

b) Prepare a brief memorandum to send to the Secretary of the Directors' meeting arranging for the item to be placed on the agenda. Send the Managing Director's copy of the report with this memorandum.   *(10 marks)*

Note: You can assume that the Secretary of the MD acts as Secretary to the Directors' meeting.   LCC PSC June 1985 *(Total: 40 marks)*

9 You work as Accounts Supervisor in the Accounts Department of Matthewson Taylor, a large publishing group. Immediately after lunch on Thursday, 3 December 19 . ., Balvinder Rai, the Financial Accountant, enters your office. Although he is not someone who is easily worried by problems at work he looks worried as he walks in. He closes your office door and asks if he can speak with you in confidence. After he has reminded you that Mary Ho, the Junior Accounting Technician, joined the Accounts Department in August this year and that shortly after that she took part in the group's induction programme, he pauses. After a few minutes he says what has been troubling him. Reports have been fed back to him that, quite frankly, Mary is not pulling her weight.

Balvinder explains the nature of the reports he has received about Mary. Harry Smith, the group's Head of Personnel, has produced a written report about her, expressing his reservations. Although she attended all the sessions in the induction programme he felt that she was less than enthusiastic about these sessions and often appeared distracted. Matthewson Taylor do not like to unsettle new employees by requiring them to take on all their duties immediately they start working for the group. Rather they prefer to have them work closely with a number of key employees in their department until they are sufficiently settled in to take up all their duties. Mary has been working with Margaret Korn, the Wages Supervisor, and Grace Philips, the Credit Control Clerk. They are both long-serving employees who have significant experience of assisting young new employees in their first days with the Accounts Department. They have indicated to Balvinder that they felt Mary was not progressing in her new job.

While they were happy to have her observe them in the performance of their duties in the initial period she was with them, they were not happy with the way in which she did not begin to take on more responsibility. Finally, Mary's apparent lack of understanding of the duties she is expected to perform has caused her to express her frustration in the form of emotional outbursts.

All in all this is clearly not a happy situation. Balvinder explains that he has a number of problems here. He says that he feels guilty that news of Mary's unsatisfactory performance had not come to his notice earlier. He thinks that if he were to approach Mary she might well feel he was disciplining her and that she could resign on the spot. He would be unhappy to have this happen given the time, money and energy which the group had already expended on Mary. But he does feel that some form of action needs to be taken to remedy this situation. You pause for a moment and then speak. You feel it would be better if you were to speak with Mary and try to find out the reasons for her lack of enthusiasm. Balvinder readily agrees to your suggestion and asks you if you would do what you propose.

Later that afternoon you call Mary into your office. You explain, in a diplomatic fashion, the nature of the reports which have been made about her behaviour. Once Mary understands what it is you are talking about she makes a half-hearted attempt to excuse herself but then breaks down in tears. You reassure her and once she has calmed down, ask her what the matter is. She explains that she has been distracted by a number of long-running problems of a domestic nature at home, that she has been struggling in her work as a result of this, but that she feels the problems at home have now been resolved. By the time you conclude your interview with Mary you are convinced that she is genuine in her stating that her problems are now over and are persuaded by her promising to commit herself to the efficient performance of her duties at work. After Mary has left your office you go to Balvinder's office. You explain what has taken place. He is grateful that matters appear to have been resolved but asks you to do two things for him. Firstly he asks you to produce a written report containing full details of the incident. Secondly, as this matter cannot pass without some formal comment, he asks you to produce the draft of a letter, written on his behalf, to Mary stating that he is pleased that she is now determined to commit herself to her job but that she will have to be closely monitored in the near future to ensure that she does not fall back into her old ways. You go back to your office to produce these two documents.

Write the detailed report about this incident. You must include background information about Mary's poor performance, an account of the interview you conducted with Mary and an explanation of the action you took.   (20 marks)

Write the draft letter to Mary thanking her for her promise to commit herself to her job but warning her that her work will be closely monitored for the next few months.

AAT P Dec 1987 (20 marks)

10   You are personal assistant to Philip Grant, Director of Comlon International plc, and his responsibilities include Reclamations and Small Works. Mr Grant has followed discussions concerning the building of specialised accommodation for the elderly with interest. He believes that such a development could be a part of the 'Docklands Redevelopment' scheme currently planned for the town of Shieldport.

A large proportion of Comlon staff is reaching retirement age and Mr Grant has collaborated with the Director of Personnel to provide a staff conference on this issue. The venue will be the Royal Hotel, which is situated next to the Docklands area under development in Shieldport.

All Comlon employees who are soon to reach retirement age have been invited, and those who have accepted the invitation will arrive at the hotel on the evening of 17 June. Mr Grant, Mrs Forbes and several other members of Comlon staff will welcome people as they arrive. Dinner will be provided. The main conference sessions will take place on 18 and 19 June, and a number of specialist speakers have been invited. These include a medical practitioner specialising in the Health of the Elderly, the Comlon Chief Accountant – who will speak on Pensions and Related Issues, the Principal of an Adult Education Centre, a nutritionist from the local hospital and the Bishop of Shieldport, who will close the conference after tea on 19 June. Some speakers will give formal talks to the assembled group, but most sessions will have informal discussion in small groups.

The keynote speech on the morning of 19 June will be given by Dr H Burton-Wood OBE, Chairman of ACE ('Action and Care for the Elderly'), a national charity which, among other things, provides sheltered accommodation for the elderly. After lunch Mr Grant and Dr Burton-Wood will visit the Docklands site to consider its suitability for sheltered housing provision. Mr Grant hopes to gain much useful information on housing and other needs of the elderly from the conference.

You have been responsible for making most of the detailed arrangements for the conference which is now only one week away. Using a format with which you are familiar, prepare a report for Mr Grant listing these arrangements. (A suggested answer is given in Appendix 1.)

LCC PESD June 1987 (30 marks)

11 You are personal assistant to Mr R. W. Wayland, managing director of a firm employing four senior secretaries and eleven other secretaries in its head office situated on five floors of a high-rise building. Following a lunchtime discussion with two of the senior secretaries you have asked Mr Wayland to agree to the holding of a half-day internal secretarial seminar next September. The idea is that as many of the firm's secretaries as possible will meet to hear common work interests and problems outlined, to discuss methods of reducing such problems, to broaden their understanding of the firm's internal functioning and, in the longer term, to enhance their own efficiency.

Mr Wayland is somewhat unsympathetic to your plan but grudgingly agrees to consider it further if you will

a) measure the degree of support for the seminar among the secretaries and those for whom they work,

b) explain to his satisfaction how essential office services can be maintained during the seminar, or at least how disruption can be minimised,

c) justify the seminar in terms of benefits to the firm.

  i) Explain concisely how you would complete task a) economically. Explain also why other ways of collecting this information are unsuitable. *(5 marks)*

  ii) In about 300 words write an informal report for Mr Wayland, tabulating your findings for task a) and meeting his other stated requirements. *(15 marks)*

RSA DPA June 1981

12 You work as personal assistant to Mr Michael Chalmers, Managing Director of Enamellon Utensils Limited, a small company manufacturing a range of cooking utensils which it sells to wholesalers and chain stores in the UK and in a growing export market. The company's factory is situated at 196–8 Surrey Road, Exwell, London EW3 6SR. The factory employs 50 skilled, 100 semi-skilled and 200 unskilled employees, while its adjacent offices employ 38 administrative personnel.

The company's products are being sold in increasingly competitive markets, so any cost-savings would be welcome. At present, some 60 per cent of UK sales are made to customers located south of the line from Bristol to the Wash.

This morning, Mr Chalmers called you into his office and had this to say:

'As you know, our lease on the Surrey Road premises comes up for renewal in six months' time. Preliminary negotiations have confirmed that we shall find it difficult to meet the expected increase in rent without shedding factory and administrative staff, which could seriously affect sales.

'I've had another look at the Winsfield Estate prospectus. Winsfield's about 20 miles from the major port of Mereport and some five miles from the M58 motorway spur. The area is in the North West and so qualifies for government development aid, and it looks as though we could save up to 25 per cent of our manufacturing and administrative costs by moving up there. The area is one of higher than national average unemployment and is traditionally trade-union conscious – something we've not much experience of.

'At present there's not enough office accommodation on the site, but there's plenty of land included with the factory. The trouble is, we couldn't wait for buildings to be put up.

'If we *did* decide to move, lock, stock and barrel, the whole thing would need to be handled carefully. I'd certainly like to take our skilled people with us at the very least, but you can't just uproot people at the drop of a hat. In any case, the office staff could probably find something similar round here if they had to.

'Now this is what I'd like you to do. Get up to Winsfield and have a look round. See what you think of the possibilities. Weigh up our present situation as it obtains here. Then I want you to write a report for me outlining the pros and cons and supplying your own recommendations. I've a Board Meeting in a fortnight and I'd like another view of the subject, reached independently, before any initial discussions. I'll need to have your report on my desk in a week's time.'

Compose a report, based on the above information, but including any additional material you consider appropriate, to meet Mr Chalmer's requirements. Your report should not exceed 500 words.

RSA DPA June 1980 (*25 marks*)

4 Miscellany

Advertising

> **Divorcee aged 38 seeks gent with car. Has own house, old banger and child. Blonde, rather chubby – likes dining out. Only gentlemen with pensionable positions, please. Send photo and address to Box 967.**

How would *you* sell yourself? It's not only in interviews that this happens, for some people (the 'lonely hearts') do advertise themselves through the personal columns of newspapers. Sometimes they manage it with humour and originality without giving a self-description that might offend against the Trade Descriptions Act. The above advertisement actually appeared as:

> **ROMANTIC Divorcee aged 38. Still dreaming of Knight in Shining Armour. Charger need not be white, but prefer it paid for. This damsel in distress has own castle, aged steed and heir. Tresses are long and golden, though slightly rounded form – have a love of banquets. Only heroes on pensionable crusades. Send likeness and turret number to Box 967.**

Even in the classified columns where display possibilities are virtually non-existent, the key word 'ROMANTIC' attracts the eye and sets the tone both by its position and capitalisation. What in the first advertisement might have been off-putting has been made appealing by someone who knows that not only what you say is important but also how you say it.

This practice should be followed by exam candidates who may be called upon to compose advertisements, leaflets, notices or posters for a variety of purposes. Sometimes their primary aim will be to sell (an article, a holiday, a social function); at other times they may be mainly informative (a leaflet on a college course) where any 'selling' or 'persuasive' elements are subdued.

All, however, have a number of techniques in common. Generally, their authors seek to achieve readability and visual impact by considering some of the following:
- an eye-catching heading or title
- good use of layout and spacing
- the best possible order for the information
- the highlighting of detail
- the correct register for the intended reader
- the right balance between over-compression and continuous prose
- the position and content of illustrations (which may be indicated in exams but need not be drawn)

Common faults in exams are to use:
- slabs of congested prose
- excessive colouring
- over-elaborate lettering
- lettering at all angles
- an inappropriate or lifeless style

Talking point

Comment on any points of interest in the advertisements in Figure 3.

You'll be doing it for Mencap.

Collect £125 in sponsorship and you land a free parachute jump.

For a refundable £67.50 bond, qualified instructors will train you at an airfield near you, and Mencap will give you a free parachute jump.

For the brave, it's a chance of a lifetime. For people with a mental handicap your sponsorship will help give them a better chance in life.

Send a first-class stamp for more details (one stamp per pack required) to MENCAP SPONSORED PARACHUTE JUMP, P.O. BOX 336, SOLIHULL, WEST MIDLANDS B91 1NZ.

Or tel: 01-2501537. (Answerphone after office hours.)

NAME
ADDRESS
POSTCODE
SES5

RECEPTIONIST

What we do need is a bright, personable receptionist with accurate typing skills. Someone of smart appearance, who can demonstrate self confidence, initiative and work under pressure.

WE ARE one of the Midlands fastest growing advertising agencies dealing in TV, Press and Radio.

OVER 21? Interested? The right rewards await the right person. Apply in writing with full C.V. to

Edward Rowan.
Managing Director
Rowan Advertising.
Rowan Court.
512 Etruria Road.
Basford. Newcastle.
Staffs. ST5 0SY

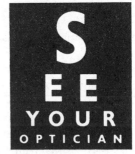

Figure 3

In the following examples the suggested answers were all produced by college students whose work illustrates some of the above techniques.

Example **A job advertisement**

Miss Sandra Kearsley, private secretary to Mr David Pearson, Regional Manager of Mignonne Cosmetics Ltd, is shortly leaving the company to get married. Mr Pearson's office is in central London, and the company's Head Office is at 20–8 Ardingley Road, Birmingham BN14 3GR, telephone Birmingham 56734/5/6. Recently, Mr Pearson attended a meeting at Head Office with Mr Roy Jackson, Sales Manager, and Mrs Irene Simpson, Personnel Manager, and discussed the appointment of a replacement private secretary prior to display advertisements being inserted in London evening newspapers. Reproduced below is an extract from the discussion which took place:

Mr Pearson: Well, I must have someone who can look after the office while I'm away. As you know, I'm out a lot travelling round the region. I'm also looking for someone who can get on with things without having to be given constant instructions.

Mrs Simpson: What about the telephone? I imagine you must be kept busy with enquiries and calls from customers and your own staff.

Mr Pearson: I don't mind telling you there are days when the 'phone seems red-hot and Sandra isn't always good at saving me from my friends!

Mr Jackson: What about shorthand and typewriting? You always seem to be talking into your pocket dictating machine.

Mrs Simpson: As a matter of fact, it's been company policy that private secretaries at regional management level should possess minimum speeds of 100 words a minute shorthand and 50 for typing. And they need to be proficient at audio-typing. Each regional office is equipped with Adona electronic typewriters and audio-transcription equipment.

Mr Jackson: I take it that your secretary will work the 38-hour week, Monday to Friday, and is eligible for three weeks' paid holiday?

Mr Pearson: That's so. But there are times when something has to be typed to go out at the last minute. I must have someone who's prepared to pitch in – Sandra is very good in that respect. And she knows the cosmetics business – she's been invaluable in coping with queries.

Mrs Simpson: And she always looks fresh and well-groomed. Makes such a difference! And she's always helpful over the telephone.

Mr Jackson: Now about salary. According to my records, the job falls into the £8500– 9000 range, depending of course on age, qualifications and experience. Are we still operating the luncheon voucher scheme?

Mr Pearson: Oh yes, certainly in my region.

Mr Jackson: Right. Well we seem to have agreed on all the qualities needed – all that remains is to advertise for this paragon of virtue! I'll leave you to make the arrangements, Mrs Simpson. The usual drill – applicants to write to you, here. You'll contact the newspapers? Fine, well, let's hope we find another Sandra!

Assignment

Using information in the above extract which you think appropriate, design a display advertisement for the position discussed. You should use the whole of one side of answer page bearing in mind that it will be reduced to a 6-inch double column.
                                                              RSA CIB Stage II June 1978 (*17 marks*)

Commentary

The components of a standard job advertisement are as follows:

1 **The Heading**
   This is usually the job title in bold type. Sometimes extra information is included, such as the salary and location:

   SENIOR SECRETARY
   London   £15 000

2 **The Company**
   If included, a brief description is generally sufficient: 'This major UK electronics company requires ...' or 'Expanding advertising agency seeks ...'

From real advertisements

PERSON FRIDAY
for Sundays only

WANTED: Kennel person to work in large boarding kennels and cattery. Could live in.

Opportunity for receptionist/telephonist with good telephone manner and akurutt typing.

EXPERIENCED legal shorthand/audio secretary for partner in busy practice. Criminal experience preferred but not essential.

NURSERY NURSE
This post is temporary to cover the maternity leave of an exciting member of staff.

Job ads – a guide to interpretation

'Perfect opportunity for school-leavers': *Pathetic pay*
'Pleasant working manner essential': *Must be subservient*
'Salary negotiable': *Downwards*
'Excellent travel opportunities': *Sub-branch in Wolverhampton*
'Earn £££s': *Sell doubleglazing*
'Earn money at home': *Be exploited at home*
'Person Friday required': *We're not sexist about who does the boring jobs*
'Must have sense of humour': *Boss specialises in telling dirty jokes*
'All the advantages of a big company': *Nobody knows anybody else's name*

By kind permission of *YOU, The Mail on Sunday* magazine

SECRETARY/RECEPTIONIST
for expanding contracting company.

PART-TIME cleaner required – 24 hours a day.

Assistant required, aged 20 to 30. Applicants must be reliable and conscious.

EMPLOYMENT FOR DEAF & DUMB
Phone Mr Smith for an interview.

Figure 4

3   **The Job**
    An indication of the main duties is given. Words such as
    'challenging', 'stimulating', 'varied' are used to arouse interest.

4   **The Person**
    The qualifications and experience required should be stated and
    age limits (if any) given. NB Reference to the sex of the applicant
    should be avoided – here and elsewhere in the advertisement.

5   **The Rewards**
    Apart from the salary and holidays, a post may offer such things as
    luncheon vouchers, company car, BUPA membership and non-
    contributory pension schemes.

6   **Method of Application**
    Precise instructions are given on how candidates should apply
    (with deadlines).

This conventional approach does not, of course, have to be followed – there is always scope for originality[1] But the best procedure when faced with a question such as the above is to *select* the relevant information, *order* it and then *display* it to its best advantage. Figure 5, despite occasional omissions (what are they?), shows a good sense of balance, position and highlighting of detail to create an attractive image of the company.

Example   **Notices, posters, leaflets**

You work for Mr Keith Heywood, Warehouse Manager of Marklands Ltd, a department-store chain. The company have decided to expand the ladies' fashion departments in all stores, starting with a major promotion in the spring. A contract has been signed with a local manufacturer for an exclusive, and expensive, range of very up-to-date holiday clothes and beachwear for the 'younger set'.

Samples of all garments are available in the warehouse in standard sizes 10, 12, and 14, and it is intended that all six stores will be supplied with poster-size card-mounted full colour photographs of selected lines, for counter display during the period of the promotion. A famous professional photographer, David Henry, is being employed, but it is hoped that volunteers from the staff can be found to model the clothes.

Volunteers will not receive additional pay for this, but will be allowed to keep any clothes they model, free of charge, and they will also be given free enlargements of all their photographs.

Mr Heywood informs you that he hopes to get models who reflect a 'girl next door' image. He does not want applications only from aspiring beauty queens – although they will be very welcome – but also from fairly 'ordinary' girls. He agrees that the latter will probably need a lot of persuasion.

Any girls who are interested should initially apply to him by letter, giving their age and other relevant information. They can 'phone him on extension 28 for further details. David Henry will interview all applicants during the week commencing 18 February. The latest date for applications to arrive is 14 February.

Any staff may apply: sales, clerical, or others, from within any department.

[1]One employer, tired of tearful young secretaries, advertised for a 'fiery dragon' to keep his office in order. He wanted applicants over 45, able to throw their weight about and tell him off if he stepped out of line.

Mignonne Cosmetics Ltd,

Require a

Private Secretary (London)

Salary £8,500 – £9,000 A Year Depending On Age, Qualifications

* * * * * * * * * * * * * *

MUST BE ABLE TO WORK ON OWN INITIATIVE
EXPERIENCE ESSENTIAL
MINIMUM SPEEDS – TYPING 50 w.p.m.
SHORTHAND 100 w.p.m.
PROFICIENT IN AUDIO TYPING
GOOD TELEPHONE MANNER
KNOWLEDGE OF COSMETIC BUSINESS AN ADVANTAGE
WORKING: MONDAY – FRIDAY – BASED ON 38 HOUR WEEK –
FLEXIBLE APPROACH TO HOURS

* * * * * * * * * * * * * *

LUNCHEON VOUCHERS EXTRA

INTERESTED?

APPLICATIONS IN OWN
HANDWRITING TO:

The Personnel Manager,
Mrs Irene Simpson,
20–28 Ardingley Rd,
Birmingham.
BN14 3GR

* * * * * * *

TELEPHONE: Birmingham 56734/5/6

Figure 5

Assignment

Design a notice to be displayed on all staff notice boards. It should be eye-catching and well laid out, making good use of spacing, proportion, and other devices which make it visually attractive and easy to comprehend. Give all the necessary information.

For your answer use a single side of A4 paper. The text of your notice should not use more than 150 words.

RSA CIB Stage I Jan 1980 (*22 marks*)

Talking point

Discuss the merits of the suggested answer (Figure 6).

Example **A notice for office display**

Imagine that you are the secretary of Mr F Simpson, office manager of Excelsior Finance Co. Ltd.

Your company has its typewriters serviced every quarter by Advance Typewriter Services Ltd. Their technician is due to arrive in ten days' time, on Thursday 22 June, to carry out routine servicing.

Experience has shown that staff using typewriters tend to forget to report faults unless reminded and the company incurs extra costs when Advance have to make a special visit. In addition, some typewriter faults, if left unrepaired, lead to poorly typed documents being produced and despatched.

Assignment

You have therefore been asked by Mr Simpson to draw up a notice to be displayed on the office noticeboard reminding secretaries and typists of the impending visit of Advance's technician. Any defects are to be reported to Miss K. Rogers, office services supervisor. Miss Rogers likes to have enough time to inspect reported typewriters before the technician's visit.

Design a notice suitable for display which you think will produce the desired effect.

RSA CIB Stage I June 1978 (*10 marks*)

Commentary

This type of notice requires a clear indication of the intended readership at the beginning with the source and date of posting at the end. The notice serves the dual purpose of *informing* staff of the forthcoming visit and *persuading* them that it is in their own interests to report faults by a given deadline.

COULD THIS BE YOU?

YOU don't have to be a glamour girl to
be photographed by the world-famous

DAVID HENRY

COME and model the store's new range
of holiday and beach wear for our
MAJOR PROMOTION IN THE SPRING

This line is

! **EXCLUSIVE** !
EXPENSIVE

with

! **SPECIAL APPEAL TO** !
THE YOUNGER SET

WE feature your pictures, poster-size
and in full colour in all our stores.

YOU KEEP the clothes you model AND
enlargements of your photographs
FREE

THE only qualifications you need are to work
in this store and take size 10, 12 or 14.

FIT THE BILL?

THEN apply in writing, giving age and other relevant
details to MR KEITH HEYWOOD
OR ring him on EXT 28 for further details.

DAVID HENRY will interview all applicants in the
week commencing 18th February.

DON'T BE LATE! APPLY NOW!

Figure 6

Suggested answer

To all Secretaries/Typists

HELP YOUR TYPEWRITER TO HELP YOU

Does your typewriter suffer from hic-cups every time you try
to do a tabulation or exhaustion when you ask it to make a
carriage return?

IF IT DOES, IT'S TIME FOR A CHECK UP!

On Thursday, 22 June the Advance Typewriter technician will
be here to bring your typewriter back to health.

So if you require a sound typewriter for the future, please
report all problems to Miss K Rogers, Office Services
Supervisor, by Tuesday, 20 June.

REMEMBER - YOU can help US to help YOU and YOUR WORK.

F Simpson
Office Manager

12 June 19..

OM/ATS

Exercises

1 Comment on the effectiveness (humour, originality, use of English) of these real notices/
   advertisements:
   a) Ears pierced while U wait.
   b) Everlasting Wear – Guaranteed for 5 years.
   c) (*Builders' van of Patel Brothers*) You've had the cowboys – now try the Indians.
   d) (*Chinese restaurant*) Feel free to wok around.
   e) (*Bangkok dry cleaners*) Drop your trousers here for the best results.
   f) (*Cafe*) Hot soup to sit in or take out.
   g) (*Photographer's*) We shoot children on Thursdays without an appointment.
   h) (*Church notice*) Brush up on the Bible and fight Truth Decay.
   i) (*Boutique*) The management regrets that due to building work the ladies' changing
      booths are closed. Please bare with us.
   j) (*Music store*) Gone Chopin. Bach in a minuet.

2 Write an advertisement to be inserted in the Jolly Holidays Guide about the Golden
   Sands Hotel, Cliff Walk, Torquay. Mention its position, number of rooms, prices, etc. The
   advertisement should contain not more than 35 words.

   PEI EBC Intermediate (*16 marks*)

3 The Albert Ross Travel Agency of 12 Kingston Highway, Blackburn, Lancs BN6 4LA wishes
   to advertise in a magazine which is produced for teenagers. They aim to appeal to the
   young holidaymaker who may be wishing to go on holiday with friends for the first time.
   Albert Ross has pioneered a budget holiday for the young person who is not concerned
   about luxurious accommodation or lavish catering and would prefer modest
   accommodation at modest prices.

In the brochures you will find these budget holidays are for either a week or a fortnight in Spain, Italy, France, Austria and Germany. There are such holidays as beach camping in Italy and mountain hostelling in Austria.

Prepare a suitably persuasive advertisement. It may take up a whole sheet of A4 paper.

RSA CIB Stage I June 1982 (*20 marks*)

4 **a)** Proofread the following job advertisement (which is based on students' work).
   b) Comment on the English used and consider what changes you might make.

Condom International plc

SUPERVISER

A challenging individaul is required to deal with customers in our Service Department. They must have a pleasant mannerism, initiative and be able to help and advice customers. O' level English and Maths or equivelant.

A clean drivers license is essential as their may be liasons with customers at there homes. Experience and advantage although we will learn the sucessful applicant on the job.

Benifits

   * Negligible salary
   * Subsided meals
   * 20 days annual leave

---

5 Read the following job description, then in approximately 35 words compose an advertisement suitable for publication in a magazine or newspaper.

   The Sales Director of a small toy manufacturing company (where flexible work hours are in operation) requires a Secretary/Personal Assistant. The successful applicant for this post will have had some years' experience in a responsible secretarial post and will have excellent shorthand and typing speeds. Some experience in selling would be desirable, but not essential since training will be given. This will be necessary since the secretary will be required to negotiate with clients in the Sales Director's absence. The applicant may also be required to accompany him on business trips both at home and abroad. There are four weeks' annual holiday and the salary is negotiable around £6500.

LCC SS June 1979 (*15 marks*)

6 A recent spate of petty theft at the hospital where you are employed has made it necessary for a memorandum to be issued to all departments about care of personal property. You have been asked to write the memo and to design a poster for display in Reception, which will inform the public of the need to take care. Your notice/poster should be of A4 size.

AMSPAR C Jan 1988 (*15 marks*)

7 You are working part-time in the warehouse store of a mail-order company. Your area of the store handles household goods, including china and glassware, and electrical items. Lorries bring in goods from the factories daily. These goods are already packaged and have to be stacked on shelves up to 20 feet above the floor by hand and by forklift truck. Goods are taken off the shelves to make up customer orders. Sometimes this involves unpacking crates and large boxes.

   The warehouse manager finds out that you are a Communication student and suggests that you may be interested in helping the company improve safety standards. He asks you to have a go at three tasks, as follows:

   a) *List* five possible dangers to workers and to goods being handled.   (*5 marks*)

b) *List* four visual elements which need to be considered when designing a poster.

(4 marks)

c) Take *two* of the dangers that you have identified and *design a poster for each,* to illustrate these hazards.

   The posters should advise and warn the workers of the dangers concerned. They may be of any suitable size, and designed for display in any appropriate location within the warehouse. They may be as elaborate or as simple as is necessary to convey their message effectively.

(16 marks)

SEG GCSE Summer 1988

8 You work for Ultima Furnishings Ltd. In addition, you are a member of the company's social club committee. Recently the committee has been making plans for the Annual Christmas Dance. The following extracts record the arrangements which have to be made:

A CHRISTMAS DANCE REPORT TO THE COMMITTEE

3 <u>Ballroom</u>

The manager of the White Hart Hotel has confirmed our booking of the ballroom and dining areas. The ballroom seats over 450 people at tables around an excellent dance floor. It has a fully-equipped stage with special effects lighting. There is also a fully-licensed bar at the rear which the hotel will staff.

4 <u>Christmas Dinner</u>

The White Hart is able to provide a traditional three-course Christmas Dinner within the agreed costs.

5 <u>Entertainment</u>

The 'Blue Velvet Sextet' have accepted the engagement to play at the Dance. They proved extremely popular at last year's Police Ball. Their vocalist, Miss Julie Dee, has recently appeared on the TV show 'New Stars'. The band is extremely versatile - they can play strict tempo, rock-and-roll or beat music at will - and they have been in great demand locally. Also, Mr Dave Parsons, Showbiz Comedian of the Year, has agreed to perform a 15-minute cabaret act for a fee of £40.

B CONVERSATION BETWEEN SOCIAL CLUB CHAIRMAN AND SECRETARY

<u>Chairman</u>:

'I've just received a very generous donation from the board of directors to help cover the costs of the Christmas Dance. This means we can make a charge for the tickets of only £2.50 each! We'd best sell the tickets through the Departmental Representatives as usual, but with 450 dining places, we can allow each member of staff up to three tickets.'

C EXTRACT FROM MINUTES OF SOCIAL CLUB COMMITTEE MEETING
It was agreed that the Annual Christmas Dance should take place on Saturday, 16 December 19.., from 8.00 pm to 12.00 midnight.

As you have been involved in the arrangements for the Christmas Dance and are aware of the information in the above extracts, the Chairman has asked you to compose a leaflet to send to all company staff to advertise the event. He wants you to emphasise those aspects of the Dance which you think will encourage staff to buy tickets. He has suggested that about 140 words would be sufficient. Your leaflet should be produced on one side of A4 paper.

RSA CIB Stage I June 1978 *(28 marks)*

9 You work for Mrs Diane Kingston, Head of the Department of Business and Secretarial Studies, Lingfield Road, Rotherham. She has decided to update the leaflets that are sent to prospective students in order to make them more informative and attractive. They will give a clearer idea of the scope of each course and subsequent career prospects.

   Prepare the draft of a leaflet for your course, covering the above points and adding details of entry requirements, grants, work experience, enrolment, etc. that are relevant.

10 Your employer, Mr Don Gilford, Manager of the Accounts Department, has become concerned by a steep rise in telephone costs. He asks you to prepare a notice (incorporating six suggestions) which will encourage staff to use the telephone more efficiently and economically.

Telegrams/Telex

In his *Secret Diary*, Adrian Mole records his response to this telegram from his wayward mother:

ADRIAN STOP COMING HOME STOP

What does she mean 'Stop coming home'? How can I 'stop coming home'? I live here.

The great advantage of telegrams is speed; the major drawback is their cost (each word is charged for) which leads to a severely compressed form of communication that can confuse. Oddly, this may be because an inexperienced writer uses too many words rather than too few. Mrs Mole's telegram would have been cheaper and clearer if it had read 'COMING HOME'.

International telegrams still reach those foreign parts that other technologies have not yet reached, and British Telecom will transmit them for you (dial 100 or 193 in London). The inland service, which BT replaced with telemessage[1], has been partially restored by Couriergram (which can be reached by dialling (0604) 232828 or through one of the sub-post offices now working the scheme).

In either case, to save money, the following points should be observed:
- Keep the recipient's name and address to a minimum; use his telegraphic address (a shortened form) or his telex number if he has one on his letterhead.
- Omit all punctuation if possible: COMMA and STOP are usually unnecessary but will add to the cost.
- Omit all courtesy titles, salutations, complimentary closes.
- Express important figures in words.
- Use standard abbreviations – ASAP, ETA, REF, CIF, ETC.
- Check that the message is not obscure or ambiguous. A journalist, writing an article on Cary Grant, realised that he did not know the star's age. He immediately sent him a telegram which read:

HOW OLD CARY GRANT

to which came the reply:

OLD CARY GRANT FINE HOW YOU

---

[1]A written message that is delivered on the next working day in a distinctive yellow envelope as long as the message has been telephoned or telexed to BT before 10 p.m. the previous evening (7 p.m. on Sundays and Bank Holidays).

Example

On the day you are due to catch a plane home from your holiday in Spain, there is a strike by the aircraft crew. There will not be another flight for two days.

Compose an international telegram, using not more than 15 words, telling your parents or a close friend what has happened and when you expect to arrive home.

PEI EBC Elementary (20 marks)

Suggested answer

> **HARRISON 15 BROOK ROAD OXFORD UK**
> **DELAYED SPAIN DUE STRIKE RETURNING MONDAY**
> **PAUL**

In business, telex (a telecommunications service based on the teleprinter) has more or less replaced the telegram. The system allows immediate written communication between well over 100 000 connections in the UK and with nearly two million subscribers in 200 other countries.

Modern terminals and electronic telex exchanges give a service which is quiet, reliable and easy to use. It is available around the clock, both for dispatch and receipt of messages, and is relatively cheap to use, the cost being calculated according to the transmitting time and the distance. Messages, while still concise, are generally less severe than the skeletal telegram and normal punctuation may be used.

Example

Your Personnel Officer, Miss B. Shaw, is at present attending an EEC conference, but can be reached through your Brussels office. In view of the unrest among junior staff it is felt that her early return is imperative. Draft a telex message asking her to contact Head Office as soon as possible.

LCC SS June 1977 (10 marks)

Suggested answer

> **871721**[1]
> **888941**
>
> **3497   5 June 19..   14:22**[2]
> **TO: COMTEC, BRUSSELS**
> **FROM: COMTEC, LONDON**
> **URGENT**
> **ATTN MISS B SHAW**
> **EARLY RETURN IMPERATIVE DUE TO STAFF PROBLEM. PLS CONTACT**
> **HEAD OFFICE ASAP.**
> **RGDS**[3] **THOMPSON**
> **+ + + +**[4]
> **888941**
> **871721**

Notes

1   The first number is the answerback code of the organisation you are calling; the second is your own. The numbers are repeated (in reverse order) at the end to confirm that the full message was received.

2   The serial number, the date and the time of the message are shown.

3   Standard abbreviations (ATTN, PLS, ASAP, RGDS) may again be used.

4   This indicates the end of the message.

NB In exams only the text may be required.

Exercises

1   Using the words supplied at the bottom of the question fill in the blank spaces:

Messages sent by _____ must be as _____ as possible because the _____ is calculated on the basis of the number of _____ used.

With _____ the transmitting _____ and the _____ involved are used to _____ the cost.

A telegram should seek to convey as much _____ as necessary in the _____ words possible. It is important not to sacrifice _____ in order to be _____.

There is no need for a _____ or _____ close in a telegram. It should be typed in _____ and followed by a letter of _____.

Telegraphic _____ have been introduced to _____ the cost of telegrams. This means that _____ word may be used to represent a whole _____.

telegrams	words	complimentary	capitals
short	telex	distance	calculate
time	salutation	codes	confirmation
sentence	one	cost	information
brief	clearness	fewest	reduce

PEI EBC Elementary (*20 marks*)

2   You have discovered that an urgent box of supplies has not been posted. Send a telegram of not more than 15 words to Joseph Lokano, 151 Adelphi Street, Hong Kong, telling him that Box No. 19462 will be despatched on the same day as the telegram. Apologise for the error.   PEI EBC Elementary (*20 marks*)

3   You are a receptionist at the Majestic Hotel, Nassau, Bahamas, where a guest, Mr A.B. Jacobs, mislaid his cigarette lighter this morning just before he was leaving; he was very upset as the lighter was of sentimental value to him. Later in the day the lighter was found behind cushions on a chair in his suite.

   Send an international telegram to him at 10 Green Lane, London NQ1 2BW, telling him, in not more than 15 words, that the lighter has been found and will be despatched to him early tomorrow. Write a confirmatory letter.   PEI EBC Intermediate (*16 marks*)

4   You are secretary to Mr E.F. Holdsworthy, the Assistant Export Manager, who left the office this morning en route to Scandinavia. He is due to arrive in Stockholm tomorrow evening where he is to be met by the firm's agent, Mr E. Horsa, who has arranged a programme of visits for him.

   You have just received a telex message from Mr Horsa's secretary informing you that Mr Horsa has been involved in an accident and will be unable to meet Mr Holdsworthy as arranged.

Compose a radio-telegram, in not more than 15 words, to be sent to Mr Holdsworthy on board the ship to Scandinavia, telling him of the accident and asking him to telephone Mr Horsa's secretary on 01–6767 to discuss new arrangements.

PEI EBC Advanced (20 marks)

5   Please send a telex to the Hotel Splendide, Marbella, Spain, cancelling the two weeks' stay of the Office Manager, Mr James Last, and booking instead one week from 1 August next. You work for James Last & Co. Ltd, Newbolt House, Liverpool L6 5LM.

PEI EBC Elementary (20 marks)

6   You work for Traveltours of Bridge Street, Eastbury. Some of the new hotels at Ibiza which were to be used during the forthcoming holiday season will not be completed in time as there have been difficulties with the supply of building materials. There will, however, be sufficient vacancies for your clients in other hotels.

Compose a telex message to be transmitted to Mr Black, your representative in Ibiza, informing him that your Tours Manager, Mr White, will be flying out to meet him on 24 June. Whilst there, he hopes to meet representatives of the builders – perhaps Mr Black could arrange a meeting on the 25th. He also hopes to inspect the hotels which are now to be used – Mr Black is to arrange this. Mr White will stay for three days.

LCC SS June 1978 (10 marks)

Forms

Designing forms

The form in Figure 7 was composed many years ago and its origin has been lost in time. Yet (deliberately and humorously) it illustrates some of the problems of forms and their design.

It is at times nosy, irrelevant, repetitive; it tries to cover too many possibilities or options which may ultimately confuse; it does not give clear instructions on how to indicate the correct answer (tick? delete?) and there is inadequate space for some of the answers. It ends with a typical example of officialese.

NATIONAL HEALTH SERVICE
APPLICATION FOR PERMIT TO BE ILL

NAME. . . . . No. . . . .

ADDRESS. . . . .

When Born and why . . . .

---

1.   I hereby make application to be ill. (Permit)
2.   I declare (a) that I have a pain in my (i) head.   (ii) stomach.
                         (iii) chest.   (iv) arms.   (v) . . . .
                 (b) that my complexion is (i) ruddy.   (ii) pallid.
                         (iii) green.
                 (c) that I have broken my (i) arm.   (ii) leg.   (iii) back.
                         (iv) engagement.

(d) that during the past **12 hours** I have been sick .... times.

(e) that I expect to be sick again in .... hours.

(f) that I am afraid I shall (i) die. (ii) not die. (iii) live. (iv) not live.

(g) that I am off my (i) food.   (ii) drink.   (iii) head.

3. The name of my Doctor is ....or the name of my Veterinary Surgeon is ....

4. I have been taking (i) salts. (ii) pills. (iii) tablets. (iv) liberties.

5 I am in   (i) bed.   (ii) pain.   (iii) desperation.   (iv) my coffin.

6. What is the effect of a dose of Cascara? ....(a) How many times? ....

7. I can see (i) spots. (ii) nothing. (iii) animals. If animals state what type and colour...

8. I have spots on my ....(a) They do/do not/itch.   (b) I am/am not/scratching them.

9. I am/am not pregnant. In case of male patients further details should be given on a separate sheet. (Blankets should not be used.)

10. I am (i) depressed. (ii) elated. (iii) about to shoot myself. (NOTE: In this case a Firearms Licence is required.)

11. I would be willing to take   (i) medicine.   (ii) treatment. (iii) medicine and treatment. (iv) treatment and medicine. (v) poison. (State preference and whether fast or slow.)

12. I request admission to (i) hospital. (ii) asylum. (iii) mortuary.

13. I request the services of a (i) doctor. (ii) midwife. (iii) nurse. (State whether day, night, wet, dry, blonde, brunette, young and/or willing.) (iv) undertaker.

14. I believe my complaint to be ....

In case a permit cannot be issued for this complaint would you be willing to accept another illness, malady or disease? State Yes or No ....

This form when completed should be submitted, in triplicate, to the Local Health Officer. Should the applicant die before the permit is issued the Local Health Officer should be notified and a new application for a permit to be declared dead (Form R.I.P.) should be submitted by a relative or creditor.

Permits are not transferable, but a permit for a common cold may be used by all members of an applicant's family, provided that all the colds, up to a maximum of six, are caught within **14 days** of the date of issue.

DECLARATION

I declare that all the above answers are as true as those on my Petrol Application.

Form. ILL.   Signature..
No.9/Say./99.   Date ....

Figure 7

At work forms will often have to be designed. The first question to ask is whether the form is necessary or whether there is a better way of collecting the information. If the form really is needed, then the following points should be considered:

- **Purpose**   Why is the form being designed? The purpose should be clarified and concentrated into a title for the form.
- **Information** What information is needed to achieve the above purpose? (Do not ask for irrelevant details.)
- **Questions**   What questions will produce the information? Are they short questions and framed wherever possible so that a yes/no answer is enough?
- **Order**   What is the best sequence for those questions?
- **Length**   How brief can it be kept?
- **Wording**   Is it clear, simple and appropriate? (e.g. in a multiracial society FORENAMES is a better heading than CHRISTIAN NAMES.)
- **Display**   Is it attractively set out with sufficient space for answers? Would numbering the questions/sections make for ease of reference?
- **Instructions** Are they precise and easy to follow?
- **Action**   Is it obvious where the form must be sent on completion (and the deadline stated, if any)?

Example

You work at Phillips and Jones plc as private secretary to Mr G. Anderson, the Chief Office Administrator, among whose responsibilities is ensuring that adequate administration services are provided for the 150 staff, including mail, typing services, filing and photocopying. Yesterday Mr Anderson had this to say to you:

'Something will obviously have to be done about the photocopier in the print room – it's broken down again. That's five times in the last fortnight! Staff are always ready to complain when this happens but I'm convinced the breakdowns are caused by people not using it properly. I knew we would have this problem when it was agreed to allow staff free access to the wretched machine – people putting the paper in wrongly or being very clumsy using the controls. They don't seem to realise that an expensive machine needs careful handling. Apart from this, they don't know how to get the best out of the machine – not printing on both sides of the paper or reducing two A4 sheets onto one. And it's alarming to see how many copies have been thrown away in the waste bin! I've discussed the matter with senior staff and they agree that something has to be done – the present problems will take the whole of tomorrow to sort out – and this situation is affecting the general efficiency of the company. It's very inconvenient and frustrating for those who do use the machine properly. I want to send something out to each member of staff today, explaining the situation and getting some information from them – how often they use it, how many copies they make in an average week, whether they would like some basic training, etc – in fact, any information that may help us to sort the matter out. They may, in fact, want all copying done by a trained operator who can be in absolute control of the machine. If I can have their replies by 15 July, I'll be able to work something out to put to the next senior staff meeting.'

a) Prepare a suitable communication (using about 200 words) for Mr Anderson. *(20 marks)*

b) Prepare a reply form to accompany a) for staff to complete. This should provide Mr Anderson with the kind of information he requires. *(15 marks)*

LCC PSC June 1984

Commentary

1   Decide on the most appropriate communication for a) from the range of documents mentioned in this book – letter, memo, report or notice – and then write it in an acceptable tone – but not the exasperated tone in which Mr Anderson briefs his private secretary. Remember that not all of the staff are to blame and that appealing for their co-operation is a better ploy than harsh criticism.

2   In explaining the situation, consider how much of the background information you should include. Do you wish, for example, to tell everyone that Mr Anderson was against free access to the copier?

3   Do not forget to refer to the attached document and its purpose – to elicit information that may help produce a satisfactory solution to the problem.

4   The accompanying reply form need not be long but it should be easy to complete and process. It should be self-contained (with return instructions and deadline) and should include appropriate questions to gain the desired information. Space should also be provided for further comments/suggestions that staff may wish to make.

Assignment

Prepare the two documents before reading the suggested answer to b) below.

Suggested answer

PHOTOCOPYING

Please complete this form by ticking the relevant boxes and return it to Mr G Anderson, Chief Office Administrator, by 15 July.

1   How often do you use the photocopier?

| Every day ☐ | Several times a week ☐ | Once a week ☐ | Once a fortnight ☐ | Once a month ☐ |

2   How many copies do you make in an average week?

0-25 ☐   26-50 ☐   51-100 ☐   101-500 ☐   500+ ☐

3   Do you know how to

a) use the reduction facilities?   Yes ☐   No ☐

b) print on both sides of the paper?   Yes ☐   No ☐

4   Would you like some basic training in how to get the best out of the machine?   Yes ☐   No ☐

5   Would you prefer to have all copying done by a trained operator who would have absolute control of the machine?   Yes ☐   No ☐

6   Please add any further comments of your own

....

....

....

7   Name ....

8   Dept ....

Completing forms

When filling in any form either for yourself or on behalf of someone else, accuracy is essential and the following guidelines should be observed:
- read it through carefully before starting to complete it
- follow the instructions (BLOCK LETTERS?)
- write or print legibly
- answer fully (if forenames are asked for do not give initials)
- do not leave blanks (write as appropriate 'Not known' or 'Not applicable')
- check everything (for date of birth have you put down the current year?)

Surname of Applicant TURNER	Forenames NONE
Maiden Name VICKI	Sex: M/F Title: ~~DR~~/~~MR~~/~~MRS~~/MISS/~~MS~~

From an application form

Exercises

1   You are employed by the City Council as a trainee in the General Office of Mercia Airport. Your office is located at Mercia Airport, Old Road, Filston, Mercia SM15 4QT (Tel: 0302 3845). A new runway and passenger building extension are to be officially opened on 6 November. Your Section Head, Isobel Dundee, sends you the following message:

```
To: Assistant

Invitations to Opening Ceremony

The Director has decided that an invitation should be sent to local
organisations asking them to nominate two people to represent them
as official guests at the Opening Ceremony. As numbers will be
strictly limited we need to send with the letter some kind of
reservation form which can be returned to me by the end of September.
We will need to know the names of the representatives, their
organisation, whether they will attend the buffet and if they
require car-parking space.

    I am writing the letter of invitation. Please draw up the
reservation form, indicating clearly to whom it should be returned
and by what date.

    Thank you for your help in this.
Isobel Dundee                                             11 June 19..
```

Draw up the required form.   BTEC

2   Draft a questionnaire to be sent to ex-students of your college (e.g. those who took the same course the previous year). Establish how many are employed (full-time/part-time), how long it took them to find a job on leaving college, whether they work for one person or more than one, the kind of organisation they work for, the duties they perform, their job title and some indication of salary range, etc. Send off the questionnaires and process the replies.

3   Assume that you work as general assistant to Mr Sanjit Patel, Sales Manager of Marmoset Computers Ltd. Some employees will be going on the Staff Outing to Toms Towers, a country hotel, on the morning of Friday 11 July, departing from Deane Station, and returning on the afternoon of Sunday 13 July. All meals will be included and first-class rail tickets.

On Friday 27 June Mr Patel says to you: 'I have received a list of those going on the trip to Toms Towers. There are ten people in all. I shall be taking my wife, Alison; we will require a double room, as will Mike Tennstedt and his wife, Jennifer. You will share a twin room with Pat Toogood. Miss Mary Johnson, Mr Kevin Barlow, Miss Audrey Matthews and Mr Jan Wyczkowski will each have single rooms. We all want private bathrooms.

'I want you to make the necessary bookings on the hotel's special party booking form for the dates which you have announced. Please remember to take out the hotel's insurance for everyone. This will cost an extra £5 for each person, on top of the basic £100 each, for the weekend. Also, for first-class travel from Deane Station there will be an extra £5 for each person. Of course, as we will be going in two weeks' time, we must pay the full amount. The accounts office will give you a cheque for £1100.

'I shall be in New York for the next ten days on business so I want you to give your name as the person to whom tickets should be sent.

'I nearly forgot – Mr Barlow is vegetarian and will require a vegetarian menu. And remember, it will be full board for everyone.'

The accounts department give you a cheque, number 624868, to send with the booking form.

Make a copy of the form (Figure 8) and complete it in accordance with Mr Patel's instructions.

RSA CIB Stage I June 1986 (15 marks)

TOMS TOWERS
Weekend/Rail Relaxation Breaks
Group Booking Form

Complete in BLOCK CAPITALS

	Day	Month	Year		Day	Month	Year
Date of Arrival				Date of Departure			

	Title (Mr, Mrs, Ms, Miss)	Initial	Surname	Room Type	PB ✔ if required	Meal Requirements
Room 1*						
Room 2						
Room 3						
Room 4						
Room 5						
Room 6						
Room 7						
Room 8						

Key: (Please enter)

 Room Type: PB = Private Bathroom Meal Requirements:
        (Tick if required)

  DR = Double Room   BB = Breakfast only
  TR = Twin Room   HB = Half board
  SR = Single Room   FB = Full board

Special Requirements (e.g. special diet, ground floor room, etc.) ....

....

....

Rail Travel:

No. of tickets Outward: _____ Return: _____ Outward

Departure Station: _____ Class (Please tick) 1st ____ 2nd ____

(Note: 1st class supplement £5 per person return)

Insurance:

Hotel insurance of £5 per person will be added to your account unless

signed here: Signature _____ Date _____

Deposit required, £25 per person or, if holiday begins within 60 days, full amount payable.

     Amount enclosed £ _____ Cheque Number _____

Name of Group Leader (to whom tickets will be sent): ....

....

....

*Name of person to whom Signature _____ Date _____
 tickets should be sent
 should be given first.

Figure 8

4 a) Assume that you work for Magnet Electronics plc as assistant to Miss Tania Foss in the personnel office. The company produces components for the computer industry and is situated at Magnet House on the Whitwick Industrial Estate, Whitwick, near Birmingham WB12 WLL (Tel: 347 9863). The company has grown considerably and now has over 200 employees.

 The original form of application for jobs has never been updated and now is inadequate for the larger firm. It has been decided to redesign the form to make it suitable for all job applications. Bill Collinge, the Personnel Officer, comes into the office you share with Tania and the following conversation takes place:

Bill: Good morning, Tania. (*Nodding towards you*) Morning!
You: Good morning, Mr Collinge.
Tania: Morning, Bill. What can we do for you?
Bill: When will you be able to make a start on that application form we were talking about?
Tania: I can't do much yet. I have a job to finish for Mr Nettlecombe and you know he won't wait long!
Bill: Can you have a stab at it then? (*Looking in your direction*)
Tania: You ought to hear my colleague's views on your form! Tell him!

You:	*(Slightly embarrassed by Tania's statement)* Well, when I applied for this job I thought that the application form was very poor. It was so small it didn't look important and there was very little room to put down much information . . .
Bill:	*(Sharply)* It *was* designed ten years ago and for a very small workforce; I didn't know the company would grow so fast!
Tania:	All right, Bill, don't get cross, the form is a poor one; tell us what you want to put on it and I'll help as soon as I can.
Bill:	*(More kindly)* The usual things – name, marital status, address . . .
Tania:	Don't forget it should instruct applicants to use block capitals; some people's writing is awful!
You:	How big should it be?
Bill:	A couple of pages A4 size should be plenty to lay it out well and leave a section for personal hobbies and interests.
Tania:	We should have a space for work experience and college courses with the new schemes coming out, as well as educational record.
You:	How many referees' names do you think?
Bill:	Two should be enough. We need their addresses as well.
Tania:	Is that it, all the usual information plus the things we have talked about just now?
Bill:	Yes, I think so. *(Turning to you)* I am sure you will make a better job of it than I did! Cheerio!

Draft the application form as requested by Mr Collinge. Use two sides of A4 ignoring margins for this question. Credit will be given for sensible unambiguous questions and intelligent use of the space allowed. For this question your own knowledge of application forms may be utilised as well as the information contained in the question.   RSA CIB Stage II March 1984 *(15 marks)*

b) Get your neighbour to fill in your draft of the application form to check that you have allocated sufficient space for answers.

5   Phoenix Centres are well-designed air-conditioned multi-unit indoor shopping centres. You work as assistant to Elvet Edmonds, Manager of the Phoenix Centre at Pellingham. The Centre Manager is responsible for maintenance, security, cleaning, public relations and the promotion of the centre which is open to the public from 0830 to 2030 hours daily (Sundays excepted). Pellingham is a busy town in Staffordshire. It is 10 March.

Situation
Bill Mellors (security guard) has contacted Elvet Edmonds at 1405 hours on the two-way radio. John Freemantle, one of the centre's maintenance workers, was examining an empty unit and has fallen from a ladder and injured himself. Mr Edmonds asks you to go with him to help John as you are a qualified first-aider; he telephones an ambulance and you go down together. John, who will be 37 on 17 March, appears to have broken his left leg and is bleeding from a gash on his forehead. You make him comfortable; the ambulance arrives and you accompany him to hospital. It is confirmed that he has a broken leg, requires ten stitches in his forehead and is to be kept in hospital for some time. You return to the office; Elvet has notified John's wife and found a witness – Harry Blamair, aged 52, the supervisor of the maintenance team. His address is 17 Willoughby Bank, Ashurst near Pellingham, and John lives at 92 Cornwall Terrace, Pellingham. Harry called Bill Mellors to report the accident. Mr Edmonds asks you to complete an accident form and to write a brief memo to go to all centre staff. Inform them of John's accident and make them aware that safe practice must be observed when working anywhere in the centre – if members of the public are involved, compensation has to be made.

Copy and complete the accident form (Figure 9) *(13 marks)* and then compose the memo *(7 marks)*.   RSA CIB Stage II March 1986

PHOENIX CENTRES

Head Office: Phoenix House
              11-21 Ashrise Road
              London SW2 WS4
Telephone: 071-337 5987 (6 lines)
Telex: 795737
ACCIDENT REPORT FORM
PLEASE USE BLOCK CAPITALS THROUGHOUT

1 Address of centre reporting accident ....

2 Name of Manager ....

3 Date and time of accident ....

4 Did accident occur inside centre? Yes/No*

5 If no, give details of location ....

6 Details of people injured; if more than two, please continue on back
   of this page.

   a) Name .... (Mr Mrs Ms Miss)*

      Address ....

      .... Date of Birth ....

      Employee Yes/No* If yes, please state department ....

   b) Name .... (Mr Mrs Ms Miss)*

      Address ....

      .... Date of Birth ....

      Employee Yes/No* If yes, please state department ....

7 Injuries sustained by a) ....

                         b) ....

8 Action taken; (i)   First aid given   Yes/No*
                  (ii)   Sent to hospital   Yes/No*
                  (iii) Sent home   Yes/No*
                  (iv)   Returned to work   Yes/No*

9 Witnesses: a) Name .... (Mr Mrs Ms Miss)*

   Address ....

   ....

   .... Age ....

Employee Yes/No* If yes, please state department ....

        b) Name .... (Mr Mrs Ms Miss)*

Address ....

.... Age ....

Employee Yes/No* If yes, please state department ....

10   How did accident occur? ....

      ....

11   Draw diagram if possible

12   If employee, give time finished work on day of accident ....

13   What was employee doing at time of accident? ....

14   Would this be considered part of his/her normal occupation? Yes/No*

15   If not, give reasons ....

      ....

      ....

16   Damage sustained to centre property ....

      ....

      ....

17   If member of public involved, have you obtained their written statement?
                                                                                         Yes/No*

18   Any other details which you consider should be reported at this time

```
19   Signature of Manager .......................................................

20   Signature of first aider (if employee) .................................

21   Date of writing report if different from date of accident ..............

NB   Details of all accidents must be reported within 12 hours of occurrence.

* Delete as necessary
```

Figure 9

Programmes

Programmes are required for visits and conferences and should contain details of
- where the visit/conference is to be held
- where visitors should assemble
- the day's events (with time and place for films, demonstrations, seminars, etc. and, additionally, for talks, the name of the speaker and the topic)
- times of tea/coffee/lunch breaks
- excursions or entertainment (for conference delegates or their guests when a conference lasts for several days).

Example

```
Conference 1992

A guide for businesspeople to opportunities in the new
European marketplace.

Carlton Hotel
Sloane Square
London SW1

Friday, 9 May 1990

Conference Room

PROGRAMME

0930          WELCOME
              Sir Raymond Carver, Chairman CBI

0945          A BIGGER MARKET THAN THE USA
              Denise Robbins, Director of Astra

1015          THE IMPACT OF THE CHANNEL TUNNEL
              Alistair Martin, Co-Chairman of Eurotunnel
```

1045	Coffee
1100	LABOUR RELATIONS IN THE 1990s Gavin Lord, OBE, Chairman of ACAS
1130	MAINLAND EUROPE – RETAILING Freda Keays, Vice President of Mart & Spender
1200	OPEN SESSION
1230	Lunch in the Tennant Suite
1400	A COMMON CURRENCY FOR A COMMON MARKET Mark Kroner, Chairman of MidWest
1430	BUSINESSMEN'S BAD LANGUAGE(S) Charlotte Juron, BA, Director of Polyglot Language School
1500	Tea
1530	OPEN SESSION
1630	Conference ends

Exercises

1 A local college has asked the company for which you work as a secretary to arrange for a visit by sixth-form students. They would like to see for themselves as many aspects of office, secretarial and executive work as possible

Your Head of Department has organised a one-day visit for 20 students. After welcoming them in mid-morning and giving an introductory talk, he wants them to tour the offices and ask questions about what they see. After lunch they will be permitted to attend either a sales conference for senior executives or a training session for new secretarial staff (these two events occur at the same time).

Your Head will be attending a meeting himself from 3 p.m. onwards, but after tea his Deputy Head will be able to answer general questions. Meals will all be served in the Directors' Dining Room and will be complimentary.

The college would appreciate receiving 20 copies of a detailed and informative programme for distribution to the students, who will arrive separately at the company's premises.

Draft a suitable day's programme, basing your answer on the foregoing details and inventing additional points where necessary to make your answer realistic.

LCC PSC June 1973 (*25 marks*)

2 Your employer, Miss K. Finch, FAMS, General Secretary of AMSPAR, is organising a one-day education conference for teachers of Medical Secretary courses in colleges of FE. The conference will be held in the Trades Hall, South Street, Liverpool 8 on 1 September 19.. She says, 'Let's do the programme now. Luncheon will be at 12.30 p.m., tea followed by dispersal at 3.30 p.m. and we'd better give them a cup of coffee when they arrive at 10 a.m. The Chairman, Dr A. R. Stout, FRS, FRCP will open the proceedings at 10.30 a.m.; Mr C. Parkes, LLB will speak about the medical secretary and the law at

10.45 a.m. and be followed by Mrs M. Bradley, SRN, MRSH, talking about confidentiality and the medical secretary at 11.30 a.m. At 2.00 p.m. Mrs P. Porter, M.Phil. will speak on organising new courses and we'll conclude with Mr S. Lever, BA talking about AMSPAR and the NHS at 2.45 p.m.

I'd like you to set that out as a programme, then draft a suitable covering letter informing course tutors in college of the conference (cost for the day – £12.00, including lunch). Put a tear-off acceptance slip at the bottom. Oh – would you also design a straightforward notice of the conference that we could get printed and sent to colleges for display there.'

AMSPAR D June 1984 (*20 marks*)

Forms of address

'Call me Dr Rock,' joked Paul McCartney after receiving an honorary doctorate from Sussex University.

Titles are commonplace in most areas of public life, including business (and showbusiness). This is a dauntingly complex subject on which books have been written, the most authoritative being Black's *Titles and Forms of Address*. Below are a few simple pointers to good practice which will enable students to cope with the titles that occur most regularly in exams:

- 'Mr' is now the same as 'Esq' and either may be used – but not both.
- A medical consultant is also addressed as 'Mr' but both a medical doctor and the holder of a doctorate (such as a PhD) are addressed as 'Doctor'.
- Use 'Ms' if you do not know the marital status of a woman.
- Husband and wife are jointly addressed by the husband's forename and surname, e.g. Mr and Mrs Paul Hammond.
- If you are writing to a knight or dame, the forename is always used with the title, e.g. Sir Stanley Matthews, Dame Edith Evans. (The correct salutation would then be 'Dear Sir Stanley' or 'Dear Dame Edith' – not 'Dear Sir Matthews' or 'Dear Dame Evans'.)
- When addressing a lord, the forename is not used: the late Sir Laurence Olivier became Lord Olivier.
- When addressing the wives of knights or lords, the forename is not used: e.g. Lady Sinclair. When the forename is used, the lady holds the title in her own right, e.g. HRH the Princess of Wales was formerly Lady Diana Spencer.

Letters after names

A glance back at the last section will show numerous examples of letters and qualifications after names. Care should always be taken in placing them in their correct sequence and in general the order of precedence is as follows:

1   The two highest decorations for valour – the VC and the GC
2   Orders of chivalry or knighthood, starting with the highest – KG, KT, GCB
3   Other decorations, starting with the highest – MBE, MC, DFC
4   Degrees and diplomas, starting with the lowest – BSc, MA, PhD
5   Membership of professional bodies – AMBIM
6   Other titles – MP, JP

Example: The Rt Hon Sir Winston Churchill, KG, OM, CH, FRS

Exercises

1 The following letters have all been mentioned in this or the previous section. Explain what they mean and say which, if any, confer a title on the holder:

BA	LLB	KT	MP
OBE	SRN	MC	JP
Ph.D.	VC	DFC	KG
FRS	GC	MA	OM
FRCP	GCB	AMBIM	CH

2 Consult a suitable reference book to discover how to address the people below in the ways indicated:

a) The Queen — envelope/verbal address
b) A Royal Prince/Princess — opening of letter/verbal address
c) The Prime Minister — envelope/opening of letter
d) The President of the USA — envelope/verbal address
e) The Pope — envelope/verbal address
f) Ambassador – British — envelope/opening of letter
g) Nigel Carlton, KG — place card/opening of letter
h) wife of the above — envelope/opening of letter
i) Richard Armstrong, CBE — envelope/verbal address
j) wife of the above — place card/verbal address
k) Edna Everage, DBE — envelope/opening of letter
l) Michael Jackson, Ph.D. — envelope/verbal address

3 There are two titles that are similar: Hon. and Rt. Hon. Give a brief explanation of each title.

4 Rearrange the following letters in their correct order:

a) MP Ph.D. M.Sc.
b) KT MBE VC
c) JP OBE LLB
d) MA OM DD
e) DSO CH FRS KBE

Visual communication

These days we are used to 'picture language' – on road signs, lavatory doors, car windscreens (disabled stickers) and notice-boards (cartoon safety strips).

Open any magazine, newspaper or report and the chances are that you will see a variety of tables, charts, graphs and diagrams to reinforce the text. A recent eight-page supplement to *Woman* entitled 'You and Your Home' included a cartogram[1] with house prices all over the UK; pictograms accompanying a section on 'What kind of mortgage is for you?'; pie charts showing who gets a 'slice of the action' when a house is bought or sold; a table showing how house prices rise in various parts of the country (by the month, week, hour and minute!); and, most dramatically and ingeniously of all, a bar chart representing the weekly price-rise with the bars portrayed as a series of bank notes literally going 'through the roof' of a house.

[1] A map with superimposed symbols, shading, figures, etc.

Such graphic display is effective in communicating simply and concisely. It breaks up continuous prose to add variety and impact, and it is often the most vivid way of showing comparisons or trends. It is vital, however, to remember to add the following (where appropriate), without which any presentation, however attractive, is likely to be meaningless:

- an explanatory title
- labels for axes/columns (e.g. units of measurement)
- different colours/shading/lines for different data
- a key
- the source of the data.

Ultimately, the choice of the most appropriate form of visual communication will depend on the type of information to be conveyed, the intended reader and the purpose. Some of the forms most commonly used in business (and asked for in exams) are considered below:

- **Organisation charts:** A 'family tree' of the organisation showing the status, responsibilities and relationships of its various members (*see* Exercise 1, page 98).
- **Tables:** A simple and accurate method which lacks visual impact; difficult too to show trends.
- **Bar charts:** Good visual impact and useful for comparing quantities; not as accurate as tables, however. (For examples of dual and composite bar charts, *see* Exercise 3, page 99.)
- **Line graphs:** These vary from simple line graphs to complex ones showing several pieces of information. They are useful for showing trends and making comparisons; again, not as accurate as tables.
- **Pie charts:** Visually attractive and easy to 'digest' if the pie is not cut into too many slices, but the total must be known if this method is to be used (*see* Exercise 4).
- **Pictograms:** Appealing to the eye but liable to oversimplification and distortion. These last two methods are probably the least accurate and are more suitable for the house magazine or the layperson rather than a board of directors.

Example

The following statistics analyse bankruptcies in England and Wales in 1980 and 1981.

Bankruptcies – Industrial Analysis of Net Cases Administered

ENGLAND AND WALES	NUMBERS		PERCENTAGES	
Industry	1980	1981	1980	1981
SELF-EMPLOYED				
Agriculture & Horticulture	50	70	1.4	1.4
Manufacturing, Construction & Road Haulage	1204	1498	32.5	31.1
Wholesaling & Retailing	683	960	18.4	19.9
Financial & Professional Services, Hotels, Restaurants, Garages, Other Consumer Services, Other Industries	873	1161	23.6	24.1

	NUMBERS		PERCENTAGES	
	1980	1981	1980	1981
OTHER INDIVIDUALS				
Employees, no occupation and unemployed	510 ⎱		555 ⎰	
Directors & Promoters of companies	313 ⎰ 894	1131	486 ⎱ 24.1	23.5
Occupation unknown	71 ⎰		90 ⎰	
TOTAL	3704	4820	100.0	100.0

[Source: Department of Trade]

Your employer is producing an article on 'Insolvencies: Current Trends'.

a) Prepare the above data for him in an easily assimilated visual form.

b) Prepare for 1980 and 1981 pie charts for that part of the table headed 'Other individuals'.

RSA DPA June 1983 (*20 marks*)

Commentary

1   No form is specified for (a) and while a line graph would be acceptable it would not be as impressive as a bar chart, which is the ideal method for illustrating comparative totals. Separate bars should be drawn for each entry, using either the percentages or the individual totals as the units for the vertical axis (*see* Figure 10).

2   For the two pie charts it is necessary to work out the angles (or 'slices') that can be measured with a protractor. The pie or circle has $360°$ to represent the total for 1980 of 894. So the first 'slice' is calculated as follows:

Employees, etc. 510 $Angle = \dfrac{510}{894} \times 360° = 205°$

Similar calculations give the other 'slices':

Directors, etc.   313 $Angle = \dfrac{313}{894} \times 360° = 126°$

Occupation unknown   71 $Angle = \dfrac{71}{894} \times 360° = 29°$

Total   894 $360°$

The angles for 1981 can be worked out similarly using the known total of 1131 (*see* Figure 11).

Suggested answer

a) **Bankruptcies – industrial analysis of net cases administered 1980–1 England and Wales**

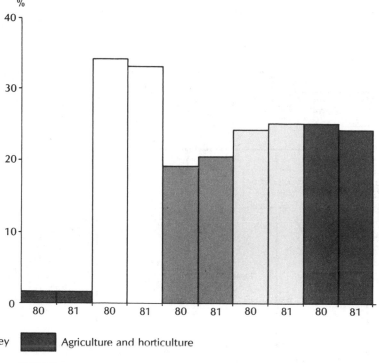

Key
- ■ Agriculture and horticulture
- □ Manufacturing, construction and road haulage
- ▨ Wholesaling and retailing
- ▨ Financial and professional services, hotels restaurants, garages, other consumer services, other industries
- ■ Other individuals

Figure 10   Source: Department of Trade

b) **Bankruptcies – other individuals**

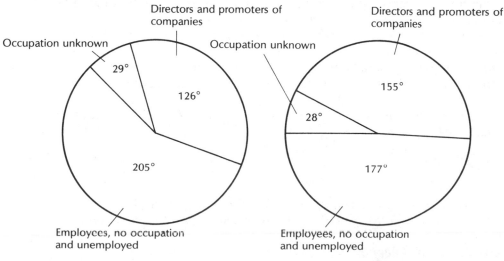

Figure 11   Source: Department of Trade

Exercises

1   Look at the organisation chart below, then answer the questions that follow.

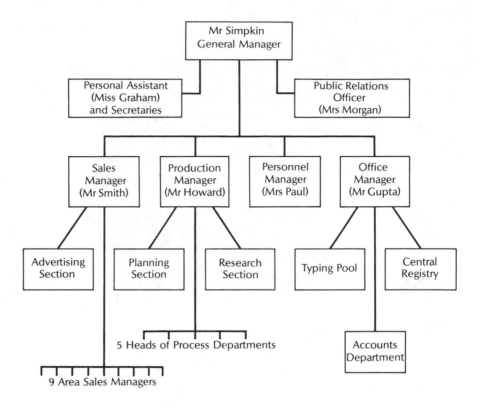

a)   How many sections does Mr Howard control?
b)   Who is responsible for Public Relations?
c)   Who handles the General Manager's correspondence and telephone calls?
d)   To whom do the members of Advertising Section report?
e)   Why should Central Registry come under Mr Gupta?
f)   Which of the four managers appears to have the least responsibility for other groups?
g)   Is Mr Smith responsible to Miss Graham?
h)   Through whom should the Heads of Process Departments approach Mr Simpkin?
i)   To whom does Mr Smith give responsibility for selling the company's products?
j)   Can Mr Smith give direct instructions to the members of Research Section?
k)   From whom should Mrs Paul seek clearance to interview a member of Planning Section?
l)   Which three rectangles contain the common support services which the whole company can use?

(15 marks)

LCC EFB First Level Sample Paper

2   You are helping to prepare a printed programme for an opening ceremony. Your Personnel Manager has written to three firms to obtain quotations for programmes printed in:
a)   one ink colour on white paper;
b)   two ink colours on white paper;
c)   two ink colours on coloured card.

A committee will then consider prices and decide which style of programme they prefer. It has been agreed that a minimum of 5000 copies of the programme will be required because as well as being given to guests they will be available to members of the general public, large numbers of whom are expected to attend the opening.

The Personnel Manager gives you the following table of information extracted from the replies she has received from the printers.

Printing costs

Printer	One ink colour/ white paper	Two ink colours/ white paper	Two ink colours/ coloured card
Carew & Sons	£55 for 1st 1000	£60 for 1st 1000	£90 for 1st 1000
	£50 for each 1000 of next 2000	£56 for each 1000 of next 2000	£82 for each further 1000
	£40 for each further 1000	£40 for each further 1000	
King Print	£116 for 1st 2000	£115 for 1st 2000	£199 for 1st 2000
	£35 for each further 1000	£50 for each further 1000	£62 for each further 1000
Beaumont and Fletcher	£65 for 1st 1000	£72 for 1st 1000	£93 for 1st 1000
	£60 for each further 1000	£64 for each further 1000	£80 for each further 1000 up to 3000 then 7p per copy

She asks you to use the above information to find out the lowest price for 5000 copies of the programme for each of the variations mentioned. You must also inform her of the names of the printers who offer the lowest prices.

BTEC

3 **a)** From the bar chart printed below, state:
   i) in which years home sales exceeded £10 000;
   ii) in which years home sales exceeded 50 per cent of total sales;
   iii) in which years total sales exceeded £35 000.

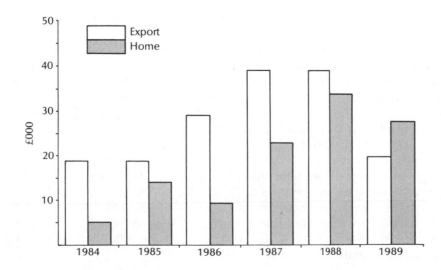

b) From the bar graph (shown below) give the following information:
  i) In which year was the greatest net dividend paid?
  ii) In which year were no profits retained?
  iii) In what years were the retained profits approximately equal to net dividends paid?
  iv) In what year was there a marked rise in the cost of administration?

RSA Secretarial Duties Stage II

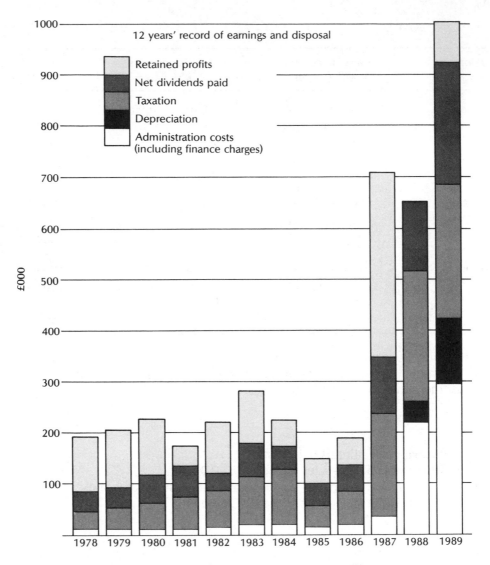

12 years' record of earnings and disposal

Legend:
- Retained profits
- Net dividends paid
- Taxation
- Depreciation
- Administration costs (including finance charges)

4 You work as assistant to Mrs Rita Thames, General Manager of Cartland & Co. Ltd, a large store which puts on special displays for periods such as Christmas, Easter and Summer. Extra space is required by certain departments for these, and this causes friction, especially between the Toy and Carpet Departments. Recently the Toy Department asked for extra space for a special display during Guy Fawkes' Week – 'It will mean taking a bit from Carpets but they won't sell any in November,' said Mrs Gellatly, Buyer for Toys. She also wants extra space for the Christmas toy display, but is meeting with opposition from both Carpets and Soft Furnishings. The Buyers for these departments feel strongly that each department should keep to its own area and not disturb others.

Somewhat concerned by the possibility of confrontation between the Toy Department, the Carpet Department and Soft Furnishings which between them occupy the whole of the Top Floor, Mrs Thames decided to make herself acquainted with some facts. She took the monthly sales figures for the previous year for the three departments and gave you the totals. These were:

Toy Dept	Jan.	£3 000	Feb.	£2 000	March	£10 000
	Apr.	£8 000	May	£5 000	June	£11 000
	July	£8 000	Aug.	£9 000	Sept.	£7 000
	Oct.	£8 000	Nov.	£14 000	Dec.	£25 000
	Total for the Year £110 000					

Carpet Dept	Jan.	£5 000	Feb.	£6 000	March	£9 000
	Apr.	£8 000	May	£8 000	June	£5 000
	July	£4 000	Aug.	£3 000	Sept.	£15 000
	Oct.	£16 000	Nov.	£13 000	Dec.	£8 000
	Total for the Year £100 000					

Soft Furnishings Dept	Jan.	£2 000	Feb.	£3 000	March	£10 000
	Apr.	£9 000	May	£6 000	June	£7 000
	July	£4 000	Aug.	£3 000	Sept.	£8 000
	Oct.	£10 000	Nov.	£11 000	Dec.	£7 000
	Total for the Year £80 000					

a) On a sheet of graph paper plot all three sets of monthly figures, superimposing the second and third sets on the first. Draw them so that each set can be clearly identified and compared. *(9 marks)*

b) Draw two pie charts, one showing the division of sales in September and the other in December. *(6 marks)*

c) Assume that the area occupied by the Departments is normally Toys 25 per cent, Carpets 55 per cent and Soft Furnishings 20 per cent. List the conclusions that Mrs Thames might reasonably draw from the graph and pie charts you have made to support or reject the arguments of the three Departmental Heads regarding Christmas and Guy Fawkes' Week in early November. A suitable answer will probably use about 80 words. *(5 marks)*

RSA CIB Stage II June 1981

5   The following statistics show a) the age composition of the work force of your organisation over five years, and b) pension func contributions and benefits paid out.

a)

			Year		
Age	1977	1978	1979	1980	1981
under 21	256	261	249	232	209
21–30	1905	1826	1832	1786	1928
31–40	3037	2896	2806	2780	2886
41–50	2235	2292	2091	2136	2282
51–60	1472	1466	1435	1538	1542
over 60	309	321	329	317	268

b)

(£m) Contributions	1977	1978	1979	1980	1981
by company	4.3	6.0	7.4	8.3	8.5
by employees	0.6	1.3	1.3	1.3	1.5
Benefits paid by company	4.1	6.1	8.5	9.5	9.5

Present these two sets of data in easily assimilated visual forms suitable for the organisation's 1982 Report to Employees.

(You can, if you wish, use more than one method in answering this question.)

RSA DPA June 1982 *(15 marks)*

Notes

If you are writing notes for a talk, for use at a meeting or in connection with a telephone call, it is important that they should suit their purpose. Some students' notes are either so full that they cease to be notes or so overcompressed that they become meaningless, even to the person who produced them. A skeleton outline is required – not the entire body nor a heap of disjointed bones.

All notes have one thing in common: they should be suitable for quick and easy reference. A logical sequence and effective display are therefore of the utmost importance. To achieve this, you should consider using:

- headings/sub-headings
- numbered points
- good use of space
- capitals/underlining for key words
- the dash in preference to other punctuation marks
- common abbreviations (wd, shd, ∴, e.g., NB)
- abbreviated expressions rather than complete sentences.

Example

You are employed as Senior Accounts Clerk in the Accounts Department of the Overseas Trading Company plc. The Accounts Manager, Mr Grey, has met with you and voiced his displeasure regarding a certain problem which has arisen with regard to staff in the Accounts Office. He suggests you could handle it by holding a meeting with all staff in the office.

The problem is as follows: there is a small room in the corner of the office where files and records of previous years' work are stored pending computerisation. Over the past couple of years this room has been used to 'brew up' tea and coffee for the office instead of staff having to go across the Despatch yard and up two flights of stairs to the canteen. The tea and coffee is better in quality, the price is cheaper and less time is wasted. The whole operation is, however, unofficial and would be frowned upon by superiors elsewhere. Mr Grey has been very tolerant and enjoys his coffee.

Due to the office's workload a lot of overtime has been worked. Consequently some of the staff have jointly purchased a small mini-grill to cook snacks. The result of this has been that all files and records taken from the room give off the odours of hamburgers, toasted sandwiches and other foods. Mr Grey fears that these smells may even permeate upstairs to the Directors' Boardroom.

Everyone enjoys good work relations in the office. No one would want to 'make a mountain out of a mole-hill'. Nonetheless the time has come for a reprimand and appropriate remedial action.

The problem is: what would be the most appropriate course of action to be taken? On the one hand Mr Grey does not want to lose the goodwill of staff in working voluntary overtime. On the other hand a reprimand must be given.

Prepare yourself for the staff meeting by making out *useful* notes on the problem.

You should concisely summarise all the information available to you, outline your suggested solution to the problem and offer reasons for your suggested solution. Any solution should be realistic and appropriate within the context of the office and the firm.

The notes should be organised in such a fashion that you can quickly and easily refer to them in a staff meeting chaired by yourself.

AAT P June 1986 (*20 marks*)

Suggested answer

Notes <u>for</u> staff mtg re Store Room

ACTION(S)	REASON(S)	PROBLEM(S)
1 Past practice		
tea/coffee	- more convenient	<u>unofficial</u>
last 2 yrs	- better quality	(tho tolerated)
	- cheaper	
	- quicker	
2 Present practice		
snacks	- overtime	SMELLS!!!
mini-grill		- on files/records
		taken elsewhere
		- may reach Dirs'
		B/droom
3 Future		
cooking <u>must</u> stop	- Mr G compromised?	
	- Dirs may w/draw <u>all</u>	
	unofficial facilities	
	- fire hazard?	
	- other depts jealous?	
SOLUTION(S)		
- use canteen	good relations	
- buy take-aways	preserved (no fingers	
(time allowed?)	burnt!)	
- revert to tea/		
coffee making only		

Exercises

1 You are a practising secretary and have been invited to speak on 'The Role of the Private Secretary' to secretarial students at a local college. Your talk will last for about 30 minutes and will be followed by a period for students' questions. Prepare the notes you would use during your talk.

2 Assume that you are working as general assistant to Mr Joseph Gilbert, Manager of the Imperial Ambassador Hotel, who is organising a conference for the International Institute of Contemporary Dance, Music and Art.

   Mrs V. S. Nijinsky, Secretary of the Institute, rings the hotel on Monday, 13 August. Mr Gilbert is out of the office and you receive the call. She says:

   'As you know, we have booked our conference at your hotel for the first week in October, and there are a number of extra things which I would like the hotel to organise if this is possible.

'First of all, is it possible to arrange a platform in the conference hall, if there isn't one already? This should have a long table on it, with chairs for ten people. Can you arrange a rostrum with a stand for speakers' notes? Some speakers will want to show slides: do you have a screen, a slide projector, and can you black-out the conference room easily? Do you have an overhead projector available for speakers? Do you have a video-system available for showing videotapes? Do you have a sound system for playing cassettes and records? If you don't have any or all of these items, please let me know by the beginning of September, and I can arrange for us to bring our own.

'Could you let me have some maps of Edgeley-on-Sea which I can copy and send to delegates? Do you have details of buses and taxis from the railway-station to your hotel? Have you any information about facilities in the town?

'I am pleased that you can organise the special dinner we requested. I wonder whether you could arrange to have a toastmaster available? What would be his fee? Also, could you arrange a stand for speakers to use for the after-dinner speeches? Could you organise buffet lunches rather than set meals?

'Have you a photocopier and duplicator available for use in the conference office, or do you wish us to bring our own? Is there a telephone in that office?

'I can now confirm that we will need 73 double bedrooms for the conference. We shall also need a single room for Dame Nanette Poliakov just for the evening of 5 October. Could you please make sure this is a good one? It may be helpful to you to know that 22 of our delegates are vegetarians: this will obviously be important for the special dinner.

'If there are any problems, please let me know by Friday, 7 September.'

Organise the relevant material of Mrs Nijinsky's telephone call into a set of notes. These should be set out logically and in such a way that Mr Gilbert can immediately grasp the points which demand his attention. A suitable answer will probably use about 150 words. (A suggested answer is given in Appendix 1.)

RSA CIB Stage I June 1984 (20 marks)

3   Your employer is attending a conference next week to introduce the company's latest word processor. From the information given below, select suitable headings and reminder points for him to use in a talk.

We are pleased to announce our latest model, The Screenwriter. This is a modular screen-based system, priced at £4800, which incorporates single disc drive and a golfball printer. It is by far the cheapest screen machine on the market and has already proved a big success in America. Previews are being held up and down the country – simply ring your local office to make an appointment for a demonstration. The two key features of this machine are its modularity, which enables you to build it up, and its programmability, which means that it can be programmed in various different ways. It does also have automatic centering and justification facilities, decimal tabulation, pagination and automatic carriage return. The machine is made in Italy, displays 80 characters across and 25 lines down, and tilts and adjusts position.

PEI EFB Advanced (20 marks)

5 Composition

I'd really like to learn how to write . . .
The Beatles, *Paperback Writer*

The article

There are more than 2000 company or house magazines in this country with an estimated circulation of 17 million. They exist as a communication medium in their own right and vary from cheaply produced news-sheets to the professional 'glossy' magazine. Their contents range from domestic news for employees (sports items, births, marriages, deaths) to company news suitable for the wider audience of customers, shareholders and the press.

Some exams ask for items for one of them – or for other magazines and newspapers. The key to success is to identify your audience and then adopt a suitable approach and technique. A news-story should give the main facts straightaway and then amplify them in the rest of the piece, the least important information coming at the end. (*See* p. 108 for a fuller discussion.) The article, however, often has an introductory paragraph (or two) to lead up to the main points before an incisive conclusion.

Impact and readability are prime requirements for this kind of writing and the following journalistic techniques will help to inject these qualities into your work.

Titles

Usually it is the title that first catches the reader's eye and decides whether or not he will pause and begin reading. An article entitled 'A Male Secretary' might get scant attention; the same article entitled 'Confessions of a Male Secretary' is more arresting.

Titles can be made appealing by the use of

- 'you'/'your' – *Your Next Interview*
- the question – *Who Wears the Trousers in Your Office?*
- the exclamation – *Meetings, Bloody Meetings!*
- twists in well-known sayings – *For Richer, for Porsche*
- an unusual or provocative note – *Man Cannot Live by Chips Alone* (on the silicon chip)

Puns, alliteration and repetition are all used to strengthen titles as can be seen from the above examples.

The beginning

The first paragraph is vital for it determines whether or not the casual reader will read on. A striking opening captures the attention and, if the early paragraphs are kept brief, a sense of quick and easy reading is created.

Effective ways of whetting the appetite are by using anecdotes, dialogue, exclamations, questions or challenging the reader's preconceptions in some way – anything in fact that creates reader-involvement.

The following openings were written by students on the theme of 'the male secretary'. They achieve that sprightliness of style which will encourage most readers to go on:

1   How many bosses would like their secretaries turning up for work complete with 'designer stubble', wearing trousers and smelling of Brut?

2   'Take a letter, Mr Smith.'
    Yes. *Mr* Smith!
    Well girls, it looks as if we'll have to curb our language in future now that there's a man
    in our office.
3   Most people know that the role of the secretary has changed dramatically over the last
    few years.
        But how many know that the *shape* of the secretary has changed too?

Structure

Once you have gained the reader's interest you must keep it, and a well-structured piece
(with a beginning, middle and end) stands a better chance than an accumulation of stray
thoughts, however amusing.

It is sometimes in the middle section that interest begins to wane. Dialogue, well-chosen
quotes, anecdotes, colourful metaphor will all help to rekindle it, and a strategically placed
sub-heading will not only aid the display but also sign-post what is to come.

> ## GARETH DAVID of *The Sunday Times* advises on how to handle job interviews
>
> Not everyone can be as lucky in interviews as was 30-year-old divorcee Marianne Herion when she went for a secretarial job. Bournemouth business-man Martin Forster, 28, told her: 'The post's yours, but only if you marry me within seven days.'
>
> At first she thought he was joking. But he wasn't. It was love at first sight, and the candidate got the job and a husband into the bargain.
>
> Whatever your chosen career path, it is a sure bet that from time to time you will have to face the grim prospect of going through job interviews. These can vary dramatically – from the relatively informal one-to-one discussion, to a full-blown grilling by an appointments panel or two days of character assess-ment at a specialist residential centre.

An effective 'lead', courtesy of NatWest *Moneycare*

The conclusion

Some excellent articles end not with a bang but a whimper and undermine the impression
that the rest of the piece has worked hard to create.
    Successful ways of ending are to:

- emphasise the point of the article
- save a striking example or illustration for the end
- exploit a well-known phrase to good effect
- introduce an unexpected twist, the 'sting in the tail'.

The following paragraph illustrates the first method. It was written by a student to conclude an article on how highly skilled secretaries are wasted in positions calling for little use of initiative and responsibility:

> One day I'll type a memo in spaced capitals and send it around the company. It will say: 'I'M HERE. I HAVE A BRAIN. I WOULDN'T MIND BEING GIVEN THE CHANCE TO USE IT ONCE IN A WHILE!'

Example

Write an article for a staff magazine describing favourably your recently completed year attached to an overseas office of the firm.

RSA DPA

(The article that follows, written by a student, illustrates many of the points made in the foregoing pages.)

GLOBE-TROTTING GLORIA RETURNS

by Gloria Richards, PRO

'Are you wearing clean underwear?'
   You know the feeling – there you are, standing at Heathrow trying to look like an experienced jet-setter who gets sent abroad every other week, while your mother fusses about, asking embarrassing questions. You could cheerfully bonk her on the head!
   Despite having studied French at school, I had never actually visited the country, so when TRIXO offered to let me work in our Paris branch I seized the opportunity with both hands. I was now regretting it. They were not butterflies I could feel in my stomach – they were more like elephants doing the quick-step!
   Although I had bought a 'useful' phrase book, I still doubted my ability to make myself understood. And would I be safe? I'd heard that civilisation ended at Dover.
   I need not have worried. My flight was not hijacked; the plane did not develop engine trouble; and my luggage and I touched down at the same airport on the same day.
   Paris! Once I was through customs I could hardly wait to see all the sights and landmarks that I had looked at only on postcards before. I arrived early on Saturday, and that gave me two whole days to take in the flavour of France before starting work. I climbed the Eiffel Tower (1572 steps up – I had to come down by lift); stood under the Arc de Triomphe; walked down the Champs Élysées; and sat drinking coffee at a pavement cafe just watching *le monde* go by.

SACHA DISTEL

Of course there was work to do as well and I soon settled down in the small comfortable office with its view of the Seine. There were five other girls there – all French – and the boss, Monsieur Flautré, who looked just like Sacha Distel!

TRIXO have only just moved into Europe and most of my work was in the public relations field – contacting possible buyers, briefing representatives and putting advertisements in suitable journals – generally making people aware of us.

Language presented a problem to begin with, especially slang and jargon, but after just a few weeks I began to think in French, and I believe that many of the customers took me for a native. In fact, when I came home for Christmas I had to stop myself spouting French at my parents – it seemed the natural thing to do.

As my time in Paris drew to a close, I began to wish that I could stay for good – Stoke seemed rather tame in comparison. But I had to leave, and as my plane winged its way over the Channel sadness was mixed with pleasure at the prospect of seeing family and friends again.

Looking back, I can see that my year abroad taught me a lot, not only about the company but about life in general. I feel sure that TRIXO have a great future *sur le continent* because there seems to be no competition to rival us in either quality or design. With a bit of luck I shall soon be flying out to help in new TRIXO branches in Germany, Australia, America, Japan . . .

Harlem Globe-Trotters – eat your heart out!

The press release

Many of the stories that we read in newspapers, hear on the radio or see on TV originate as press releases. These are issued by organisations to tell the media of anything they consider newsworthy – such as gaining a valuable export order, opening a new branch or staging an important event. They may be directed at local or national media (or both) and gain the best kind of publicity for a company – free publicity.

Not surprisingly, editors receive hundreds of press releases every week, of which only a small proportion will be used. It is therefore essential to maximise the chances of any release not only by convincing the editor (or examiner) that it is genuinely newsworthy but also by presenting it in the correct format and style.

How to present a press release

- Double-spaced typing is essential and wide margins are preferred so that an editor can make changes on the original. (In an exam which is handwritten it is best to write the release as normal and add a note on typing conventions at the end.)
- The release should tell the editor when he can use the information; for example, 'For immediate publication' or 'Embargo: Not for publication before . . .' should precede the heading.
- A brief factual title (in capitals) should indicate the theme of the release. (This will usually be changed by the editor.)
- Only one side of the paper should be used. If there is more than one page 'more', 'm.f.' (more follows) or 'continued' is added at the end of each page. The word 'ends' is used to indicate the final sheet.
- Nothing in a news release should be underlined as this conveys instructions to the printer to set that part in italics.
- The date of issue should be given and a reference number may be added to make the release quickly identifiable.
- The source of the release should be given together with the name and after-hours telephone number of the person who can give further information if required.
- The availability of photographs may be mentioned at the end of the release.

How to write a press release

- Short paragraphs are ideal.
- The first paragraph(s) should give the gist of the story at once and answer the questions *Who? What? When? Where?* and usually *Why?*
- The paragraphs that follow amplify the story and give the additional details in *descending order of importance*. (If an editor lacks sufficient space for the whole release, he will start cutting it from the end.)
- The style should be simple and factual; overwriting of any kind should be avoided.
- A release for local media must generate local colour – by naming local people, places and organisations.

Example

The following press release from British Coal was sent to both the local and national press. Among other newspapers, it was used by the *Wigan Evening Post* and Figure 12 shows how it was tailored for that particular medium. Comment on any changes that have been made by the editor.

IMMEDIATE

          JIM 'FIXES IT' FOR DISABLED PITMEN

    Top television star Jimmy Savile has 'fixed it' for hundreds of disabled

mineworkers to spend a holiday by the seaside.

    The ex-pitman turned celebrity will officially open new purpose-built

holiday accommodation at Blackpool on Saturday (April 9th).

    Jim, a tireless charity worker, who has a keen interest in the severely

disabled, was invited to open the new 'Sherwood' holiday unit by Trustees

of the Lancashire Mineworkers' Paraplegic Fund.

    Said trustee Brian Talbot, Industrial Relations Officer for British Coal

Western Area: 'Jim's achievements in the charity field are well known and

as an ex-miner we thought he was the perfect man to open the new unit.

    'We are delighted that he has agreed to interrupt a busy schedule to "fix

it" for us.'

                                                                    m.f.....

...2

The new holiday unit, which has been built adjacent to the Miners'
Convalescent Home on Blackpool's North Shore, comprises six self-contained
flats, each sleeping two people.

The flats, which are complete with bathrooms and kitchens, open out into
a glass-covered, landscaped courtyard. There are panoramic views of the sea
front from a communal television lounge.

In addition to the new unit, which will open all the year round, three
existing bungalows for the disabled on the site have been modernised and
improved to provide family accommodation.

'All these improvements, coupled with the opening of Sherwood, mean that
we can now offer unrivalled facilities for our paraplegic mineworkers at
Blackpool,' said the fund's longest-serving trustee, North West NUM Agent
Bernard Donaghy.

The opening of 'Sherwood' is being tied in with celebrations to
commemorate the Sixtieth Anniversary of the Miners' Convalescent Home.

Opened by HRH The Prince of Wales in June, 1927, the home was the first
miners' convalescent home to be built in Britain, and it was funded from a
levy of 1d. per ton on the coal raised in the Lancashire and Cheshire
coalfields.

The home, which can accommodate 155 people, has fully equipped medical
services, a sun lounge, two television rooms, a library, writing room,
games room, and an outside bowling green.

Providing entertainment at the joint opening and anniversary
celebrations will be the Bold Brass Band, from St. Helens, and the Parkside
Male Voice Choir from Newton-le-Willows.

Ends

WA 2211

Thursday, March 31, 1988.

Public Relations Department
British Coal, Western Area
Staffordshire House, Berry Hill Road
Stoke-on-Trent ST4 2NH
Telephone 0782 744201 or 411741

After Office Hours:
Rod Crossley, Alsager (09363) 3466
John Harris, Leek (0538) 373262

Jim'll fix it for unit

Miners get TV star for opening

EX-MINERS from Wigan are set to enjoy modern new holiday homes after a major revamp of their famous "pitman's paradise" at Blackpool.

Jimmy Savile will travel to the resort on Saturday to open officially the Sherwood holiday unit for the disabled at the seafront miners' home.

And North West NUM agent Bernard Donaghy, of Astley, near Leigh, said today the new accommodation meant miners were now able to spend a well-earned holiday in luxury.

As well as the Sherwood development, next to the convalescent home, three more existing bungalows for the disabled have been modernised and improved to provide family accommodation.

"All these improvements, coupled with the opening of Sherwood, mean that we can offer unrivalled facilities for our paraplegic mineworkers at Blackpool," said Mr Donaghy, the Lancashire miners paraplegic fund's longest-serving trustee.

Trustee

Jim was asked along to open the new development in recognition of his charity work for the disabled.

And, as he stressed in accepting the request to travel to Blackpool on Saturday, the "fix-it" TV star is an ex-miner himself.

Fund trustee Brian Talbot, industrial relations officer for British Coal's Western Area, explained: "Jim's achievements in the charity field are well known and as an ex-miner we thought he was the perfect man to open the new unit.

"We're delighted he has agreed to fix-it for us."

The new unit at North Shore comprises six self-contained flats, each sleeping two people.

And the flats, which are complete with bathrooms and kitchens, open out into a glass-covered, landscaped courtyard.

"There are panoramic views of the seafront from a communal television lounge," said a spokesman for the trustees.

Diamond

The opening coincides with the diamond anniversary celebrations at the home.

It was opened by the Prince of Wales — the first of its type in Britain — and was funded in the 1920s from a levy of one old penny on the coal raised in Lancashire and Cheshire coalfields.

It can now accommodate 155 people and also has an outdoor bowling green.

Figure 12 (Courtesy of the *Wigan Evening Post*)

Example

Comlon International plc is an Entertainments Group which owns theatres, concert halls and leisure complexes in Europe and Australasia.

You are secretary to Mr Peter Barton, Managing Director of Comlon International plc (Europe). It is June 1987.

Since next year has been designated European Music Year, a year to demonstrate the richness of European music, Mr Barton and his fellow directors have agreed that the Company should stage a music conference to celebrate the event. The conference is to be held on Friday 8 January 1988 in Comlon's London Concert Hall (Comlon Hall) with an exhibition in the foyer, followed by a concert in the evening.

Various speakers have been contacted and have agreed to take part in the conference; invitations have been sent to 1000 leading people in the music business, including promoters, impresarios, performers, music shop owners and managers.

At a meeting to discuss the arrangements, Mr Barton agreed that Comlon should gain maximum publicity from the proposed conference and decided that a suitable press release should be sent to the national press for publication immediately before the conference.

Mr Barton has asked you to draft the necessary press release and you have made the following notes to help you in the task:

<u>European Music Year</u>

Idea of music campaign   - European Parliament's - 1980
                                      - to 'push' European music throughout
                                         year: concerts, dance performances,
                                         operas, publications, recordings,
                                         festivals, exhibitions,
                                         competitions, conferences on
                                         musical themes in many European
                                         countries.

<u>Comlon Conference</u>

Date: January 8 1988
Times: 1000 to 1700

Speakers (include)   - music critics, composers, artists;
                                         - Humphrey Littler, famous jazz
                                         musician and broadcaster;
                                         - David Jacobson, well-known radio
                                         and TV personality;
                                         - Ted Manlove, composer - will discuss
                                         'Symphony Orchestra and Electronic
                                         Music'.

                                         Mr Barton will welcome guests.

<u>Exhibition</u>

                                         - All day - in foyer - other rooms in
                                         building
                                         - important developments in European
                                         music
                                         - pictures, tapes, records,
                                         instruments, performers
                                         - all types of music

```
Concert

                        - 1930
                        - compère Mr David Jacobson
                        - performers various
                        - all types of music - classical,
                          light, jazz, pop
                        - London Symphony Orchestra to play
                          using electronic sound
```

Draft a press release 200 to 280 words long. You may invent detail if necessary.

LCC PSC June 1987 (*40 marks*)

Commentary

1   In the 1987 exam many candidates were unfamiliar with this document and some answers gave no release date (here an embargo is required), heading, source or person to contact. One candidate told the editor that the release was 'To be printed immediately on the front page'!

2   The main problem, however, was finding the correct register. Some examinees chose styles more appropriate to:
   a) a gossip column – 'Rumours are that an all-day exhibition is being held at Comlon Castle. . .'
   b) a company's AGM – 'Notice is hereby given that Comlon International's Conference will be held on. . .'
   c) a handbill – 'Don't miss your chance to see the most spectacular Music Conference ever. . .'
   d) a football programme – 'Comlon will kick off with a conference. We have a great line-up. . .'
   e) a pop show advert – 'Fantastic knock-out concerts. . .'
   f) a frenetic sales leaflet – 'Hurry soon as tickets are selling like hot cakes. . .'
   g) an order from an official authority – 'Report to the foyer for the exhibition. . .'

3   Some candidates copied the given information wholesale, adding little to it except their own errors (Humphrey Litter, Ted Madlove). Two misconceptions recurred: *European Parliament's* was often read as a plural while *1930* became not the time of the concert but either its theme ('music produced in 1930') or a description of David Jacobson ('famous compère of the 1930s'). To achieve good marks candidates should use the notes accurately and imaginatively to produce fluent prose which is suitable for the required business document.

Assignment

Compose a press release of your own before reading the suggested answer that follows.

Suggested answer

COMLON INTERNATIONAL plc

PRESS RELEASE

EMBARGO: Not for publication before 4 January 1988

COMLON'S CONFERENCE TO CELEBRATE EUROPEAN MUSIC YEAR 1988

Comlon International plc is to celebrate the beginning of European Music
Year by staging a grand music conference in Comlon Hall, London, on Friday,
8 January 1988. It will last from 1000 to 1700 hours and over a thousand
prominent figures from the music world will be there, including promoters,
impresarios, performers, music shop owners and managers.

   Guest speakers at the conference will include many distinguished
critics, composers and artists, among them Humphrey Littler, famous jazz
musician and broadcaster, and David Jacobson, the well-known radio and TV
personality. A discussion on 'the Symphony Orchestra and Electronic Music'
will be led by the composer Ted Manlove, to introduce one of the themes of
the evening concert. This will be held at 1930 hours when David Jacobson will
compère a concert whose musical range is all-embracing - from Beethoven to
the Beatles. All types of music, including classical, light, jazz and pop,
will be played by a host of star performers. The highlight of the evening
will be a performance by the London Symphony Orchestra using electronic
sound.

   Throughout the day an exhibition will be held in the foyer and other rooms
of the building to show the important developments that have contributed to
the popularity of European music. All types of music are to be represented -
from classical to pop - and the exhibits will include pictures, tapes,
records and instruments.   m.f....

In the audio-visual studio there will be the chance to see and hear specially produced videos and recordings and to meet some of the musicians.

European Music Year, originally conceived by the European Parliament in 1980, aims to promote European music throughout the year with concerts, dance performances, operas, publications, recordings, festivals, exhibitions, competitions and conferences on musical themes in many European countries.

Ends

(Photographs of guest speakers are available on request.)

9 June 1988
PB/LCC

Comlon International plc
Comlon House
West Street
London
SW1Y 2AR
071-920 0261

After office hours:
Peter Barton 071-3752371

Exercises

1 Write an article for your company's monthly magazine, which is distributed free to all employees, giving your views on whether or not men and women should have equal opportunities for promotion in commerce. Your article should be *interesting* and *persuasive*.

LCC EFB Second Level 1988 (*40 marks*)

2 Using the following notes and adding any information you may think suitable, compose an item of not more than 200 words to be considered for inclusion in the local newspaper:

Midchester Chamber of Trade – golden jubilee – charity football match – exhibitions, gala procession – series of events – special activities for local schools – gala – opened by famous TV personality – theme 'value to the community' – organisers hope for local TV coverage.

AEB EBU Specimen Question Paper

3 Super-Temp is a secretarial agency which supplies temporary staff for local firms which are short-staffed owing to holidays, illness overwork or other reasons. Temporary secretaries are employed by and paid by the agency, which engages them on a permanent basis, either full-time or part-time, and sends them to work in the offices of local firms as the need arises.

When the temporary secretary first arrives a firm explains her exact duties, although she is usually full trained. She will work at a given firm for a period from half-a-day upwards, but seldom spends more than two or three weeks there. this might be unsettling for some girls, but Super-Temp tries to employ staff who enjoy variety. The girls sometimes need to travel fairly long distances, though fares are refunded by the agency. Full-time staff can earn up to £120 per week and part-timers *pro rata*.

Super-Temp plans to distribute hundreds of copies of a recruiting leaflet to local houses. The object is to find housewives with secretarial training and/or experience who would like to join the staff of Super-Temp. An open evening will shortly be held on the agency's premises so that interested persons can learn more about the life and work of a temporary secretary. They will be able to meet some of the staff, listen to a talk by the Manager, and so on. There will be suitable light refreshments.

Attempt *one* of the following exercises, inventing any necessary *minor* details:

Either

a) Prepare the full text of a suitable recruiting leaflet. You need to present all the relevant particulars attractively but crisply. Circular letter format should be used.

Or

b) As a junior reporter for a local newspaper, you have attended the open evening. Draft a brief feature article about Super-Temp and its activities. You must assume that your readers do not know anything about temporary work.

Note

You may choose whether the evening was a success or failure, provided you clearly indicate *why*. This exercise tests your ability to report and put forward reasoned views. (A suggested answer to b) is given in Appendix 1.)

LCC PSC June 1974 (*30 marks*)

4 Write an article of about 500 words for a staff newspaper issued fortnightly to 180 office and factory employees on the findings of a survey of attitudes to the firm's proposal that the standard lunch break should be reduced from 1 hour to $\frac{3}{4}$ hour, with compensation at leaving time.

RSA DPA June 1976 (*25 marks*)

5 Write an article of about 400 words for the house magazine of a large office organisation, entitled Safety in the Office.

RSA DPA June 1981 (*20 marks*)

6 (Some examining boards ask for the more traditional essay, but the points made in this section concerning structure, openings and conclusions, etc. still apply. Candidates are often asked to show an awareness of current affairs and the reading of quality newspapers and magazines such as *The Times*, *Guardian* and *New Statesman* is highly recommended.)

Write an essay on one of the following:

a) AIDS. Is the State doing all it can, or all it can be expected to do?

b) Napoleon once described the British as a 'nation of shopkeepers'. Recent government policies seem to be turning us into a nation of shareholders. Do you see this as a good thing or a bad thing?

c) There is continuing concern about the social (and economic) problems of decaying inner cities. What do you think could or should be done about them?

d) A most moving experience.

e) 'Over the hills and far away'.

AMSPAR D June 1987 (*30 marks*)

7 In about 500 words prepare a press release for a British firm, announcing a large export order gained in the face of considerable home and overseas competition.

(Consider how and why the order was gained – quote particularly the customer's reasons; give details of the order and describe the likely benefits for the firm in the light of the country's present economic situation. The contract was signed on 30 May.)

RSA DPA June 1977 (*25 marks*)

8 In about 400 words prepare a press release for local circulation on the following:

Each year your town's Carnival Committee, supported by many local organisations and interests, holds its Family Day in one of the parks. Profits from the venture go to local charities. This year the event will be on Saturday, 4 July. The Carnival Queen will be crowned, there will be a procession from the town centre to the park where the main entertainments will be staged and a very well-known person will open proceedings which include organised displays, competitions, amusements, stalls and sideshows.

RSA DPA June 1981 (*20 marks*)

9 The following information describes a recent experiment in shopping methods:

Computerised shopping experiment – involves Fransco Foods and Wallsfoot Borough Council. Postan Street branch library, Wallsfoot, used since May 3rd. Two Fransco staff attend there four mornings a week – use a side room. Wallsfoot Social Services Dept co-operating – they picked out 60 local folk who find it hard to get about – the old, the sick, the handicapped and mothers with young children. These people all shop at library. Fransco has at Postan Street library a data terminal cash register with memory and Prestel viewdata Fransco price lists – customers order from these. As 'background' – slide projection scenes from Fransco's town centre store – to make customers feel they're in the supermarket. Deliveries free the same day. All very successful. Fransco plans follow-up: three KcT 47 microprocessors to connect two branch libraries and Social Services Dept direct to Fransco's town centre store – up to 700 handpicked 'customers' this time. Their shopping orders go down phone as digital data to supermarket – faster service follows. Overall customer saving – no fares to town centre, shorter trips, avoidance of expensive corner shops, less congestion in supermarket.

a) Using *all* of the details provided write a press release of about 300 words designed for business editors of national newspapers. (*15 marks*)

b) Using *some* of the above details write an article 300–350 words long for the *Wallsfoot Chronicle*, bringing out the 'human interest' features of the computerised shopping experiment. Give the article a title and add your name. (*20 marks*)

RSA DPA June 1983

10 **Assignment: 'Press Gang'**

Learning outcomes
This assignment enables the student to:
1 Draft a memorandum, forms and an informal report
2 Make notes of an interview
3 Give and receive a telephone message
4 Design a poster
5 Proofread and correct a typescript
6 Compose an item for a newsletter
7 Design a page of a newsletter
8 Write a letter of congratulation.

Resources
- Task 4 would be more realistic if telephones were available
- Task 6 requires a copy of the article

- Tasks 7 and 8 would be easier if copies of local companies' newsletters/house magazines could be consulted
- Task 8 might require typewriters, Letraset or black felt-tip pens and paste.

Situation

You are the assistant to Ken Pemberton, the Public Relations Director of Renshaws, a large manufacturing company. He has just returned from the July directors' meeting and tells you that they have decided to introduce a staff newsletter to improve communication and morale within the organisation.

'Staff don't know what's happening in the next office,' he says. 'In fact they often don't even know the *people* in the next office. So we're going to put everyone in the picture. And I mean everyone.'

Mr Pemberton, who has journalistic experience, has been given the responsibility for implementing the project. 'Obviously I shall need a lot of help,' he says. 'It's been suggested that I find someone in each department to act as a "reporter" and send on titbits of news, features, ideas that we can use. I need four or five people with their ears close to the ground, who can write well themselves or get others to write. They'll be given time to do this properly and there'll be a special all-expenses-paid training week in August at a London college for those chosen. It will cover everything from sub-editing to desk-top publishing – we're going to print it ourselves. Then we're all going to meet regularly as an editorial team. For anyone with a bit of nous and creative flair, it should prove an exciting prospect. But we must get cracking. The first issue's to appear in three months' time.'

Task 1

'First I'd like you to draft a memorandum to the staff and tell them what we're proposing. Encourage any potential "reporters" to apply. Don't make the content sound too "heavy" – it's meant to be a lively read. Besides company news we'll have space for sports, hobbies, holiday travel, cartoons, competitions – that sort of thing. But don't make it sound like a "soft option" either. I want people who are keen as mustard, literate, and who can produce the goods on time.

'Would you also draft a simple application form to go with the memo. Find out more about those interested – how long they've been with us, any writing experience, etc. Put a deadline on it – I'd like to interview those who apply at the end of the month.'

Task 2

There is a good response to the memorandum and an encouraging number of applications. 'The place seems full of budding writers,' comments Mr Pemberton.

As he is working under considerable pressure, he asks you to sift through the forms and assess applicants' likely suitability. 'Let me have a brief report,' he says, 'with a profile of the four people you would recommend for interview (with your reasons).'

Task 3

On the day of the interviews Mr Pemberton tells you that he has invited along a Miss Jane Greer, who joined Renshaws shortly after the deadline for applications. 'I've heard she may be just what we're looking for,' he says. 'But as she didn't fill in your form I'd like you to sit in on the interview and take a few notes that I can refer to later if necessary. As you selected the shortlist, I'd also like your opinion of her.'

The interview proceeds as follows:[1]

Ken Pemberton:	Good morning, Jane. Take a seat. Are you settling in all right?
Jane Greer:	Yes, fine, thanks.
Ken Pemberton:	I invited you for a chat today because I heard on the grapevine that you'd be very interested in applying. Can you say why?

[1] To make it a more realistic exercise, two members of the group could role-play the interview while the remainder take notes.

Jane Greer:	Yes. At my former employers, Swift House, I helped with a house magazine that was circulated among all 800 employees. I did a fair bit of sub-editing – some of the contributions really did need a lot of polishing – and I also tried my hand at writing. I've brought several pieces that I produced. (*Hands over magazines.*) I enjoyed the work.
Ken Pemberton:	Thank you very much – I look forward to reading them. How often was the magazine produced?
Jane Greer:	Quarterly. We also published an occasional news-sheet of information that couldn't wait.
Ken Pemberton:	Have you always been interested in writing?
Jane Greer:	Yes – I think it first started at school and when I went to Standon Sixth Form College I took an optional course in creative writing.
Ken Pemberton:	Was it any good?
Jane Greer:	Oh yes – we dabbled in most things: poetry, short stories, descriptive writing, and so on. I was toying with the idea of journalism as a career at the time. My father used to work for the old *Evening News*.
Ken Pemberton:	What other subjects did you study?
Jane Greer:	I took A-Levels in English Literature and Spanish as well as their secretarial course.
Ken Pemberton:	And you finally decided that you preferred secretarial work to journalism?
Jane Greer:	Yes – partly because the *Evening News* was being taken over at the time and there was a lot of uncertainty about job prospects. But I've managed to keep my hand in ever since – I write in a modest way for the *Herald*, the free weekly paper.
Ken Pemberton:	What sort of thing do you write for them?
Jane Greer:	Well, some time ago they advertised for correspondents for their *Down Your Way* page who could produce a column about the area where they live. I volunteered and write about Heron Cross. Anything of interest that is happening locally – from bingo to break-ins.
Ken Pemberton:	Do you write every week?
Jane Greer:	No, not quite. But sometimes if they're short of contributions they ring me up and ask me to produce something at short notice.
Ken Pemberton:	So you're used to working under pressure?
Jane Greer:	Oh yes – in fact working against a deadline often seems to help.
Ken Pemberton:	What other hobbies and interests do you have?
Jane Greer:	I like most sports – and photography. I also sketch a little when I get time.
Ken Pemberton:	Would the fact that you've only just joined us and don't really know many faces or the organisation be a handicap for this type of work, do you think?
Jane Greer:	On the contrary – I think it would help me meet people and get involved with the company's affairs so much more quickly.
Ken Pemberton:	And would there be any problems in attending the week's training course we're going to run in London in August?
Jane Greer:	None at all. It sounds quite exciting.
Ken Pemberton:	Any questions you would like to ask me?
Jane Greer:	Yes. Who has the final say with regard to what is published? For instance, if a very good article was received which was slightly critical of the company and the editorial team wanted to use it but you were not very keen on the idea, who would make the final decision?
Ken Pemberton:	As editor, I would ultimately decide. But I don't see myself as the censor for the company. I should be quite happy to use the kind of article you describe. I hope we get some. Anything else?
Jane Greer:	No, I don't think so.

Ken Pemberton:	Fine. Well, whatever we decide today I hope that you'll contribute to the newsletter in due course. Perhaps, as a newcomer, you might like to write a short piece on yourself?
Jane Greer:	*(laughing)*. Certainly – I'll try not to make it boring!
Ken Pemberton:	Thank you very much for coming. I'll be in touch later this afternoon.

Task 4

Mr Pemberton is delighted with the interviewees and later that afternoon asks you to telephone them. 'Tell them they've been successful,' he says. 'Confirmation in writing with details of the training course in the next day or two. The first editorial meeting will be held in the Board Room on the first Monday in September. Two o'clock. In the meantime they should start rustling up contributions. Tell them you're sending them a poster.'

Working in pairs, members of the group should take turns in giving and receiving the message.

Task 5

'As soon as you've finished the calls would you design the poster as a matter of urgency,' Mr Pemberton asks. 'Announce a competition for the best name for the newsletter – £20 for the winner. Request contributions – no matter how brief. *Anyone* can write for us – they don't have to be William Shakespeare. Indicate the range of material we're after: news of sports events, articles, features, photographs, cartoons, advertisements, etc. But items *must* be readable. I don't want any boring committee reports or out-of-date information.

'Suggested names/contributions to the "reporters" or direct to me as soon as possible so that we'll have some material to consider at our first meeting.

'Don't forget to make it eye-catching and try to involve as many people as possible.'

Task 6

Your poster obviously does the trick as a steady trickle of contributions comes in. However, their quality varies greatly and Mr Pemberton draws your attention to one in particular that has come directly to him. You read the following:

The Lonliness of the Long Distance Runner

For several years now the local marathan has taken place in July. John Lawton, our Supperman in Sales, has always taken part. This year was not exeption.

And if you were watching & blinked you make have missed him! For John is getting faster by the year. In 1989 when he was still a tenderfoot (no pun intended! John spent a grewelling 3 hours 50 minutes in completing the 26 mile Course.

But this year he crossed the line in 3 huors dead.

'"Dead" being the right word,' Groaned John, when I spoke to him. 'Its to soon think of doing another. Everyyear when I hit "the Wall" I ask myself, "Why am I doing this?"'

One reason is the money that John rases for his pet charity, the NSPpC, which this year amounted to £570. At the end of the race not only he but also the pockets of his sponsers were several pounds lighter!

Not bad for someone who, by his own admition, a was 40-cigarettes-a-day, 5-pints-a-night 12-stone weakling a few years ago. But now

---

this "Weight-Watchers' reject if the manestay of our squash and
ba^{dmington} teams and a vetteran marathan man to boot (or rather, to
running shoe).

So if you see him running home from work during the coming winter
months, dont take pity and offer him a life. Either his wife's run
off with the car or he's in training for next year.

So congratulations John on a marvelous performance! Keep up the good
wrok!

(Enclosed: photograph of John on his knees at the end of the race)

a) 'Can you do anything with this?' Mr Pemberton asks. 'I like the photo – we can use
   that – but the typescript's full of mistakes. Doesn't anyone proofread any more? I can
   see at least 25 errors, but your English is better than mine and you may well find
   more. Would you indicate any corrections that need to be made? Standard
   proofreading marks, please.'

b) He goes on: 'The title isn't quite right either. It was OK for Alan Sillitoe's story – have
   you read it? You should – but there's nothing lonely about marathon running! Can
   you think of anything better?'

c) 'Also I'm not very keen on the opening paragraph – it's dull where it needs to be
   snappy. Can you jazz it up? What about developing the Superman image: "Is it a
   bird? Is it a plane? No, it's our Superman from Sales. . ." Just a thought. You can
   probably improve on it.'

d) Finally he says: 'What about the conclusion? Do you think it's strong enough? I don't
   like the repetition of "So" and the cliché right at the end doesn't help either. See
   what you can do with it and make any changes you think fit. When you're happy
   with it would you type out a fair copy for me so that I can get copies made for the
   meeting?'

Task 7

As employees of Renshaws submit contributions on any of the following topics (or short
pieces on topics of your own choice which would be of interest to fellow employees):
● Births, Marriages, Deaths
● New Appointments, Promotions, Retirements
● Sports news (fixtures, results, personalities)
● An advertisement inviting staff and their children to visit an ice-skating rink
● Company sales figures for this year and the previous year
● Display advertisement for a Hallowe'en Party
● An interview with the MD on his recent trip abroad
● Forthcoming visit by a VIP
● Proposal by company to introduce a flexitime system
● The Staff Restaurant: Healthy Eating?
All members of the group should also suggest a name for the newsletter.

Task 8

Imagine that you are at the editorial meeting in September. After the initial discussion
(during which you decide on the best name for the newsletter) you consider the
contributions already received and start to put the first issue together.

   In pairs or groups, compose *one* page of the newsletter based on the work produced
for the previous exercises. If desktop publishing facilities are not available, contributions
should be typed – in columns – and then 'pasted up' on the page in order to achieve the
most effective display. Space should be allocated for photographs and captions should
make clear what is to go there. Black felt-tip pens may be useful for bold lettering.

Task 9

After the meeting Mr Pemberton asks you to write a letter of congratulation to the person who suggested the winning name and enclose a cheque for £20.

Task 10

In October the first issue is published and widely circulated. 'But how did it go down?' asks Mr Pemberton. 'I know the MD liked it, but did anyone else? Can you do a spot of market research and find out if people have seen a copy and if they have read it? Find out if they liked it and what they liked most. Ask if they have any criticisms or suggestions for future issues. You know the kind of thing. I can take the results to the next editorial meeting.'

Draft the questionnaire you would use to sample opinion.

6 Summarising

Help!
The Beatles

As summarising is at the heart of many business tasks (telex/telephone messages, minutes, job descriptions, advertisements) it is not surprising that it often appears on exam papers.

It tests comprehension, the evaluation of relevance and the ability to write good English within the confines of a word limit. Examinees usually find it demanding.

The following guidelines should prove helpful in tackling this question:

- Read through the passage several times – you will find it difficult to summarise something you do not understand.
- Ensure that you know *exactly* what you have to do and why your summary is required.
- Keep in mind the intended reader(s) of the summary who may influence its style, content and display.
- Select a working title which states the main theme of the summary. (Sometimes the original title will serve, but often it will need to be changed.)
- Select the main points and organise them logically. *NB* It is often a mistake to work through the passage summarising paragraph by paragraph as some paragraphs may be irrelevant or misleading. If in doubt, test for significance against your title.
- Omit examples, illustrations, quotations, questions and names. Figurative language should be reduced to factual statement ('an avalanche of protests' = many complaints).
- Do not add any ideas or comments of your own.
- Decide on the most appropriate display. One paragraph of continuous prose is less likely in communication exams than two or three headed paragraphs, notes under sub-headings, arguments for and against, etc.
- Write your first draft *using your own words* whenever possible. But do not go to extremes: a student once paraphrased 'overmanning' with 'too many people working for the company' – seven words instead of one!
- Check that you are not over (or well under) the word limit. 'In *about* 130 words' allows you a little leeway; 'in *not more than* 130 words' does not.
- Check against the original for any omissions or change of emphasis. A common error is for examinees to run short of words and then omit or over-compress the last part of the original.
- Polish your draft, paying attention to correct English. Then make a fair copy.
- State the number of words used at the end. Do *not* give a false word count!
- In secretarial/business exams the summary will sometimes need to be accompanied by a short covering memo with details of author, title, date and source. This is excluded from the word limit.

The examples that follow show the most common problems of summary work and illustrate some of the layouts at your disposal.

Example

You work for a Citizens' Advice Bureau and have been asked to prepare a brief summary, in approximately 130 words, of the following extract (taken from *Money Which?*) for inclusion in a leaflet to guide the ordinary citizen who has a bank account.

BANK REFERENCES

How private is my account?
'. . . A customer's affairs are treated in the strictest confidence, every member of the Bank's staff being pledged to secrecy. Even if your employers pay your wages or salary direct into your account they will know nothing more about your finances than the amount they pay you.' (A bank leaflet)

Do you realise that if you've a bank account your bank manager will give references on your creditworthiness, if asked to do so by another bank manager? He doesn't have to let you know or get your approval.

If you apply for credit – to buy a car, for example, – the lender may ask his bank to get a reference on you. Getting a poor or not-so-good reference could well lead to your being refused credit.

Under the Consumer Credit Act, you can ask a lender for the name of any credit reference agency he approaches. But the lender doesn't have to tell you of any bank reference he gets on you. So you might be refused credit because of a poor bank reference without ever knowing the reason!

What you can do about it
To make sure that you always get the best possible bank reference:
a) Keep your manager fully informed about your financial position. For example, if you've got your money put away in a different bank account or in a building society, make sure that your bank manager knows about it – otherwise he might not realise how creditworthy you are.
b) If you're asked to give the name and address of your bank as part of any transaction, it probably makes sense to discuss the matter with your bank manager first (because a reference is likely to be involved). By speaking to your bank manager before he writes your reference you may be able to remove any doubts he has.

If you object in principle to bank references being given on you, you could write to your bank manager and ask him never to give one. But this has its dangers. Getting no reference at all could be as harmful to you as getting a poor one.

Improving the bank reference system
Money Which? has been unhappy about the system of giving bank references for some time. We hoped that things might improve as a result of the Younger Committee Report on Privacy, which recommended:

'. . . that the banks should make clear to all customers, existing or prospective, the existence and manner of operation of their reference system, and give them the opportunity either to grant a standing authority for the provision of references or to require the bank to seek their consent on every occasion.'

If these sorts of changes were made, bank references would still be confidential, but the customer could have some say about who could get one.

What has been done to implement these proposals?
Very little.

We looked at the leaflets the High Street banks give to prospective

> customers. None of them makes it clear that a customer may have a reference given on him without his permission. And some of the leaflets stress the confidentiality of dealings with the bank – for example, see the extract at the beginning of this article.

LCC PSC Dec 1979 (*30 marks*)

Talking point

The following answer, written by a student, illustrates a number of typical faults. Try to establish what these are before reading the commentary:

MY BANK ACCOUNT

How Private is my Account

A banks staff have been sworn to secrecy, so you can be sure that you are treated with the strictest of confidence.

Your bank manager is allowed to give references on your creditworthyness to another bank, without your approval.

When applying for credit, the lender could ask for a reference on you, without you knowing. The lender must give you the name of any credit referance agency, but you may not know the reason for refusal.

How to get a good Bank Reference

a) Always inform your bank manager of any other bank accounts you have.
b) Always discuss your reference with your bank manager to remove any doubts he has.

Improving the bank reference system

Banks should give the oppotunity to grant authority for references or to seek customers consent.

Bank references would still be confidential with these changes, but the customers could control them.

Very little has been done to implement these proposals

Many leaflets in High Street banks, still do not make it clear that a reference can be given without a customers permission.

Commentary

1   The title of the original is apt and should be retained. By changing it the student fails to highlight the main theme.

2   The instructions refer to the correct form and style to adopt – 'a leaflet . . . to guide the ordinary citizen who has a bank account'. Sub-headings are a feature of most leaflets and some of those in the original could be adapted. (Are the student's headings crisp enough?) The style should be simple and direct – words like 'implement' are out of place here.

3   To summarise this passage paragraph by paragraph is disastrous as can be seen in the above summary where the second statement totally contradicts the first. The opening of the original is a misleading quotation from a bank leaflet and should be omitted.

4   The third paragraph of the summary typifies the poor English that is evident throughout. It begins with a misrelated participle which makes it sound as if it is the lender who is applying for credit. 'Knowing' is a gerund which requires the possessive 'your'. The final sentence contains a copying error ('referance') and loses the point of the original by over-compression. The 'ordinary citizen' might well wonder what a credit reference agency had to do with his bank account.

5   Elsewhere there are many traces of repetition and wordiness, exemplified by the advice:

   Always inform your bank manager of any other bank accounts you may have (13 words)

   in which 'bank' is repeated (as it is throughout the summary) and 'bank accounts' (taken from the example in the original) is too narrow to convey the meaning of 'financial position' – what about bonds, stocks and shares, and property? Far better advice would be to:

   Inform your bank manager of any other assets (8 words).

6   Even at first sight an examiner could tell that the summary was far too long. Although no word count has been given, it turns out to be about 180 words – 50 words too many. This would be little short of suicidal in an exam. With a crop of punctuation, grammatical and spelling errors also to be taken into consideration, the candidate would undoubtedly fail.

Assignment

Draft a summary of your own before reading the suggested answer.

Suggested answer

```
BANK REFERENCES

How Private is Your Account?

Your bank manager may give references on your creditworthiness to other
bank managers without telling you.
```

A lender may ask his bank to get such a reference. If it is poor, he may refuse you credit and need not tell you the reason.

What You Can Do

* Inform your bank manager of any other assets.
* Speak to him beforehand if a reference is likely to be required.
* Ask him never to give references on you if you feel that this in itself is not harmful.

Improving the system

Banks should explain the system to their customers and allow them more control over it.

But none does, and some bank leaflets assure everyone that their business is strictly confidential - which is untrue.

Adapted from *Money Which?* (127 words)

Example

You are the personal secretary to Mr John Alexander, Manager of the Information Department, Comlon Advertising plc, Cannon Street, London EC4 5AB, head office of a large advertising agency which has branches throughout the world. One of the reasons that Comlon has become so big is that it is able to offer clients the benefits of a very efficient information service based at head office.

One of Comlon's biggest clients is the giant car manufacturing company, International Cars plc. This company is planning to launch a new electric car, 'The Electron', which has several revolutionary new features. It is planned that the launch will be virtually simultaneous in Great Britain and other EEC countries. The management of International Cars plc presented the plan to Comlon Advertising plc and requested that a meeting should be held to discuss the problems involved.

Mr Alexander, who will represent Comlon at the meeting, decides that it is important that the launch of the new vehicle should be preceded by a conference in order to brief dealers and to create in them a feeling of enthusiasm.

You notice an article in a business magazine about staging a conference and you show it to Mr Alexander who immediately asks you to summarise the main points so he may use it for the meeting. The article is printed below. Write your summary in *not more than 180 words*.

Talking point

Before reading the commentary, answer the following questions:
1   Can the original title be used?
2   Is every paragraph relevant to the theme?
3   What is the best display for this summary?
4   Can you suggest any possible sub-headings?
5   Do you need to write a short covering memo?

STAGING A CONFERENCE

In the commercial world in the 1980s, business organisations often operate on a global basis.

Even in Great Britain, companies are no longer as insular as in the past. Many are subsidiaries of foreign giants; for instance Ford in Great Britain is a subsidiary of the American parent company. Others, which are solely British, now regard Europe as part of the home market since the time when Great Britain joined the European Common Market.

The tendency towards internationalism in the business world means that there is a requirement for companies and their personnel to be outward looking and aware of market conditions in every continent. This presents managements with a communication challenge which is almost as big as the organisations themselves.

The most effective way to provide that communication is to bring important personnel and clients together at one time and in one location. Besides providing managements with the opportunity to disseminate information formally, it also makes informal meeting between company personnel possible which can only be beneficial to the organisation as a whole. In addition, there is the likelihood that the meeting together of people from different backgrounds will generate its own 'group dynamic' as the Americans often call it. In the long term, this too is likely to be of value to the company when the delegates at a meeting pass on to their dealers their enthusiasm for the company's products. Even in the electronic age with modern communications networks such as telex, telephone and, in the not too distant future, computer controlled electronic mail, there is still no substitute for personal contact.

Increasingly companies are turning to the conference as a fast and effective way of briefing their personnel and clients. International conferences are, of course, also held for political purposes and the exchange of information by professionals. For instance, leading doctors might meet, say in Paris, to discuss the latest research into and treatment for a particular illness.

The planning of such international conferences presents the organisers with a mammoth task but nowadays travel agents and hoteliers are aware of the requirements and do their best to facilitate conference arrangements. Initially, certain fundamentals have to be established. The venue must be chosen and decisions made about the dates and budget for the conference and, of course, its theme – whether it is to be about office technology in the 1980s, the exploration of the seabed, the prevention of pollution or whatever. Currently many conferences by commercial companies are convened to launch a new product or put over a management message. On the successful launch of a new product may depend the fortunes of a company for some time to come; if the product succeeds, favourable results will show up on the balance sheet. If the launch is badly handled (even if the product is likely to be successful) at best that will not help the company; at worst, the organisation may go out of business. Whether or not the product sells successfully may ultimately depend on the way it is presented to its potential customers, on its image.

It follows that putting across a good image for the product is of vital importance for its commercial success and it is for that reason that managements put so much time and effort and indeed so much financial weight behind the launch of a product. The benefits of bringing together at a conference clients and personnel outweigh the organisational difficulties and seem to be justified by subsequent sales figures.

Adapted from an article by Leonie Grayeff in *2000*, March 1982
LCC PSC Dec 1984 (*30 marks*)

Commentary

1 The title can be retained.
2 Very little of the first three paragraphs is needed – someone in Mr Alexander's position would know all of this.
3 The context tell you that your principal will be using your summary at the meeting with International Cars plc when he presents his case for holding a conference. A suitable display would therefore be one to which quick reference could be made (i.e. headings and numbered points). A traditional précis would be useless.
4 Paragraph 4 mentions some of the *advantages* of staging a conference while paragraph 6 raises the problems of *planning* conferences.
5 A brief covering memo is required.

Assignment

Prepare rough notes (assessing whether you need to reorganise the information you select) and then draft the summary before consulting the versions below.

Suggested answer

Rough notes:

STAGING A CONFERENCE

paras 1–3: **Trend towards internationalism = a communication challenge**

para 4: ***Advantages* of conferences:**
– formal and informal meetings
– enthusiasm generated/passed on
– personal contact

para 5: **Companies now favour international conferences = quick efficient means of briefing staff/customers**

para 6: ***Planning***
Formidable problems but
1. travel agents/hoteliers will help
2. early decisions must be made on place, date(s), theme and financial provision
Many companies use the conference to launch a new product on which its future may depend
'Right' image can be created – essential for success

para 7: **Advantages outnumber problems – seen in increased sales**

Draft summary:

MEMO

To: Mr John Alexander   Date: 8 December 19..

From: Sally Bowles   Ref: SB/SAC

Staging a Conference

I enclose the summary you requested for the forthcoming meeting with
International Cars plc.

The original article was written by Leonie Grayeff and appeared in *2000*
(March 1982).

Enc

STAGING A CONFERENCE
1 Current Trends
   1.1 Companies, which today have to be aware of what is happening in
        markets world-wide, now favour the conference as a quick, efficient
        means of communication and sales promotion.

   1.2 This is particularly true when they launch a new product on which the
        company's future may depend.

2 Advantages
   2.1 Personal contact is maintained.

   2.2 Management can formally brief senior staff and clients.

   2.3 Valuable connections may be made informally by company personnel.

   2.4 Bringing together people from different backgrounds often boosts
        the enthusiasm of delegates for the product which later rubs off on
        their dealers.

   2.5 The right image of the product can be created - essential for
        successful marketing.

3 Planning Conferences
   3.1 Travel agents and hoteliers are familiar with the necessary
        preparations and will help to overcome the formidable problems
        involved.

   3.2 At an early stage decisions must be made on the place and date(s) of
        the conference, its theme and the financial provision.

4 Conclusion
   Despite the logistical problems, conferences offer many advantages and
   their success is reflected in the sales figures that follow.

(172 words)

Example

You are employed as a secretary by a firm which makes toys and a range of fireworks (firecrackers, rockets, sparklers, etc.). The firm is thinking of closing down its fireworks factory. For the benefit of one of the firm's executives, summarise in not more than 160 words the following correspondence which has been published in a national newspaper during the last few days. You need to write a short covering memo to the executive, explaining to him (or her) where you saw the correspondence and why you think it is significant.

Sir

My daughter Mary took part in a local fête at our village last week, and at the end of the day she joined in the firework celebrations. There were a number of children and young people roaming around, letting off fireworks. One of these hit Mary in the face. As a result, she is now blind in one eye and has a permanent burn scar on the left side of her face.

Isn't it time the government banned fireworks? How can manufacturers be so wicked as to sell these dangerous things?

Your faithfully
(Mrs) Elizabeth Onslow

Sir

How hypocritical can one be?

Maurice Morgan is *paid*, I repeat *paid*, by his Association to utter platitudes defending his members. Fireworks are lethal – he admits it himself! I hope the government will take immediate action to put an end to this trade in death and disfigurement.

Yours disgustedly
Paul Simon

Sir

On behalf of my Association may I reply to the letter from Mrs Onslow which you recently published?

I naturally sympathise deeply with the very great distress which her daughter's accident has caused. However, I am sure your correspondent would not wish to ban kitchen knives, or even building bricks. Yet these, if thrown indiscriminately by reckless persons, can be just as lethal as any firework.

Your readers will know that the sale of fireworks is strictly controlled so that only responsible persons of a certain age can buy them. The solution to tragedies such as Mary Onslow's is better education and more stringent control. Fireworks bring enormous pleasure to many people and it seems a pity to allow a very tiny irresponsible minority to deny this pleasure to the public.

Yours faithfully
Maurice Morgan
Secretary, Association of Chemical Processors

Sir

As a plastic surgeon at one of London's biggest hospitals, I should like to comment on the correspondence which has recently appeared in your columns.

Every year I treat a large number of cases of firework burns. The majority of patients are children, often quite young children. The pain and suffering which these patients have to endure is very considerable, and although it is often possible to repair much of the damage by means of plastic surgery there is an inevitable legacy of disfigurement and impaired function. And, of course, plastic surgery is of no avail in the many cases where there has been eye injury.

My colleagues and I have pressed for many years for very strict controls on the sale of fireworks, and your recent correspondents have convinced me that only a complete end to the manufacture of these dangerous toys will be effective.

For professional reasons I prefer not to sign my name, and remain

Yours faithfully
London Surgeon

Sir

'London Surgeon' makes a very good case, but like your other correspondents he is in danger of throwing out the baby with the bathwater.

Fireworks do indeed give much pleasure. Why then should we allow an irresponsible group of people to deprive us of that pleasure?

Mr Morgan wrote that the sale of fireworks is strictly controlled, but your readers will all know that children can get hold of fireworks – perhaps through contact with older children. The answer would be to prohibit the sale of all fireworks to the public, but to license local authorities and other responsible bodies to hold firework displays under carefully controlled conditions.

We have done this locally for several years and public support has been most encouraging.

Yours etc.
Jennie Staples
Youth and Recreation Officer, London Borough of Bridgenorth

Dear Mr Editor

My Mum won't let me have any fireworks for my birthday party because she has been reading your newspaper and I don't think it's fair.

Lisa Smith (aged 9)

NOTE: This correspondence is now closed – Editor

LCC PSC June 1977 (*30 marks*)

Commentary

1   For a summary of correspondence, a heading which incorporates the names and addresses of the correspondents, the first and last letter dates and the subject is generally useful (and is not included in the word count), e.g.

> **Summary of correspondence between Dr J. Summerfield, 10 Aorta Way, Herts H15 3LT and the ABC Provident, Premium House, Dartford, Kent KT7 2RR, between 10 and 27 January 19.., about Life Assurance Policy Number 793217.**

Each letter is then summarised in a separate paragraph. (*NB* if the individual dates are important they should appear at the beginning of each letter summary.)

2   This standard heading is of little use here where there are six correspondents whose names (and addresses) are unimportant. Their roles, however, do lend significance to their views and should be mentioned in the summary. The other details – source, dates, theme – should be included in the covering memo.

3   It would then still be possible to summarise separately, letter by letter, but perhaps a more economical method would be to set out the arguments for and against fireworks followed by possible solutions.

Assignment

Attempt the summary before reading the version that follows.

Suggested answer

MEMO

To: Mr G Fawkes   Date: 12 November 19..

From: Catherine Wheeler   Ref: CW/DP

Correspondence about Fireworks

I have summarised a series of letters which appeared in the Daily Post
between 2 and 11 November.

Members of the public and the professions expressed differing views which I
hope will be of interest when the closing down of our fireworks factory is
considered.

Enc

ATTITUDES TO FIREWORKS

Against

Three correspondents condemned their manufacture: a mother whose daughter
had been seriously injured by a firework; a correspondent who described
them as deadly; and a plastic surgeon with considerable experience of the
injuries caused by fireworks – mostly to children.

For

Three correspondents disagreed. The Secretary of the Association of
Chemical Processors argued that only a few people misused fireworks and
that everyday objects, if used recklessly, could be just as dangerous. A
Youth and Recreations Officer agreed that a total ban would be against the
general interest but wanted tighter control to prevent children from
obtaining fireworks. A child expressed disappointment when denied
fireworks.

Suggested solutions

1   A total ban on the sale and manufacture of fireworks.

2   No ban but better education and stricter control.

3   A ban on the general sale of fireworks with only reputable groups
    allowed to hold closely supervised displays.

(146 words)

Exercises

1 Answer *either* (a) or (b).

   a) Your company deals exclusively with overseas customers and makes extensive use of the postal service. Your boss gives you the following information (about 400 words) from the *Post Office Guide* and asks you to summarise the points that are relevant to the company in about 120 words so that they can be printed as a guide to employees.

   b) A customer of your company who lives in London has telephoned to complain that a parcel you sent him has arrived torn and with over half the contents missing. He asks you what he should do. Using the information below, note down what you would tell him:

Complaints procedures

We want to know when customers are dissatisfied with our service so that we can try to put matters right. If, therefore, you experience any problems or are dissatisfied with the service you receive, *please let your local Head Postmaster know in the first instance.*

We aim to acknowledge all written complaints and compensation claims within one week of receipt and endeavour to deal with them all quickly. Those in respect of the inland post, unless requiring extensive investigation, are normally resolved within six weeks. *Claims concerning the overseas post may, however, need to be referred to another postal administration.* If enquiries in such cases have not been completed within six months, the Post Office, recognising that you are anxious to have your claim settled, will normally deal with the claim on its own account.

Let your Head Postmaster have full details about posting and delivery of delayed letters or parcels. He will want to try to find the cause of the problem and so help to improve the service for the future. If you can let him have the envelope or outer wrapping of the item in question, it will help to speed his enquiries. Whenever possible, he will advise you of the reason for delay.

If a letter or parcel has been lost or damaged in the post, this is what either the sender or the addressee should do in the first instance:

Ask for a form P58 'Enquiry about a missing or damaged letter or parcel' at any post office. When completed, hand it in or send it to the Head Postmaster. Where applicable, attach the certificate of posting, or clear photocopy (as explained on the application form).

If you are applying for compensation for damage under Section D of the form, the damaged article together with the cover, container and other packing, should be retained because this provides evidence of how the item was packed.

Please make your application promptly. This is because Post Office case records are retained only for a certain period, in some instances no longer than one year. Sometimes customers spend a lot of time establishing the value of an item before making an application. If this is likely to take time, it is better to make the initial application quickly, and say that the value quoted is subject to confirmation or adjustment later.

LCC EFB Second Level June 1988 (*30 marks*)

2 Summarise the following passage in about 140 words. Give your summary a title and state the number of words used.

Until recently no one seems to have thought it necessary to review the consequences of infection with the AIDS virus (HTLV3) in relation to women, nor to offer them specific protective guidelines on the special risks incurred for both mother and baby in pregnancy.

The omission was understandable when AIDS was mistakenly seen as largely a disease of homosexual men. Since 1982, however, AIDS has been recognised – at least by doctors – as predominantly a sexually transmitted disease passed on through blood or semen. Infection through simple blood to blood contact has added to the problem, with haemophiliacs and intravenous drug abusers forming other high risk groups. Now spread into the heterosexual community with women being infected, it also tragically shows that babies born to infected mothers have a very high rate of infection.

It was against this background that the Scientific Advisory Committee of the Royal College of Obstetricians and Gynaecologists last year requested two British doctors, an immunologist and a virologist, to report on the consequences of HTLV3 virus in pregnancy. Their recommendations and guidelines were published in a recent issue of the British Journal of Obstetrics and Gynaecology and they have important implications for society as a whole if the AIDS epidemic is to be contained.

Dr Anthony Pinching and Dr Donald Jeffries, the authors of the report, both work at St Mary's Hospital Medical School, Paddington, London, which is in the front line of the battle against AIDS. Dr Pinching made it clear that he felt some sections of the media had not always handled the AIDS problem well. 'They have concentrated on stigmatisation of special risk groups,' he explained, 'and on inappropriate ideas that AIDS is a casually spread infection. It is not and there has been failure to address the real issue of containing sexual and blood-borne spread, which rests on individuals in society.'

Dr Pinching, the immunologist, was anxious that the report should not be used to whip up any fresh AIDS panic but he stressed that it contained important protective guidelines to be followed as the best way at the moment of containing the disease.

'Risk of infection with this virus for women in the UK at present is very low,' he said. 'But we need to keep it that way and that means more prudent sexual activity, reducing the number of partners preferably to one. If and when that is not done, then at least there must be recognition and protection against high risk contacts.'

The report makes it clear that this is particularly vital for women of child-bearing age. The risks for both mother and baby are so great that if the woman even carries the HTLV3 virus, pregnancy should always be avoided. The report actually recommends that any pregnant woman found to have been infected with the virus, even where there are no symptoms of disease, should be considered for and counselled about termination.

From a *Guardian* article by Wendy Cooper, published 4 February 1986

AMSPAR D June 1986 (*22 marks*)

3   You are the secretary to Mr Charles Greenaway, the Chairman of a publishing company. Mr Greenaway has been sent a review of a book on Communications and wishes to send a brief summary to the Managing Director. Read the review carefully and then, by summarising, reduce it to approximately a third of the length of the original.

A professional's guide to writing professional communications

As its title conveys, this book is geared towards the professional. Therefore, about two-thirds is concerned with writing about computers and programs. While there are some good ideas in the book, it may not be the best book for the word-processing professional. However, I do not have an alternative recommendation. The book might be a good starting-place if you can get a few leads from it, and then go on to do some additional research at the library on the specific subjects that interest you most.

The first section of the book, the first 80 pages or so, is the portion that will probably be of the most use to you. It is devoted to communication skills in general, and includes the mechanics of professional writing. Targeting the writing to your reader, the steps of outlining the manuscript, laying out the work, and graphics, are a few of the topics covered in this 225-page book.

The remaining two-thirds of the book can be divided into two parts. The first of these sections examines writing documents related to data processing systems and investigates progress report procedures and systems studies. The final part discusses technical proposals, policies and standards manuals, and technical articles.

The book practises what it preaches. It recommends using many section, sub-section and paragraph titles, and the author does so. Placing a title alone in the margin really makes the various sections stand out. Consequently, the text has rather wide margins and is liberal in its use of open space. Many publishers object to this technique, but I find that it makes reading much easier.

PEI EFS Advanced (*25 marks*)

4 You are employed as a journalist by a magazine read by young businesswomen. Summarise the following extract in not more than 150 words, to make a brief item for publication as an 'end filler' (i.e. to fill up a small gap on a page). The passage is from a journal read by members of the National Association of Local Government Officers (NALGO).

You may believe that in this age of Women's Liberation and heightened awareness of the 'feminine mystique' we are making rapid progress along the path towards equal opportunity in career structure. That, I am afraid, is a myth, certainly so far as local government is concerned. There is no evidence to suggest that local government is any better than anywhere else in this respect. The higher grades in the civil service, for instance, are virtually a male preserve.

True, in some areas things are improving slowly, but there is so much room for improvement that these small advances only draw attention to the extent of inequality. It is easy to be misled by all the talk about Women's Lib on the media and all the plays written around the theme that there is a notable lessening of discrimination. When one appreciates what is really happening, a couple of women news readers and a 'statutory woman' on a discussion panel can only be seen as mere window-dressing.

Regrettably, nobody has compiled up-to-date figures of the way top local government jobs are distributed between the sexes, but a rapid scanning of the Municipal Year Book produces the following . . .

From 887 local authorities in Britain
One chief executive
Six secretaries and directors of administration
Four legal officers
Five personnel officers
Two planning officers
18 housing directors
13 directors of social services

I could not find a single woman chief financial officer or treasurer, no woman holding office as chief architect, chief environmental health officer or chief public health inspector, and scanning the list of directors of technical services again revealed nothing but males.

On the other hand, women predominate in the lower (and more poorly paid) grades.

This explains why one is surrounded by a mass of male decision-makers at local government conferences, where more often than not the only feminine influence is provided by those ladies who hand round the microphones, make the coffee or serve the lunch. Frequently women are found manning the reception tables, charged with greeting delegates with a warm smile and handing out conference literature. Occasionally you may even meet a woman public relations officer as they do seem to be more readily accepted in this profession than elsewhere.

Sheila Smith, chairman of NALGO equal opportunities committee, told me that with women comprising more than half its membership, the association had to be very concerned that so many of them were in the least responsible and lower-paid jobs and that so few of them held top jobs.

There were many reasons for this, she said, mainly historical and cultural, but she claimed that the situation was changing. More women are being appointed to senior posts at supervisory and lower management levels, and in due course we can expect this shift to spread to more senior posts.

'Perhaps the most important development has been the improvement in maternity leave arrangements, coupled with a wider recognition that having a family need not mean the ending of a career.

'But that is only the beginning. There is much more that individual local authorities could do to encourage and help the women they employ.'

Perhaps the biggest obstacle to the creation of greater opportunities for women at managerial level, she rightly says, is the interruption of their working life in those years when they might expect to be promoted into jobs where they would gain wider experience in preparation for their further promotion.

Keeping married women at work at this time is therefore vital for their overall prospects. For this reason it is equally important that nursery provision for the children of women at work is greatly improved and that employers are pressed to provide work-place nurseries on a much wider scale.

'These are matters on which NALGO has been campaigning vigorously and will continue to campaign.'

From *PSLG* for May 1980

LCC PSC Dec 1982 (*30 marks*)

5 You work as the personal secretary to Dr J Kenney, the Public Relations Director of Comlon International plc, a pharmaceutical company. This morning Dr Kenney asks you to begin to summarise the contents of a number of articles that have been published on the pharmaceutical industry. He has agreed to appear on a television programme, and be interviewed by the press, on the subject of how the industry deals with claims for compensation. He will be away from the office for a few days and will expect the articles summarised by his return.

Produce a summary of the following article for Dr Kenney using about 160 words.

Drugs: The road to compensation

Under English law, a manufacturer has a duty to take reasonable care in researching, designing, making and promoting products. If his product is defective and, as a result, causes loss or injury to a person using it, the manufacturer may be liable to compensate the user. The user needs to collect and present evidence to support his case and the manufacturer will usually present his own case in defence. The final judgement will be that of the court.

However, proving that a product was defective and caused loss or injury may not be easy. In a simple case there may be strong evidence of the existence of a defect. For example, if an unopened bottle explodes in your hand causing severe cuts, there is little doubt that the bottle caused the injury and, unless some other explanation for the explosion is known, the fact that it happened at all suggests that the bottle or its contents must have been defective.

But with drugs it is usually much more difficult. Firstly drugs are inherently hazardous. Secondly there is often no obvious link between the drug and the injury. You take the drug because there is already something wrong with you. At that time, or some time later, you suffer unexpected problems which may or may not be caused by the drug. Even if the problems disappear when you stop taking the drug, it does not follow that the drug was the cause. But if enough people taking the same drug suffer similar problems it may be that – on the balance of probabilities – the drug will be judged to be the cause of the problem.

Even when a drug is widely suspected of causing certain side-effects, it may be impossible to sort out whether the unexpected symptoms are due to the drug, or to the illness being treated, or to another drug, or interaction between a combination of drugs, or to some totally unrelated cause. Even where it can be proved that a defect in a product did cause the loss or injury, a person claiming compensation still needs to show that the manufacturer failed to take reasonable care against such a defect occurring, or that he continued to allow people to be exposed to the defect once the risks were known.

Gathering evidence of negligence is likely to be a difficult task for the person seeking compensation. In essence, he has to show that there was some carelessness in the research, manufacture or marketing of the product. To do this, it may be necessary to get detailed access to the manufacturer's records. The individual will often need expert help in seeking out all the relevant information, and in understanding and interpreting it. The process is usually extremely long and expensive.

(460 words)

Adapted from *Which?* magazine
LCC PSC Dec 1986 (*35 marks*)

6 A programme has to be prepared for a music conference to be staged by Comlon International plc on 8 January 1988 to celebrate European Music Year. Mr Peter Barton (Managing Director, Europe) wishes to include, inside the front cover, a brief résumé of what European Music Year 1988 entails. He hands you a copy of the following article which he wants you to summarise in a suitable form for inclusion in the programme.

European Music Year 1988
European Music Year, to be inaugurated by the Vienna Philharmonic Orchestra's New Year concert, conducted by Lorin Maazel and broadcast on Eurovision, will be the first cultural venture to be carried out jointly by the Council of Europe and the European Communities. Support totalling 600 000 dollars has been provided for 32 multinational projects proposed by the national committees of 24 European countries.

These projects, which are both imaginative and bold, were selected by a European organising committee, chaired by Walter Scheel (a former President of the Federal Republic of Germany), for their relevance to the Year's aims, which are as follows:

● to give a prominent place to music of all types and periods;
● to encourage composition;
● to foster public participation;
● to improve musicians' working conditions;
● to further the teaching of music;
● to protect the musical heritage.

Other musical initiatives have been launched by the hundred, and the Year's turnover could exceed 60 million dollars if one adds together the contributions from national and regional authorities, international organisations, the music and tourist industries, radio and television, commercial sponsors and private foundations.

The Year will include the widest possible variety of events, from the most modest to the most spectacular, and its musical range will extend from Gregorian chant to jazz via classical music, folk music and opera.

One of the major events will take place on 21 June when, on the lines of an initiative recently started in France, 'Music Day' will be celebrated in towns and villages throughout Europe.

The Year will provide an opportunity to study such questions as the influence of music on related arts (dance, painting, literature) and its role in medicine (Norway will be organising a seminar on music therapy).

Music year will also demonstrate the richness of Europe's many musical cultures.

It is with great pride that Comlon International will help to celebrate the beginning of European Music Year 1988 by bringing together many leading personalities in the music business at a conference to discuss many important musical issues.

(336 words)

Source: 'Forum, Council of Europe'

Make your summary in not more than 140 words. (A suggested answer is given in Appendix 1.)

LCC PSC June 1987 (*30 marks*)

7 The Board of Comlon International Banking is considering giving further support to the Government enterprise agency movement.

The Bank currently holds the Queen's Award for Export, and it is felt by the Chairman that the Investment Division might well provide a member of its experienced personnel to give help of a practical nature to a specialist entrepreneur or small export company.

The scheme which is designed to assist small businesses to expand and improve their expertise, and to develop their future potential in the market, relies for success on the response of large companies to the project.

Mr David Moss, as head of the Trust and Investment Division, has been asked for his views on the possibility of a member of his Division being placed with the selected company for a period of at least 12 months. He has seen the following article in *The Financial Times*, entitled 'Seeking to Meet a Vital Need', and has asked that you compile a suitable summary in no more than 200 words so that he may use the information in his report to the Board.

Seeking to meet a vital need

by Ian Hamilton-Fazey

If ever there was an idea waiting for its time, the enterprise agency movement must be it. Almost from inception, agencies have become key factors in small business formation and growth. They are still mushrooming.

Sheer need for what they offer has been the main reason for their growth, but although the principal function of an enterprise agency is to give advice, that alone hardly accounts for their increasing importance. After all, advice is available from many sources, including the Government, local authorities and the banks. So what is special about the agencies? The answer appears to lie not so much in the advice itself but where it is given and by whom – in other words the key is the very nature of the agencies themselves.

The typical enterprise agency will have been set up jointly by the private sector and a local authority. The Government now helps fund start-up, but that money is more about pump-priming than taking a stake and demanding part-control or even a return. The local authority may well help with premises and cash but what makes enterprise agencies different is the involvement of the private sector. This may take the form of money but the most widespread type of help is through the lending of experienced managers or specialists – and for significant periods ranging from nine months to several years.

Almost invariably only large corporations or financial institutions can afford such secondments. Increasingly, they are used for the management development of able people in mid-career but there is also a significant portion who are highly experienced senior managers, either coming up to retirement or in the early stages of it.

This begs the question of whether people from big company backgrounds can really understand the needs of life as a business tiddler.

Independent surveys suggest that they can. After all, the principles of management are the same whatever the enterprise. Small business – where the entrepreneur does everything – can be regarded as an extreme case of general management; what better advisor than a general manager from the big league? Indeed, one school of thought in the enterprise agency movement is that a similarity in thinking between big and small arises because of the nature of business itself.

Whereas most middle managers are usually concerned with operational matters and their impact on the trading account, senior managers in large companies have to focus on the securing of capital and ensuring its efficient use. This latter role is much closer in principle to what small business owners have to do. By the same token, middle managers from, say, large manufacturers gain useful insight into general management principles through a period of secondment.

The experience with secondees from the financial sectors is also interesting. Some of the most useful have been young accountants from large practices. Because of their professional discipline they home in on agency clients' balance sheets. By contrast, secondees from the banks concentrate on cash flow. The combination can provide some of the best consultancy anyone could wish for – and it is free, independent, non-political, and not given by anyone trying to lend you money, or working for officialdom or housed in offices where you have to pay the rates.

The Financial Times, 30 April 1985
LCC PESD June 1986 (*30 marks*)

8 Comlon International plc is an international group of 5-star hotels. The Board recently made a decision to use guard dogs in some hotels with extensive grounds. Mr Jeremy Robertson, Head of Security, often uses the company's staff newsletter to give information or ideas on security matters and he has decided to contribute to the newsletter on this subject. He has given you the following extract from a book on security recommended by a colleague, with this instruction:

'Please let me have a summary in continuous prose of this for the newsletter. The editor has allowed me a maximum of 150 words – remember that it will be read by all types of staff.'

Guard dogs

It is only in recent years that the recognised qualities of guard dogs have been applied to police and security purposes. Even now they are often not used to their full potential, possibly because most countries now have various laws limiting their use.

The Alsatian, or German Shepherd dog, is generally recognised as one of the most intelligent breeds of dog in the world. This is the essential quality to ensure that in addition to being fearless without being aggressive, they can be trained to act as guard dogs or working security animals.

The Alsatian has an appearance which is consistent with the general idea of what a guard dog should look like: sturdy build, combined with a physical ability and strength to work hard in all types of weather. Other types of dog have been tried for the same purpose, and after the Alsatian the most widely used type is the Doberman. Experience has shown that the Doberman is less predictable in its behaviour, and breeding is less likely to guarantee the qualities required of a guard dog.

There are characteristics of the Alsatian which render them to be of particular value to users; these are of a hereditary nature arising from their origin in pack life, hence the alternative name, wolf-hound. They have a real sense of self-preservation, quick reaction to danger with an alertness to every sight and sound; loyalty to those with whom they are in regular contact, coupled with a suspicion of strangers and a quickness of supple movement.

They are comparatively short-sighted, but their range of hearing covers 7 octaves above the human ear and is infinitely more acute. Their power of scent is even more greatly developed in comparison; it can warn them of the presence of intruders or strangers even when they are motionless and cannot be seen or heard. Having an ancestry associated with cattle and sheep herding under all conditions, they can pass instantly from sleep to alertness. It is no hardship for them to work for up to 14 hours a day if this should be necessary, although for humane reasons they should not be worked for periods of this duration.

While they may be used every day, they will reflect the benefit if one clear night's rest each week can be allowed. There is no difference whatsoever between dogs and bitches in security usage; they are equally efficient.

Security dogs can now be obtained from well-established breeders whose reputations are built on reliability. Also, there are many opportunities for the training of dog handlers. Thorough training of dog and handler can ensure the perfectly safe and highly efficient use of dogs as an enhancement of security.

(396 words)

Adapted from *Practical Security in Commerce and Industry* by Eric Oliver and John Wilson (Gower Press).
LCC PESD June 1988 (*30 marks*)

9 John Enright, the newly appointed Personnel Director of a large manufacturing concern with a poor record of labour relations, is trying to devise a more effective employee communications policy for the firm. You are his personal assistant and see the following article. In 300–350 words prepare for Mr Enright a summary which evaluates Kellogg's approach to their communication with employees.

Giving employees something to chew on

A 10-week strike at Kellogg all but removed the morning plate of cereal from millions of British breakfast tables last year.

The dispute was essentially over pay, but a confidential poll of workers' attitudes conducted by the company revealed that a contributing factor could have been the poor standard of communications with its 3000-strong workforce.

According to the workers, management hardly ever kept them informed about the company's performance or plans; neither were they told the reasons for major decisions. The opinions of staff were also generally ignored and there was seldom any consultation when changes were made in conditions of employment.

In general, the local and trade Press and radio were quicker to publish information than the company was to inform staff.

To make no bones about it, the company – as it now admits – had no employee communications policy to speak of and, as the poll demonstrated, morale was at a very low ebb.

In an attempt to reverse this situation Kellogg has recently established a procedure to keep all employees informed about the company's activities, performance and personnel policies.

Within a remarkably short space of time, Kellogg claims, its new communications policy had created 'a much better spirit' in its six factories scattered around the country and has brought it several benefits.

In the first place, Kellogg says the improved level of communications helped smooth the latest pay negotiations, which resulted in an 18 per cent award for most workers. 'We got through the settlement without any trouble at all,' a spokesman said.

Secondly, the company believes that the new policy has been instrumental in staving off the approaches of an additional trade union. The

Association of Scientific, Technical and Managerial Staffs (ASTMS) had been recruiting among the 600 non-unionised administrative staff and subsequently appealed to the Arbitration and Conciliation Service (ACAS) after the company refused to recognise it. Three months ago, however, ASTMS suddenly withdrew its application because it had attracted insufficient membership.

'We think we are now satisfying the communications needs of our staff, which means that they have one less reason to join a trade union,' the company says.

Kellogg's new policy represents a departure from the common British practice of using trade unions as one of the vehicles for disseminating certain company information among their members. In effect, the new policy establishes a procedure that bypasses them in this. But it is not intended to affect the company's traditional relationship with existing unions over such issues as pay and conditions.

The new policy has been generally welcomed by Kellogg's unions, the largest of which is the Union of Shop, Distributive and Allied Workers.

George Cheetam, USDAW's branch chairman at the company, described communications as 'an awful lot better' since the dispute last year. 'All that the company is doing is informing the workforce direct. It saves us a job actually.'

The man brought in to implement the new policy under the title of manager, public affairs, is Nicholas Cole, a former public relations executive.

For a man more used to calming controversy he is surprisingly forthright about the role of unions. 'Unions have taken away from management the duty to communicate and that was wrong,' he says. 'In the past the company's hourly paid workers usually got their information either on the grapevine or through their union. This method sometimes led to misunderstandings. We are now asserting our duty and right to communicate. Unions still have a distinct function in representing their members but that does not include communicating company information.'

Cole says that shop stewards will get such information on the basis of their function as employees, rather than as officials of a trade union.

The implementation of the policy revolves round a monthly departmental meeting chaired by a director and attended by all 24 departmental managers. Company information such as trading performance and sales projection is systematically released for communication to employees. Each manager provides the meeting with departmental information, either verbally or in briefing notes. The managers then communicate this information at one or more meetings with the members of their departments. Department heads subsequently pass the information to the foremen who, in turn, inform the company's 2600 part-time workers.

So, information which basically used to be communicated through the unions will now be passed through the foremen after a chain of meetings. The procedure can also operate in the reverse direction, as an upwards channel of communication.

Under the new communications policy Kellogg is also providing a two-way forum for the company's administrative staff, none of whom belong to a trade union. Through a staff committee, which meets regularly, they are able to contribute ideas and opinions about their work and conditions of employment and to have prior discussions about major changes affecting their jobs.

Kellogg describes the meetings as 'tending to be a bit of a bitching session, so they are not proving to be particularly useful yet.' But the company is confident that 'they will settle down in time and become a constructive forum.'

While the staff committee is able to discuss many aspects of staff employment, it does not have any negotiating rights; Kellogg makes an annual pay award to its administrative staff.

In addition the company is considering involving the total workforce in its annual management conference. One way of doing this would be to extend the gathering into an all-employee conference, but apart from the wider policy negotiations, Cole says this is still being appraised because of the logistical problems.

An alternative would be to videotape the proceedings and make the tape available to all workers – an experiment tried out with some success at the latest annual meeting in February this year. A decision will be made later in the year, says Cole.

The company also intends to disseminate information in other ways. An employees' annual report will be published and the coverage of *Kellogg's News*, the company's monthly newsletter, will be enlarged. The company feels that there should also be a weekly bulletin of general news to be posted on all notice boards. Thus, the recent visit of Trades Union Congress general secretary Len Murray to the cereal packaging plant outside Manchester was announced before it was revealed in the local press.

The employees' annual report will be an uncomplicated review by the management and will contain reports from all departments such as human resources (personnel, etc.), logistics (distribution, purchasing), marketing, finance and production. It will be the only report produced by the company in the UK. Usually any account of UK activities is referred to briefly in the US parent company's statutory annual report. The first UK document is expected to be circulated in February next year.

Having implemented its policy Kellogg is clearly experiencing the first flush of success after a period of low morale. The policy is less than a year old and its effectiveness will naturally depend on whether it can stand the test of time.

It hinges on two uncertainties. Can the staff committee evolve from being 'a bitching session' into a more constructive forum? Secondly, will the series of meetings down the line lead to fewer misunderstandings than in the past?

Arnold Kransdorff, *The Financial Times*, 24 September 1980
RSA DPA June 1981 (*25 marks*)

10 Your firm is considering making a substantial cut in its 3000 strong work-force (located on several sites) and is keen to implement redundancies as smoothly as possible. You see the following article describing Whitbread's handling of its own redundancies and note both the policy's apparent success and the fact that the special problems posed by Whitbread's work-force (long service staff, etc.) reflect the composition and background of your firm's own work-force.

As the personnel manager's PA complete the following tasks:

a) in not more than 250 words outline under suitable headings Whitbread's approach to dealing with redundancies and the benefits achieved by all parties

b) in about 100 words set out the case for forming a resettlement team to deal with your own firm's forthcoming redundancies and make a formal recommendation

c) write an explanatory memorandum to the personnel manager covering the two tasks you have just completed.

A little extra effort eases the pain of redundancy

When making workers redundant most British companies are conspicuously negligent in providing employees with anything but their statutory rights – ie a redundancy cheque. At Whitbread Bridget Litchfield goes much further. A modest 32-year-old, Litchfield has a sympathetic ear and a smile that would disarm even the most belligerent of redundant shop stewards.

In fact, this is exactly what she does. She leads a special team – highly unusual in British industry – which tries to make life as easy as possible for workers made redundant.

Apart from offering a counselling service designed to help people overcome the domestic and psychological problems of redundancy, she arranges for employees (if they want) to see financial advisers; with redundancy payments of up to £40 000, Litchfield feels that some employees may well require sound investment recommendations. In addition, she organises an extensive job-search programme to place the redundant workers in positions with other local companies – with notable success. Alongside this she runs training courses on how to find other jobs.

In recent months, when the company has announced closures at Luton, Tottenham and Lewisham (affecting almost 500 people) she has been one of the first to be mobilised. As soon as those to be made redundant have been told she has been ready to move in with a team of three others, including a company psychologist.

Litchfield is no stranger to handling redundancies. This time last year, as personnel manager of Whitbread London, scores of people had passed through her hands. The effects of redundancy worried her, so she decided that something more should be done – if only to demonstrate that Whitbread was a 'caring company.' Up to then, any redundancy programme simply amounted to offering limited advice.

In Whitbread's case there were special problems to deal with. First, many of those being made redundant had been with the company all their working lives and were unused to dealing with the 'cold hard world outside the factory gates'. Secondly, the company often employed more than one member of a family and redundancy therefore was especially difficult. In many cases the people affected were not particularly literate.

On the other hand, she reasoned that there could also be spin-off benefits for the company if the redundancy problem was handled well. Apart from good-will, problems arising out of the run-down might be curtailed, with consequent saving.

Whitbread gave her programme rapid approval. Within months and with a new title of resettlement manager she was putting her ideas into practice at the company's Oakley Road brewery in Luton, a town where Whitbread was one of the largest employers. There, it had been decided to cut the work-force by 50 per cent at all levels, first through voluntary redundancies and then compulsorily, on the basis of last in, first out.

The redundancies were announced on 1st April. Three months' notice was given but those affected were not required to work more than four weeks. In the event of future vacancies at the brewery the company, as part of the package, offered to re-engage people who had not found jobs.

Redundancy pay-offs were generous – varying according to age and length of service but ranging from a minimum of a third of gross salary for those with less than four years' service to a maximum of three-and-a-half-years' salary.

Litchfield observes: 'At the beginning there were the inevitable tears and recriminations. Because we are basically a young team and most of those being made redundant were middle-aged, it took time to get their confidence. The informal atmosphere helped. But as time went on there was a dramatic change. People became more cheerful. They saw that we were genuinely interested in helping them – and this made them feel less alone. Quite apart from anything else there were virtually no problems during the run-down period; quality control, for example, was not affected.'

Litchfield's counselling services are designed to help the redundant workers overcome any social and financial problems. The loss of a job can often affect a family's domestic relationships and there is often a psychological problem caused by loss of status. Again, as Litchfield notes: 'Many of the people involved are totally unskilled in money matters and the redundancy payments are often the largest sums they will ever receive at one time. Frequently, for the people involved, it will be the first time that there will be no income coming in and this is often difficult to handle.'

Employees can therefore see a number of advisers, including representatives from two banks, two building societies, two insurance companies, a Whitbread tax adviser, the company's pension adviser, an unemployment benefits officer as well as a supplementary benefits officer.

Some workers wished to become self-employed. To help them, Litchfield called in advisers from the Small Firms Centre, run by the Department of Industry. Whitbread is also setting up its own New Ventures Board, to give employees advice on how to set up their own business.

The third aim of the redundancy programme – and perhaps the most revolutionary – involves the job-search scheme. Armed with a file for each employee, Litchfield and her team try to marry their skills with available jobs in the area. This involves using the Yellow Pages to ring up local companies, keeping in close touch with nearby government-run Job Centres and even writing to the local MP to check if there are any new businesses opening in the neighbourhood. 'Seventy-five per cent of local jobs are not advertised,' says Litchfield.

'In Luton, more than 250 companies were contacted and more than 1000 vacancies identified. A total of 21 people got job offers.'

Litchfield's success rate in Tottenham has been significantly greater. Up to the end of last week, more than 2000 vacancies had been identified and there had been 50 job offers.

All job vacancies are categorised and brief details included on a daily summary sheet posted on notice boards, on which also appear government announcements on financial benefits and training schemes. Employees are encouraged to browse around at any time of the day and consult the counsellors.

The other part of Litchfield's programme involves training courses on how the employees should go out and get another job. Two basic courses are offered – one for manual workers and the other for supervisors. The former is a relatively short course lasting just two hours, which illustrates how a potential employee should 'sell' himself on the telephone, fill in an application form and conduct himself at an interview. The supervisors' course lasts three days and covers instruction on how to prepare a *curriculum vitae*, fill in application forms and develop interview techniques.

One reason for the programme's success is the amount of co-operation gained from the main union involved – the Transport and General Workers. Shop stewards were consulted from the beginning.

Of equal importance has been the attitude of the Whitbread London board which has supported Litchfield's team; with an £8000 budget in Tottenham (excluding her own and one other counsellor's salary) she reckons that the whole exercise has also been cost-effective.

But perhaps the best measure of the programme's success can be judged by the reaction of those people made redundant. Robert Callow, secretary of the local Tottenham branch of the TGWU, who was himself one of the casualties, is full of praise for Litchfield and her team. While regretting the necessity for layoffs, he said his members had been impressed with the help offered. 'People are quite cheerful and there has been no trouble,' he said.

Adapted from an article by Arnold Kransdorff, *The Financial Times*, 25 September 1981

RSA DPA June 1982 (*30 marks*)

11 Assignment: 'The Move'

Learning outcomes

This assignment enables the student to:

1   Draft a summary and a memorandum
2   Design a notice
3   Draft a circular
4   Write a letter of apology

Information base

Pilson and Doorbar Ltd was formed in the mid 1960s by the amalgamation of two family businesses. In 1956 Arthur Pilson inherited a large and very profitable arable farm just south of the county town of Norwich in Norfolk, England, and while the farm manager continued to oversee the day to day running of the farm itself, Arthur Pilson developed a fertiliser production and distribution business in Norwich. In 1967 he went into partnership with his brother-in-law, Jack Doorbar, whose long-distance haulage business based in Lowestoft on the East Anglian coast some 28 miles south east of Norwich, was looking to expand.

At that time the farming side of the business had a considerably larger annual turnover than the haulage, but the combination of the two businesses suited both men. Pilson was able to provide capital and Doorbar had a new and reliable fleet of heavy goods vehicles which could transport the fertilisers more quickly and efficiently across country to the Midlands and the rich farmlands of south-east England.

The development of the North Sea oil industry and British entry into the European Economic Community furthered the expansion of the long-distance haulage side of Pilson and Doorbar's business so that by the late 1980s this is now significantly the larger and more profitable side of the business and the fertiliser production side of the business has been sold.

Since the company's formation the Head Office has been situated at 'Norfolk House', Cathedral Square, Norwich, Norfolk NR7 4GH with branch offices in Lowestoft and Ipswich. Ipswich is some 44 miles south west of Lowestoft and it is some 43 miles south of Norwich.

This division between the three centres, once favoured by Pilson and Doorbar Ltd, is now seen as being unsatisfactory and the company has decided that the time has come to streamline the workings of their organisation before they meet the challenges of the 1990s.

Thus over the last year, negotiations have taken place with all concerned and Pilson and Doorbar Ltd are looking forward to August 1989 when they leave their offices in Norwich, Lowestoft and Ipswich and take possession of their new centralised offices located in Lowestoft. Their address will be 12–16, Cranley Place, Lowestoft, Suffolk IP27 4EB. The telephone number will be 0502 735928.

You are employed in the centralised Accounts Department at Head Office in Norwich where you work as an Assistant Cashier. Among the full-time staff employed in the Accounts Department with whom you come into regular contact are:

Michaela Smythe	Accounts Department Manager
Tanvir Dobie	Departmental Secretary
Ben Mapperley	Accounts Supervisor
David Plaistow	Supervisory Cashier
Susan Flint YOU	Assistant Cashiers
John Bartlett	Wages Supervisor
Irene White Harold Quantock	Wages Clerks
Grekha Fahmid	Ledger Supervisor
Mike Hopkins Ali Alaqat Nye Deal	Accounting Assistants

Narrative

It is 21 June 1989 and you have just returned from a two-day course. You fill in the 'feedback form' as instructed by Mr Mapperley and, having left it in his secretary's office, go along the corridor to Mr Plaistow's office where you ask him what you are to do until it is time to deal with your usual Thursday afternoon duties.

Mr Plaistow says that as Susan does not seem to need any help with her morning's tasks he would like you to do something a bit different for a change.

'Let's see if you can put those communication skills you've been learning about over the last couple of days to some practical use, shall we? This article's been sitting in my in-tray for days now. It's about office design. Apparently the new offices in Lowestoft aren't going to be like these. There's even some talk of the whole Accounts Department being in one room instead of the senior staff having their own offices and other staff being in section offices! I can't see that working myself. Anyway, apparently this article compares two types of office design and the advantages and disadvantages the styles have. I'd like you to summarise it for me and present the information in an easy-to-read format. Do you think you could do that before lunch? By the way, if there's anything you think I don't need to read just leave it out and if there's anything really important let me know!'

You assure Mr Plaistow that you can do as he asks and you return to the office which you share with Susan to read the article.

Two types of office design
by Carolyn Farmer

One hundred years ago

The term 'Office Design' would have meant nothing to an office worker 100 years ago. Indeed, purpose-built offices were themselves rare. Generally companies either bought or rented space in a building which had been constructed for some other reason, maybe as a house or a shop. Thus the earliest offices were of a TRADITIONAL design – they were made up of small rooms. Every room would have a desk or two with some storage space and shelving. The occupant generally kept his door shut so that he was not easily in contact with other people. Privacy was valued by the office workers and the managers believed that people concentrated harder and worked better if they were on their own as much as possible. Certainly there were few opportunities for spreading gossip and time-wasting by wandering around the building chatting to anyone you happened to see. However, there was not much of a feeling of belonging to a group which is so valued today and the benefits of easily exchanging ideas which might help the workers and the company alike were not encouraged.

Changes in the 1950s

Of course changes in office design were happening all over the world and all the time but the most significant movement to occur in Europe was around 1958 when a design called OPEN PLAN was developed in Germany. One of the advantages of open plan design is that there is about 25% more use made of the overall floor space than in traditional design because you have one large office rather than lots of small offices so there are fewer walls and corridors. Heating, lighting and cleaning costs are reduced and employees can share equipment more easily. Fewer supervisors are needed for the same number of staff and, of great importance, communication is much improved between all members of staff. Of course, some supervisors might dislike their apparent loss of status as they will be in the same room as all other employees and the noise level and distractions caused by general movement may be a problem. One definite problem will be reduced security, especially where cash is concerned, and accounts section staff need to consider this problem most carefully.

When you have studied the article you realise that there is no need to summarise the first section headed 'One hundred years ago' as the traditional style is precisely what you have at the moment so you simply prepare a list of the advantages and disadvantages of the open-plan design.

You decide that you should inform Mr Plaistow why you have omitted the first section and you also think that you should draw his attention particularly to the disadvantages of open planning in so far as security matters are concerned.

To this end you write a memorandum to Mr Plaistow which you will attach to the list.

Task 1

Summarise the second section of the article, listing the advantages and disadvantages of the open-plan design.

(20 marks)

Task 2

Write the memorandum to Mr Plaistow.

(20 marks)

Mr Plaistow was appreciative of your efforts.

After much discussion and research it is decided by the management of Pilson and Doorbar Ltd that a modern variant of the open-plan idea called 'office landscape' is to be adopted with partitions using filing cabinets and purpose-built, head high, flexible room dividers separating departments and sections, one from the other. More sophisticated, modern storage equipment and other furniture will be purchased and staff will have some say in the arrangement of the decor of their area.

It is 27 July and the date for the move is approaching. Mrs Smythe has noticed that staff are already sorting out their desks and storage space in any slack moments. At a meeting with other senior staff she jots down a few rough notes outlining the general procedures to be adopted regarding packing for the move and adds a few notes about the Accounts Department in particular.

Once satisfied with the list she comes into the office you share with Susan Flint. 'Good afternoon [your name]. As you're working towards the AAT Certificate in Accounting I've got a couple of practical communication tasks that I would like you to work on for me. They should help you with the examination!

'Here's a list of procedures that staff must follow with regards to the move. (*She gives you her notes.*) They're in no particular order. I'd like you to do two things. First, our departmental secretary has an important role in the move so please write a notice which will be put on Tanvir Dobie's door stating clearly what her part in the organisation of the move is – the materials available and so on. Secondly, I'd like you to draft a circular to all Accounts Department staff informing them about the notice and giving them the extra information contained in this list. Can you do these tasks for me?'

You read through the list and assure Mrs Smythe that you can perform these tasks.

'Good, I'll ask Mr Plaistow to allocate some time to these tasks tomorrow. Let me see them when they are ready and I'll sign them.'

Reminder — all personal possessions must be moved by the owner — the company's insurance does NOT cover these items!

Staff are to collect appropriate sized boxes and labels from Tanvir Dobie to pack non-confidential stationery and materials.

Each department is being colour-coded for the move: ACCOUNTS IS GREEN — labels and heavy duty sealing tape are in this colour, so........... don't use another colour!

All fragile items must have appropriate packaging — if in doubt, leave for the removal firm to do this.

Remember to put your name on everything that you pack.

Only collect the number of labels you actually need — this is so Tanvir Dobie can keep a check on how many packages there will be.

Give Tanvir Dobie a list of the items you haven't been able to pack.

Any general problems — refer to Tanvir Dobie.

The packing of confidential items and equipment will be supervised by Mrs. Smythe.

Mrs Smythe's notes

Task 3
Write the notice to be placed on Tanvir Dobie's door. *(20 marks)*

Task 4
Draft the internal Accounts Department circular as requested by Mrs Smythe. *(20 marks)*

It is now August 1989 and the move to the new centralised offices in Lowestoft has taken place.

The adoption of 'landscape design' as the preferred office layout has caused a few initial problems, especially as regards the allocation of space and the noise levels associated with some sections. However, channels of communication are already improving and you are getting to know colleagues who, previously, were just nodding acquaintances.

The corner near to the Accounts Department is one of the 'Rest Areas' furnished with easy chairs and low tables. There are business periodicals and notice boards. It is here that staff can obtain beverages. On the other side of this Rest Area is the Personnel Department.

The areas are all separated by a mixture of filing cabinets, movable screens and large planters, some as big as a metre square, containing arrangements of foliage plants which are already helping to form a decorative 'landscape'.

In addition to these company-provided plants, some staff have brought their own pot plants and these are mostly placed on top of the filing cabinets. It is one of these plants that causes the trouble.

After work on Friday, 18 August, you, together with a few other staff from various departments, are chatting and drinking cold, soft beverages in the Rest Area. You are leaning against a filing cabinet chatting to Grekha Famid when suddenly Irene White, walking towards you, doesn't see one of the low tables in front of her and she trips over it. Fortunately she is not hurt but, as she stumbles, she knocks over one of the display stands containing periodicals and it falls towards you and Grekha. In the panic of the moment your drinks go everywhere and as you and Grekha jump out of the way the display stand hits the filing cabinet and knocks a plant pot on to the desk behind it. The plant and the desk belong to Miss Sara Coles, a member of the Personnel Department whom you know only vaguely.

Irene, although not hurt, is clearly shaken and you all make sure that she is all right. Everyone helps to clear up and assess the damage. The display stand is slightly bent and someone writes a note to the maintenance staff about this. Grekha helps Irene write the incident in the accident book and you go round the partition with Nye Deal to assess the situation on Miss Coles's desk. Fortunately it was clear of documents. The ceramic container has shattered but the plastic plant pot is all right. The azalea plant looks reasonably intact but there is damp potting compost everywhere! The only damage to the desk appears to be a few scratches where the container shattered while a note pad has been covered in compost and her plastic desk tidy, containing pens and pencils, has clearly been chipped by the container as it fell.

While Nye does his best to clear up the mess you decide to write a brief note to Miss Coles explaining how the accident happened and expressing regret for the damage.

When you read the note through you decide that although a minor incident, Miss Coles, who you have already discovered can be somewhat stern, might not treat the matter so lightly.

You therefore decide to write her a carefully worded letter instead; you feel that this will be more acceptable to her. Unfortunately the last post has gone and so you decide to leave the letter on Miss Coles's desk so that she will see it as soon as she arrives at work on Monday morning.

Task 5
Write the letter to Miss Coles.

(20 marks)
AAT C June 1989

7 Comprehension

We can work it out . . .
The Beatles

'I can't understand it' or 'I can understand it but I can't explain it' are students' perennial complaints regarding this type of question.

To get over the problem some candidates adopt what examiners call the 'shotgun' technique: they write down *everything* they can think of (or, more often, simply copy out long extracts from the text) in the hope that something will hit the target. It rarely does.

In this exercise quality not quantity is looked for. Good candidates think before they write and then go straight to the point. They do not waffle. They use their *own* words whenever possible and base their answers on the information in the given passage (except where the question asks for some point of general knowledge).

The following guidelines should prove helpful:
- Read through the passage quickly to get the gist.
- Read through all the questions. (This should help prevent any repetition or overlapping which is seldom necessary – indeed it is a sign that one of the answers is wrong.)
- Re-read the text as many times as necessary with the questions in mind. Answers should begin to crystallise with every reading.
- Concentrate on each question. Think out your answer before writing and follow the instructions ('briefly', 'stating your reasons', 'giving an example of your own').
- Do not copy out the question. This wastes time, extends the length of the answer and may lead to copying or punctuation errors. It is often a signal to the examiner that the candidate does not know the answer.
- Estimate the length of each answer by noting the number of marks allocated to it. Eight marks requires more than a one-line answer, but half a page is not necessary to explain a word or two – a synonym or short phrase will obtain full marks, e.g. 'statutory duty' = legal obligation.
- Explain every part of a phrase or sentence if asked to do so. But avoid circular answers, i.e. using words in your explanation that are used in the original ('data bank' = a bank where data are stored).
- Use the dictionary sensibly (if one is allowed) and make sure that you explain words *as they are used in the passage*. One student explained 'hash total' (in a computer context) as the amount of cannabis smuggled into Britain!
- Occasionally there will be no 'right' answer as such but your careful consideration and interpretation of the passage will be looked for.
- Check each answer for accuracy as it is completed. You still lose marks for poor English in this section.
- Answer the questions in the order in which they are set and ensure that your answers are correctly numbered or lettered.

The following examples illustrate the range of questions you may have to face. Read through each passage and the commentary that follows. Then prepare answers of your own before consulting the suggested answers at the end of this chapter.

Example

Transport strategy for a world without oil

Few people believe that we should invest in transport for the needs of today, and simply let tomorrow look after itself. But we are less

confident than we were that we know what we want, or that we can afford it as a nation and can achieve it without difficulty. The chief reason for this uncertainty dates from October 1973, for the quadrupling of world oil prices since then has had *traumatic* implications for transport planning in Britain, and no clear *consensus* about our transport future has emerged.

What we foresee is conditioned by our knowledge of past trends coupled with our view of how the *'post-industrial society'* should evolve. We must make assumptions which are neither heavily burdened with *portents* of doom nor so *euphoric* that we close our eyes to problems.

We have been warned that 'the conservation of energy must be a major national objective and in transport we must pursue it by all means that are practical and *cost-effective*' (Transport White Paper). Recent debates have underlined the balance of supply and demand, the rising rate of national consumption and the need to invest in new schemes. Frequently, the starting point is that we are *profligate* with energy in all areas.

The energy efficiency of different methods of travel varies. On the road, only about 20 per cent of the fuel used is converted to useful energy. The general trend is for fuel consumption to rise with speed, but there are interesting *anomalies*. Hovercraft are faster than power boats, yet they consume almost two-thirds less fuel per passenger-kilometre. On land, the fastest vehicle is the Advanced Passenger Train with a speed of 200 kilometres per hour, yet its fuel consumption is 70 per cent less per passenger-kilometre than that of a large car with a speed of 110 kilometres per hour. In the air, the helicopter is the most extravagant user, with a consumption per passenger-kilometre which is 2.5 times that of a jumbo jet.

However, the car has a clear advantage over rail in availability, and the helicopter over the jumbo in manoeuvrability.

Adapted from *Geographical Magazine*, September 1978

1   'The quadrupling of world oil prices' means that there was a four-fold rise. What word would replace 'quadrupling' if the rise were:
    a) Three-fold?
    b) Five-fold?
2   Explain briefly in your own words the meaning of any **four** of the following words and phrases as used in the passage:

traumatic (paragraph 1)	*euphoric* (paragraph 2)
consensus (paragraph 1)	*cost-effective* (paragraph 3)
post-industrial society (paragraph 2)	*profligate* (paragraph 3)
portents (paragraph 2)	

3   The last paragraph of the passage mentions the advantages of the car and the helicopter over rail and jumbo jets respectively.
    a) In not more than a few lines, give a simple example to illustrate each of these advantages, to prove your understanding of the writer's point.
    b) Giving your reasons, say whether from your reading of the passage you think the writer favours helicopters and cars as basic modes of transport.
4   Do you think 'anomalies' (paragraph 4) would be an apt sub-heading for the whole paragraph or not? Why?

5   Here are some simple statements. *From your reading of the passage only*, say whether you think each statement is TRUE or FALSE. You do not have to give your reasons. Simply read the passage and answer TRUE or FALSE.
   a) A car travelling at 100 kilometres per hour converts 30 per cent of its fuel to useful energy.
   b) Thanks to new transport developments, national energy consumption is stabilising.
   c) The faster the mode of transport, the more wasteful it is of fuel.
   d) Britain's transport plans are going ahead boldly.
   e) Britain is conserving energy effectively.

LCC PSC Dec 1979 (*40 marks*)

Commentary

Dictionaries have been allowed in LCC exams since 1983 and questions such as 1 and 2 are now less common. Without a dictionary they are obviously more difficult but not impossible.
1   Think of things in threes and fives with which you are familiar (triplets? quins?) and make the necessary adaptation for the answer which should be the same part of speech (a word ending in *ing*). 'Tripled' is incorrect.
2   The best answers will be a synonym or short phrase. The same part of speech is again necessary: plural nouns should be explained by plural nouns; adjectives by adjectives. Do not give more than one answer and expect the examiner to choose.
3   a) A simple illustration of your own is looked for to show that you have understood the point. Re-read the final paragraph, isolate the advantages (availability, manoeuvrability), and then illustrate them.
   b) Note that the key word is 'basic'.
4   'Anomalies' are exceptions. You must give a brief reason to support your answer.
5   Only one-word answers are needed. Pay special attention to (c).

Example

Young People and Rock

Rock music is a language that young people have made their own and which has become a global phenomenon and an industry in its own right. From its beginnings in the Fifties, it has gone through many metamorphoses which have all had repercussions on the society of the time.

   For young Europeans in 1984, rock no longer has the significance that it had for their elders in 1955. Nowadays rock is everywhere: on the radio, on television, in the shops and practically every household. Usually it is in English, but it can also be heard in one of the languages which has succeeded in adjusting to it. As a cultural bond between young people in many countries, rock is gradually losing a feeling for its origins, if not its message. That was not always the case.

   Young Americans discovered it before we did, in the spring of 1955, when Bill Haley wrote the soundtrack of the film 'Blackboard Jungle'. It was, in fact, the second stage in its development, since some young people concerned had been listening to black music which was more appealing than the variety imposed on them. It was then that a rather smart disc jockey christened Bill Haley's music 'rock and roll'.

From then on things took another turn. Listening to radios, which had been a mere pastime more or less prohibited by the prudish souls from the very religious Deep South, became the symbol of a defiance which very quickly went beyond the framework of music to redefine a whole way of life.

With the advent of Elvis Presley, a more acceptable star than the corpulent Bill Haley, people began to speak of revolt. Obviously that was not to everyone's taste: there was a flood of curses and protests against this rock and roll which 'perverts and debauches young people'. And yet young people simply wanted to have a little fun, to break out of the frightful straitjacket of puritanism which the America of the Fifties had imposed on them. And so rock become the synonym of a new language (usually coded, in order to distinguish itself from the adult world) of 'unbridled' pleasures and sexual revolution. All these ideas were conveyed in the songs as well as the private lives of the stars/models.

Europe quickly succumbed to the fascination of this new way of life. First it was England which, ever outward-looking, welcomed this beat from across the Atlantic. The first English rockers were carbon copies of their American counterparts, just as the French and Germans were to be after 1960.

The public quickly became receptive. And consequently it adopted an attitude – the word 'look' was not yet used – which resembled a need to come together in a tribe, a conspiracy, with its signs, slang and fashions. Almost 30 years later some of these tribes have scarcely changed at all; they have remained faithful to the sound and customs of their golden age. Such are the teddy boys, the great defenders of the true rock and roll of the Fifties.

Successive tidal waves have brought about far-reaching changes in these attitudes and, by extension, in the life of almost all those who have been involved in rock directly or indirectly. Scarcely anybody was spared by the Beatles and the great pop era that they ushered in. Everybody wore long hair, whether they were rockers or not, and the most obvious symbols of that period penetrated all layers of society. Rock no longer had to be the standard bearer of a new age: it was at its centre, the constant reference, the consummate form, despite its sudden lapse into decadence.

From the mid-Sixties onwards the influence of pop spread throughout Europe. It took the great upheavals of the spring of 1968 for these trends to acquire individual characteristics. Whilst at the giant pop festivals, the crowds appeared increasingly uniform from country to country, the music tended to differ. People began to speak of German rock or French rock.

They turned back to their own roots, all the more avidly in that rock was then flirting with ecological themes and folk music. Who, at the time, dared to claim that rock was passing through its last outbursts of subversion? For indeed, at the end of the Seventies and the beginning of the Eighties it ceased to be a rallying point. Perhaps because young people no longer wanted to be rallied. . . .

Source: 'Forum, Council of Europe'

1 Explain what was meant by 'Rock music . . . has become a global phenomenon and an industry in its own right'.   (4 marks)
2 Why does rock no longer have the significance for young people that it had in 1955?   (4 marks)

3   Explain fully (in your own words) what ensued following the use of the term 'rock and roll' by the disc jockey.   (8 marks)
4   Give a full account (in your own words) of the developments of rock in music in Europe up to the mid-Sixties.   (8 marks)
5   What is suggested has happened since the mid-Sixties?   (6 marks)

LCC PSC June 1987 (30 marks)

Commentary

1   The original opening has been shortened and only this abbreviated version needs to be explained. Note that there are four words/phrases that need to be covered – 'global', 'phenomenon', 'industry' and 'in its own right'. A brief answer (one sentence?) is adequate. In the 1987 exam one candidate wrote a page illustrating the 'global' nature of rock and roll and in so doing covered every other question. Dictionaries may help – but do not emulate another candidate who gave as her answer 'It means spherical body of remarkable thing and set in its own industry'.
2   From this point there is a danger of overlapping and repetition of answers. If the guidelines are followed, however, it should be possible to identify particular paragraphs as the source for each answer. 2 should be based on paragraph 2.
3   The answer is in paragraphs 4 and 5. Note the words 'fully' and 'in your own words' in the question. Eight marks suggest the longest answer so far; sometimes the mark may give an indication of the number of points required – here there may be at least four.
4   Your answer should draw on paragraphs 6 to 8. The above comments on the instructions and mark allocation still apply.
5   Your answer should focus on paragraphs 9 and 10. Six marks may suggest that there are three points to be made.

Example

Read the following extracts from a report on the European Parliament debate on 17 June 1980 (published in *EP News* No 11) and answer the questions which follow it:

> **The European Parliament held a major debate today on a wide-ranging resolution on the position of women in the Community. A point of concern in the resolution adopted on Thursday was the situation in countries which may be joining the EEC. Parliament called on the Commission to report on any disparities in those countries concerning the legal position of women, compared with the existing Community.**
>
> **Susan Dekker, rapporteur for the Social Affairs Committee, pointed out that the UN had 14 major aims to be achieved if possible by 1980. Notable among them was the desire to see an increase in literacy and the social education of women and guaranteed parity on the exercise of civil rights.**
>
> **Child allowances vary from one member state to another and (in some member states) are paid out at the rate applicable in the country where the child lives. This principle continues to apply even when the parent works in another member state. The Commission is proposing that the rate should be that applicable in the country where the wage-earner works. As of July 1979 the rates in force in the member states were as follows:**

No. of children	B £	FRG £	DK £	F £	IRL £	I £	L £	NL £	UK £
1	21	11	13	–	3	5	18	17	17
2	55	34	26	22	8	10	40	46	33
3	102	80	38	60	13	15	85	74	50
4	149	126	51	95	17	21	131	110	67
5	197	172	64	128	22	26	177	145	83
6	245	218	77	161	27	31	222	184	100
7	292	264	89	194	32	36	268	223	117
8	340	310	102	227	37	41	314	266	134
9	384	356	115	260	41	46	359	309	150
10	435	402	128	293	46	51	405	352	167

Family allowances (per month)

This view was endorsed by Willem Albers, a rapporteur for the Social Committee, who moved a resolution approving the proposal. This was adopted. The resolution also called for social security schemes for migrant workers to be extended.

In the following questions, give brief answers. Be guided by the marks obtainable.

1 The table shows nine of the member states of the EEC as they then were.
      What countries are indicated by the letters FRG and NL respectively?   (*2 marks*)

2 The extract twice speaks of resolutions being adopted. Explain what this means.
                                                                                    (*4 marks*)

3 Explain what you understand by EITHER *social education* OR *social security*.
                                                                                    (*4 marks*)

4 Explain what you understand by EITHER *guaranteed parity on the exercise of civil rights* OR *rapporteur*.   (*4 marks*)

5 The average British family has about two children. Does this fact alter the overall picture conveyed by the table at first glance? If so, in what way?   (*4 marks*)

6 After looking at the table, a cynic remarks that the EEC bureaucrats in Brussels have a vested interest in their proposal to change the rules governing the rate of child allowance payable.
   a) Explain clearly the usual business meaning of 'vested interest'. Illustrate with an example.   (*4 marks*)
   b) What do you think the cynic has in mind when he alleges this?   (*4 marks*)

7 Imagine that the European Parliamentary Elections are soon to be held. Draft the wording for a leaflet to encourage voters to support candidates who take a sympathetic line over child allowances. You hope the leaflet will bring many new members to the child welfare organisation for which you work.   (*14 marks*)

LCC PESD June 1981 (*40 marks*)

Commentary

1 The answers are not in the passage – at Diploma level a wide general knowledge is required.

2 This should be easy for anyone with a knowledge of meetings.

3/4 A brief phrase/sentence is all that is required.
5   An examination of the table is needed with two children in mind. Give reasons to justify your answer.
6   a) requires a crisp explanation and an example of your own.
    b) requires an answer based on the table.
7   Basic data need to be supplied: the name/address of the imaginary child welfare organisation for which you work (one of the leaflet's aims is to recruit new members); the name(s) of the candidate(s) you support with reasons (use the text for details of how low UK allowances are); the date of the elections. *NB* There is no need (and no time) for elaborate graphics, lettering, colours, etc. Black ink, sensible paragraphing and spacing, occasional capitalisation or underlining and an appropriately encouraging tone are all that is necessary.

Suggested answer 1

1   a) tripling (or trebling)
    b) quintupling
2   traumatic   – disturbing
    consensus   – agreement
    portents   – predictions
    profligate   – wasteful
3   a) If you wish to visit a friend your car is ready at any time, whereas trains are regulated by timetables and may be subject to delay or cancellation. In emergencies (e.g. an air-sea rescue), the helicopter has the versatility of movement that the jumbo obviously lacks.
    b) On balance the writer seems not to favour cars and helicopters as *basic* modes of transport since both are extremely wasteful of fuel; however, he does mention their obvious advantages and perhaps finally regards them as a necessary evil from the point of view of energy conservation.
4   Yes – since most of the paragraph cites modes of transport which do not conform to the general trend with regard to speed and fuel consumption.[1]
5   a) False
    b) False
    c) False
    d) False
    e) False

Suggested answer 2

1   Rock music has developed into a worldwide sensation and has become a recognised branch of business.

---

[1]The examiner's report states: 'Some candidates thought "No" and explained that the paragraph, while citing anomalies, was by no means wholly devoted to this aspect. Others pointed out that a sub-heading would be out of place unless sub-headings were also provided for the remaining paragraphs. These points were not anticipated, but were quite acceptable where cogently argued.'

2   Rock music is less significant for today's youngsters because it is now accepted and commonplace. It has become more universal, sometimes being heard in languages other than English, and has therefore slowly lost touch with its roots and what it originally stood for.

3   Young people challenged their elders by listening to radios, a pastime usually forbidden in the puritanical Deep South. Their disobedience swiftly transcended the world of music and started to change the way young people wished to lead their lives.

When Elvis Presley appeared on the scene, people started to speak of rebellion and there was a backlash against rock and roll which was said to have a corrupting influence on young people.

However, teenagers simply wanted to enjoy themselves and escape from the strict standards imposed on them. Rock became associated with unrestricted gratification and liberated sexual behaviour, ideas which were reflected in the songs and the lives of the stars.

4   Europe readily accepted this new lifestyle, first in England and later in France and Germany, with the early European rock musicians imitating the American stars.

Young people responded by seeking a group identity with their own signs, language and dress. Three decades later, some groups (such as the teddy boys) still exist unchanged.

Successive phases of rock – especially the era of the Beatles – affected everyone, regardless of social standing or whether they followed the music or not. Rock was no longer the forerunner of a new age but at the very heart of it.

5   Since the mid-Sixties pop has spread across the Continent. Although young people at the huge pop concerts dressed in similar fashion, the music developed in different ways from country to country, taking up social themes and folk music.

By the late Seventies and early Eighties rock was no longer the focal point for young people, perhaps because they no longer wished to be brought together.

Suggested answer 3

1   Federal Republic of Germany
     Netherlands
2   These are motions that have been endorsed.
3   'Social security' is the financial aid governments pay to people who become sick, unemployed, etc.
4   'Guaranteed parity . . .' is an assurance that each individual will be treated equally in all aspects of everyday life.
5   At first glance the table seems to indicate that the UK pays far less in child allowances than the majority of its fellow members of the EEC. However, where only two children are involved the differences between these payments are much less and the UK is among the five most generous states.
6   a) 'Vested interest' indicates that a personal benefit or gain is identifiable. For example, cigarette manufacturers do not sponsor sporting occasions from altruistic motives – they see them as valuable publicity and a way of circumventing TV restrictions on cigarette advertising.
     b) The highest child allowances are paid in Brussels and EEC bureaucrats would receive the top rate regardless of where their families actually lived – so a personal interest is present.

7

X MAKE YOUR VOTE COUNT X

EUROPEAN PARLIAMENTARY ELECTIONS

Thursday, 5 June

Did you know that child benefit payments in Britain are among the **lowest** in the EEC?

That a family with 3 children in Britain gets less than HALF the allowance paid to a similar family in Belgium?

HOW CAN YOU HELP?

June 5 is your opportunity to ensure that your children's welfare is protected. On this day you can use your vote to elect those candidates who will put your case before the European Parliament.

SUE EDGE and BERT KNIGHT

can help and will help if elected – just give them the chance they need and vote for a better future.

If you would like more information please write to

The Child Welfare Organisation
11 Timor Grove
Liverpool 8

Exercises

1 You have *15* minutes to read through the passage and answer the questions below.

Advertising can be thought of 'as the means of making known in order to buy or sell goods or services'. Advertising aims to increase people's awareness and arouse interest. It tries to inform and to persuade. The media are all used to spread the message. The press offers a fairly cheap method. Magazines are used to each special sections of the market. The cinema and commercial radio are useful for local markets. Television, although more expensive, can be very effective. Posters are fairly cheap and more permanent in their appeal. Other ways of increasing consumer interest are through exhibitions and trade fairs as well as direct mail advertising.

There can be no doubt that the growth in advertising is one of the most striking features of the western world in this century. Many businesses such as those handling frozen foods, liquor, tobacco and patent medicines have been built up largely by advertising.

We might ask whether the cost of advertising is paid for by the manufacturer or by the customer. Since advertising forms part of the cost of production, which has to be covered by the selling price, it is clear that it is the customer who pays for advertising. However, if large-scale advertising leads to increased demand, production costs are reduced, and the customer pays less.

It is difficult to measure exactly the influence of advertising on sales. When the market is growing, advertising helps to increase demand. When the market is shrinking, advertising may prevent a bigger fall in sales than would occur without its support. What is clear is that businesses would not pay large sums for advertising if they were not convinced of its value to them.

Now select the *one* correct answer to each of the following ten questions:

a) To achieve its aim advertising tries to:
- A   deceive
- B   increase
- C   arouse
- D   persuade

b) The word 'media' means:
- A   the press
- B   television
- C   radio
- D   all of these

c) Trade fairs may:
- A   replace exhibitions
- B   attract possible customers
- C   offer fun and amusement
- D   raise interest rates

d) The 'western world' referred to includes:
- A   only the USA
- B   all of Europe
- C   North America and Western Europe
- D   all industrial countries

e) The word 'patent' applied to 'medicines' means:
- A   pills
- B   proprietary
- C   prescribed
- D   powerful

f) Advertising is in the main paid for by:
- A   the customer
- B   the manufacturer
- C   increased sales
- D   cutting prices

g) 'Large-scale' applied to advertising means:
- A   expensive
- B   well-balanced
- C   extensive
- D   extravagant

h) The author says that advertising can increase demand:
- A   always
- B   never
- C   in a growing market
- D   in a shrinking market

i) The influence of advertising can be measured:
- A   exactly
- B   not at all
- C   by scientific means
- D   with difficulty

j) The four paragraphs deal with:
- A   the influence
- B   the cost
- C   the methods
- D   the growth in advertising

Arrange A, B, C, and D in the order used by the author.

2   You have *15* minutes to read through this passage and then answer the questions below.

Shorthand is a system of writing using symbols for sounds. It is designed to save time and labour, and particularly to enable the hand to keep pace with ordinary speech. We know that various forms of shorthand, or stenography as it is sometimes called, were used by the Greeks and the Romans in ancient times. In modern times the most successful system for English was devised in 1837 by Isaac Pitman who invented an entirely fresh method of recording the spoken word. Several other systems also have since been created.

Pitman shorthand is today widely used for parliamentary as well as for legal and newspaper reporting. It has also been applied to some twenty different languages, and adaptations have been used in countries as far apart as Japan and Argentina. Anyone who, say, knows French well can quickly learn to write Pitman shorthand, using a modified form of the English version.

Almost every top secretary learns shorthand. It is best acquired when the learner is a teenager; older people can master it, but they generally require a longer learning period. Daily practice in reading and writing, accompanied by a study of the underlying theory, is the best approach. Those who require a simpler system can learn to write PitmanScript, which is a kind of abbreviated handwriting that enables the writer to take down ordinary dictated correspondence, but is unsuitable for the verbatim recording of long speeches.

When tape-recorders first came on to the market, some people thought shorthand would no longer be needed. This prophecy has been proved wrong. Tape-recorders are indeed handy, but there are many occasions when a good shorthand writer is irreplaceable. The ambitious office worker will always do well to learn the skill. Once it has been well learnt it is never forgotten.

Now select the *one* correct answer to each of the following ten questions. (Re-arrange question j by placing 1, 2, 3, 4, against the letters.)

a) Shorthand is used for all the following reasons *except* to:
   A   save time
   B   reduce work
   C   save paper
   D   record speech

b) The author states that shorthand is used widely for reporting all but one of the following:
   A   newspaper stories
   B   parliamentary procedures
   C   legal matters
   D   television

c) Pitman shorthand was invented in the:
   A   seventeenth century
   B   eighteenth century
   C   nineteenth century
   D   twentieth century

d) The author says Isaac Pitman invented:
   A   the first form of shorthand
   B   the best form of shorthand
   C   the latest form of shorthand
   D   a new form of shorthand

e) Shorthand is best learnt by:
   A   studying theory
   B   reading
   C   writing
   D   all of these

f) Verbatim reporting means:
- A recording the actual words
- B putting meaning to words
- C putting in the right verbs
- D repeating the words

g) According to the author the best age to learn shorthand is:
- A 10–20 years
- B 13–19 years
- C 17–25 years
- D over 25 years

h) Tape-recorders in offices are:
- A useful
- B useless
- C a nuisance
- D indispensable

i) Prophecy means:
- A trying to see the future
- B foretelling future events
- C guessing about profits
- D being under God's direction

j) The four paragraphs deal with:
- A other means of recording speech
- B learning shorthand and its alternative forms
- C the history of shorthand
- D shorthand throughout the world

Re-arrange A, B, C, D, in the order of the passage by placing 1, 2, 3, 4, against the letters.

PEI EOS Elementary

3 Situation:

You are Office Manager of a small British company. Your Director has heard about the Fax service which is now available and has sent you some questions about it.

Task:

Look at the Director's questions below. Answer these questions using information from the Reprofax brochure below.

Note:

Your answers need not be written in full sentences – numbers or short answers are acceptable where appropriate. Your answers should be as helpful as possible.

Example: Can I find out more about the Reprofax service?
Answer: Yes. Call in at the local office, or phone the local office, or dial 100 and ask for Freefone Reprofax.

a) What does 'Fax' mean?
b) How does Fax transmit messages?
c) Is Fax charged like a telegram (i.e. so much per word)?
d) Is Fax available only in the UK?
e) How can we receive a Fax message if we don't have a Fax machine in the office?
f) How long does it take to transmit a document by Fax?
g) Must all documents be printed or typed?
h) Can we send documents such as maps and diagrams by Fax?
i) Do all kinds of document cost the same amount to send by Fax?
j) How can we send a Fax message if:
  i) we **don't** have a Fax machine, but
  ii) our client **does** have a Fax machine?

k) How can we send a Fax message if:
  i) we **don't** have a Fax machine, and
  ii) our client **doesn't** have a Fax machine?

l) How can we send a Fax message if:
  i) we **do** have a Fax machine, and
  ii) our client also **does** have a Fax machine?

m) How can we send a document by Fax if:
  i) it is larger than A4 and
  ii) the print is small?

(30 marks)

REPROFAX – High Speed 'Post' By Telephone

Reprofax Offices now provide a copying service (Fax), so that you can 'post' pages of text and graphics by telephone to almost anywhere in the UK and around the world in **minutes** rather than **days**.

All you do is call in to your nearest Reprofax Office and ask for your documents to be sent by Fax. They can be sent to another Reprofax Office or to anyone who owns a Fax machine. We can also deliver the 'fax' to any address within 50 kilometres (35 miles) of a Reprofax Office (at an extra charge) if the addressees can't call in and collect it themselves.

You can send as many A4 ($30 \text{ cm} \times 21 \text{ cm}/11\frac{3}{4} \text{ in} \times 8\frac{1}{4} \text{ in}$) pages as you like and it doesn't matter how much information they contain because you pay only by the **page** and **not** by the word. Nor does it matter what **type** of information you send – Fax machines can transmit all kinds of information (handwritten, typed, printed or drawn) with equal speed, ease and cost.

So you can send quick handwritten messages, urgent letters or orders, important reports, plans, maps, diagrams – the list is almost endless.

You can also use our instant reduction and enlargement facilities to make larger documents fit onto A4 pages or to clarify small print or fine detail that is difficult to read.

And if you've already got a facsimile machine in your office, you can use the Reprofax network as a quick and convenient means of 'posting' information to clients who don't possess one.

For more information about our facsimile service, call in to or telephone your nearest Reprofax Office, or dial 100 and ask for Freefone Reprofax.

LCC EFB First Level June 1988

---

4 Read the following passage carefully and then answer the questions which follow. The passage is taken from a credit card application form:

Credit Cards – Your Rights

The Consumer Credit Act 1974 covers your agreement when you apply for a credit card. It also lays down certain requirements for your protection which must be satisfied when the agreement is made. If they are not, the card issuer cannot enforce the agreement against you without a court order.

The Act also gives you a number of rights. You have the right to end your credit card agreement at any time by giving written notice (as long as you pay off all amounts outstanding on the agreement). If you have obtained unsatisfactory goods or services under a transaction financed by this agreement, apart from any purchased out of a cash loan, you may also have the right to sue the supplier, the card issuer, or both.

Similarly, if the contract financed by your card is not fulfilled (e.g. if a dealer has gone out of business), you may still be able to sue the card issuer.

If you would like to know more about the consumer protection offered under this Act, you should contact either your local Trading Standards Department or your nearest Citizens' Advice Bureau.

If your credit card is lost, stolen or misused by someone who obtained it without your consent, you may be liable to the card issuer for up to £25 of any loss. If it is misused with your permission you will probably be liable for ALL losses. You will not be liable for losses to the card issuer which take place after you have reported a theft or loss, provided that you confirm in writing within seven days.

Your answers must be complete sentences in your own words.
a) How can you end the credit card agreement? *(2 marks)*
b) If you purchased a bicycle under this agreement and it turned out to be faulty, against whom could you make a claim? *(3 marks)*
c) You have ordered goods by telephone quoting your credit card number. You then found that although the firm had charged the money against your account, it had gone out of business before your goods had been despatched. How would you be able to get your money back? *(3 marks)*
d) What action must you take if you lose your card? *(2 marks)*

AEB EFB Specimen Paper

5 Read the passage and answer the questions which follow it:

Employers report greater *productivity*, reductions in absenteeism, tardiness and *labour turnover*, together with a significant improvement in *worker morale*, when flexible working hours are offered. There are more than 100 variations of the Flexitime system, but all have in common the feature of allowing workers to show up late without penalty.

Flexitime has obvious appeal to many workers because it permits them to manage their own time. Although they are expected to be on the job during some '*core time*', such as 10.00 a.m. to 3.00 p.m., there are bands of flexible time at the beginning and end of the day during which they can determine for themselves when to begin and end their work-day. Because of the flexibility they can work when their energy is at its peak. 'Morning people' can start their day early if they so choose, and 'night people' who don't begin functioning well until, say, 11.00 a.m. can begin later. Personal errands and business, shopping, medical appointments, banking, etc., for which workers on fixed hours must take time off, can be carried out within the flexible time bands.

Many types of office work, such as secretarial, key punching, book-keeping etc., can be adapted to a flexible work schedule. Other work that appears to be particularly *amenable* to Flexitime hours includes clerical, administrative, research and service jobs. Flexible work hours are frequently used by service-oriented companies in order to maintain a greater coverage of office telephones and provide longer hours of service to the general public, particularly those people who need to contact them for assistance outside 'accepted' office hours.

Employers found a flexible work week produced more advantages than were expected. Morale and satisfaction increased, workers were better able to *integrate* work and personal life, and commuting was made considerably easier. However, the recording of hours worked is an essential feature of any flexible working hours scheme, in order to ensure that people don't abuse the new freedom to the *detriment* of their colleagues. With part of a department's work-force off each day, there is less crowding and competition for equipment and space.

Part-time work appears to be a satisfactory arrangement that offers the flexibility of hours that many women with families prefer; women seeking to combine careers with parenthood look for better ways to handle their double roles, and, perhaps, decrease their need for child day-care. Many mothers find themselves torn between their job and home responsibilities.

Alternatives to the five-day week have been considered and tried out for a variety of reasons; urban planners seeking solutions to the overcrowding of highways, parking places, recreational and commercial facilities, at certain times, and the *under utilisation* at other times; industrial psychologists who feel that job dissatisfactions on the part of employees might be lessened; and energy *conservationists* who *speculate* that petrol consumption could be reduced were all looking for a way to solve the problems they face.

Work-week variations have not been in use long enough for us to become aware of all the problems they may produce. Several studies are under way to look at such questions as what effect flexible working hours might have on families.

Do some work-week variations damage family life more than others? Do some *enhance* it? Can work-hour variability improve the economic position of women in the labour market?

Adapted from an article 'Flexitime in the USA' published by Pitman

a) The adoption of flexible working hours is under consideration at the company where you are employed as secretary/assistant to the Personnel Officer. He is at present away from the office but has asked you to send him any useful information that you have discovered on the benefits of variable working hours. Compose a memorandum outlining the advantages and disadvantages of flexible working hours from both the employer's and the employees' point of view. *(30 marks)*

b) i) Choose *three* of the following expressions and explain fully what you understand by each one as it is used in the passage:
   productivity
   labour turnover
   worker morale
   core time
   under utilisation
   conservationists

   ii) How might 'work-hour variability improve the economic position of women in the labour market'?

   iii) Choose *four* of the following words and for each give another word or phrase that conveys its meaning in the passage:
   amenable
   integrate
   detriment
   speculate
   enhance *(25 marks)*

LCC SS June 1979

6 Read the passage below, then answer the questions which follow it:

The Trade Descriptions Act 1968 requires that oral, written or visual descriptions of products and services shall be accurate, and shall not mislead 'recklessly' or 'to a material degree'. A hotel may be described in a brochure as 'only five minutes' walk from the beach': if you can only reach the beach in five minutes by clambering down the cliff face, there has been an offence under the Act. But the misleading description has to be about a physical, verifiable feature; claims like 'the holiday of a lifetime' or 'lovelier than ever before' are expected to be taken with a 'pinch of salt'. They cannot be qualified and are not part of the 'trade description'.

The Consumer Protection Acts 1961 and 1971 laid down that products be safe. They operated through regulations covering particular groups of products. The regulations specify standards for products, so that, for example, the paint on children's toys must not contain lead and the eyes of soft toys must be securely anchored and not on spikes. Over the years it became clear that more products were outside the regulations than were included within them. There was the case of a sweet made to look like a baby's dummy but designed in such a way that it might have choked a small baby. The prosecution under the Toy Safety Regulations failed because the importer's defence was that it was a sweet and not a toy and therefore not covered by the Regulations. Thus the Consumer Safety Act 1978 was passed, which incorporates the Regulations under the old Consumer Protection Acts. It requires that all products shall be safe.

The Fair Trading Act 1973 is an important piece of consumer legislation with wide powers. It set up the office of Director General of Fair Trading, with the responsibility of looking after consumers' health, safety and economic interests. This is partly done by a very active programme of consumer information, so that consumers know their rights, and by setting up *codes of practice* with industries where consumer difficulties are well known, for example, the sale, servicing and repair of second-hand cars, mail-order transactions, and a number of others.

The Act also gives the power to refer companies for investigation by the Monopolies and Mergers Commission and by the Restrictive Practices Court, both of which try to increase the competitiveness of business by preventing policies *contrary to consumers' interests*, such as price fixing, where the consumer is not paying *the true price*, and *dominance of a market* by heavy expenditure on advertising to such an extent that competition is excluded and consumers pay for the advertising in the high price of the product. The Director General investigates practices thought to be against the consumers' interests in terms of health, safety, and *economic interests*, such as prices declared exclusive of VAT (in full), and bargain offers publicised in such a way as to look much cheaper than they are. He is responsible for the Consumer Credit Act 1974. Any organisation offering loans, advice on loans, or information about creditors, must be licensed by the Director General. Any loan or agreement arranged by a non-licensed body is void. Under the Act credit cannot be refused on grounds of race or sex. When people apply for a loan, many companies check with a *credit reference agency* to see whether they are habitual bad debtors. Mistakes have been known to occur, as when an agency might classify all the people in a block of flats because of one bad debtor living there. Under the Consumer Credit Act, anyone who thinks that wrong information is being held about him or her, can, for a small fee, see the records and get them put right.

Adapted from *Consumer Education*, Marion Giordan, Methuen

a) What is the difference between a claim which *is* an offence under the Trade Descriptions Act and a claim which *is not*?   *(4 marks)*
b) Why was the Consumer Safety Act 1978 passed?   *(4 marks)*
c) What do you understand by:
   i) 'dominance of a market' (paragraph 4)
   ii) 'codes of practice'?   (paragraph 3)   *(8 marks)*
d) What practices 'contrary to consumers' interests' affect the price paid by the consumer? What do you understand by the expression 'the true price'? (paragraph 4).
                                                                         (6 marks)
e) How does the Director General try to safeguard the consumers' 'economic interests'? (paragraph 4)   *(4 marks)*
f) What do you understand by 'a credit reference agency'? (paragraph 4)   *(4 marks)*

7 Read the following passage and then answer the questions which follow it.

The lorry is probably the most flexible type of goods vehicle possible. All other modes of transport are dependent on being fed traffic by the lorry, unless, as may be the case with some large manufacturers, there is a rail, waterway or sea/airport connection. Even then, it is unlikely that the customer will be similarly connected to a private siding, inland waterway, wharf, etc. so that at least one 'leg' of the journey must be by road freight transport. At the very least this involves trans-shipment of the goods, with attendant labour or capital costs being passed to the customer or consumer. Nowadays, of course, trans-shipment is often less labour-intensive if the goods are in some way unitised, either on pallets which can be fork-lifted between vehicles (lorry and ship, barge, rail wagon, etc.) or by being containerised. Nevertheless, no trans-shipment happens without some cost being incurred, as well as the risks of breakage or pilfering arising. Thus again we can see how the very flexibility of road freight transport systems permits a very simple single control to be exercised over the goods for the whole of their transit and can appreciate how this must enhance the attractions of the system to the user.

Since the United Kingdom now boasts one of the best-developed highway networks in the world, with motorways, trunk roads and primary roads penetrating even remote rural areas and providing fast direct inter-urban connections, virtually all producers or consumers are road-connected, and most are within convenient reach of a motorway or trunk road.

The prime function of the road freight transport operator is the movement of goods, and services fulfilling this function are thus basic. The pattern of movement of the goods may be as a regular predictable flow, thus facilitating the design and implementation by the operator of a tightly scheduled regular service to deal with it, or it may be irregular and infrequent, varying in quantity, composition and destination, and thus requiring the operator to design irregular and occasional 'demand-responsive' services.

Probably the most useful service which a haulier can provide for his clients is to offer to warehouse their goods. Warehousing, as well as being profitable in its own right, also attracts and creates traffic, if only the receipt and despatch of warehoused goods. An obvious expansion of warehousing is to offer a manufacturer a 'bespoke' or tailored distribution service for his product, where the haulier collects from the production line, warehouses, delivers against orders taken by the manufacturer and passed to him, and relieves the manufacturer of all inventory control and customer invoicing. Many hauliers have the potential and experience to offer such a package and market this quite aggressively. Others provide a distribution consultancy service based on their acquired expertise, and for which they charge a fee. They may extend their package to embrace freight-forwarding activities, taking over from the customer all the arranging and documentation of his export traffic. Because they are often able to arrange to consolidate such traffic with similar traffic from other customers for the same destination, the service they can offer in this way can prove very attractive to customers.

It is up to the goods vehicle operator to market his service by finding out his customers' needs (market research), providing a tailored or 'bespoke' service to meet those needs, advertising this to customers, and then constantly monitoring both his undertaking's performance in meeting these needs and any potential variation in demand. For example, if a customer is expanding his production he should seek to tender for the new traffic.

Reprinted from *The Business of Transport* – Bell, Bowen and Fawcett, MacDonald & Evans by permission of Pitman Publishing

a) Why is the lorry an indispensable part of the transport system?   *(4 marks)*

b) What are the attractions of road haulage to the user?   *(6 marks)*

c) What is the advantage of the road network compared with transportation by rail, waterway or sea/airport? *(4 marks)*

d) Explain what you understand by the expression '"demand-responsive" services'.

(4 marks)

e) What are the advantages of warehousing and the expansion of warehousing to the
   i) haulier? *(6 marks)*
   ii) manufacturer? *(8 marks)*

f) Why would consolidating similar loads for the same destination enable the haulier to offer attractive terms to customers? *(2 marks)*

g) What is the importance to the haulier of research and constant monitoring? *(6 marks)*

LCC SS June 1988 *(40 marks)*

8 Read the passage below and answer the questions which follow.

Car manufacturers may liaise more

European car production in the 10 years from the mid-1960s sped along at an average annual rate of increase of 5.8 per cent. The impact of two oil supply shocks, the rapid rise of the Japanese car makers and the growing reluctance of developing countries to take built-up cars as imports all helped slow that pace considerably.

In the period between 1973 and 1982 the trend growth in car output was only 1.7 per cent.

For most of the decade, however, the *automotive industry* remained a key element in the economies of the major European countries. In 1980 it was still absorbing 20 per cent of steel production and of machine tool output, more than 5 per cent of glass production and around 15 per cent of rubber production.

So, apart from employing 2 million itself, the industry also created roughly 4 million more jobs in the supply and raw material sectors.

But the industry is now undergoing a major *transformation*. After years of *evolutionary development* it has entered a revolutionary phase as the manufacturers race against one another to introduce new machines incorporating *new technology* and to modernise their production plants to improve productivity.

This would have been a fairly difficult process at a time of high demand. During the current recession it has proved particularly painful.

The low level of sales – most markets are well below their best – has depressed prices. In any case, they have been significantly influenced in recent years by the fact that the Japanese can charge relatively low prices because of their highly-efficient production methods and for much of the time have had the benefit of *an undervalued yen*.

As a result, the European industry is not generating the cash it needs for its investment programme.

Ford (Europe) believes the loss of profitability in the face of major new capital investment requirements remains one of the really significant challenges to a successful completion of the transition by the European industry in the 1980s, that the capital requirements for the European industry are close to $10 billion a year, and that this annual requirement is likely to persist throughout the decade.

The European Commission estimates that the industry will spend £35 billion in the next three to five years and this will have to be provided by shareholders, banks or governments if the rate of investment is to continue at the same pace.

Many people believe that financial difficulties will at last force the European manufacturers to co-operate more among themselves.

So far there is no 'European motor industry', just several national companies competing against one another. Whereas in the US the 2 biggest car companies account for 75 per cent of the total sales, in Europe five producers share this percentage.

A recent European Commission document pointed out: 'Thanks to mergers, several European companies have reached a size which now puts them among the top world producers. But the resulting *infrastructures* are understandably very cumbersome and require a substantial effort of harmonisation before they can be used to *optimum effect*.'

The Commission also claimed that the industry's research effort is too weak, is unco-ordinated and that the results are too slowly put into practice. At the industrial level, greater co-operation must be encouraged between European companies in the face of world-wide competition. Competition between European companies is supervised by the European Commission in accordance with the Treaty of Rome. Community surveillance would help avoid overpricing and waste, encourage contacts between member states and ease the required industrial changes by preventing non-competitive companies from being responsible for over-production.

Adapted from *The Financial Times*, 13 December 1982

a) Explain briefly in your own words what you understand by any five of the following, as used in the extract:

automotive industry (paragraph 3)

transformation (paragraph 5)
evolutionary development (paragraph 5)
new technology (paragraph 5)
undervalued yen (paragraph 7)
infrastructures (paragraph 13)
optimum effect (paragraph 13) *(15 marks)*

b) Why is the manufacture of cars so important to the European economy? (paragraph 3)

(5 marks)

c) What grounds are given as the major reasons for shortage of investment funds?

(7 marks)

d) Discuss the solution the article provides. *(8 marks)*

e) What caused the growth in European car output to decline from 5.8 to 1.7 per cent during the 'seventies'? *(5 marks)*

LCC PSC June 1983 *(40 marks)*

9 Read the passage below and then answer the questions which follow:

Mention electric vehicles and Englishmen think of milk floats, Frenchmen of Parisian garbage trucks and Americans of golf carts. Our plans to make battery-powered, urban runabouts in volume from next year have startled car makers who had virtually written off the possibility of mass-produced electric cars this decade.

'If it were anyone but International Cars,' said one competitor, 'we'd say they were mad.' But can we be so crazy?

On the face of it, yes. *The tide has been out for electric vehicles* – especially passenger cars – *since 1981.* Recession in the car industry, falling oil prices and cuts in government money (especially in America) have slowed *the 'drive electric' momentum built up during the oil-hungry 1970s.*

Plodding progress in developing light, long-lasting and powerful batteries led many motor manufacturers to concentrate their short-term ambitions on urban delivery vans and trucks, where the weight and limited range and power of conventional lead-acid batteries are less of a drawback than they would be in private cars. Karrier Motors (with Dodge trucks), Land Rover Leyland and GM's Bedford Commercial Vehicles have led the way in Great Britain. Grumman Aerospace has recently produced electric vans for the American post office. Other electrically-minded truck and van makers include Daihatsu, VW and Renault. Chrysler, having struggled back from the brink of bankruptcy, is now talking of introducing an electric version of its new mini van next autumn.

But sales and production are not inspiring. In Great Britain, which has more electric vehicles on the road than anywhere else (33 000–40 000 – mostly milk floats), new registrations dropped from about 1200 in 1979 to 900 in 1982. In America, where the number of electric vehicles being used is about 10 000, production fell from 1500 in 1981 to 1100 in 1982. Three of the most important manufacturers in the United States have switched products, collapsed or been bought out in the past 18 months. The problem is how to make electric vehicles cheap enough to justify their limited performance. It is hardest with non-commercial vehicles.

Volkswagen has experimented with electric versions of its Golf/Rabbit for years. The best Volkswagen models now being tested by West Germany's biggest utility company, RWE, can accelerate from 0 to 30 m.p.h. in 12 seconds, drive on the flat at top speeds of just over 60 miles per hour, and travel (with battery top-ups) about 60 miles a day. Even if VW could make and sell 100 000 of these a year, the purchase price would be at least 20 per cent above that of petrol-powered cars, according to the head of VW's electric vehicle programme. And even if petrol costs 50 per cent more than it does now, the running costs of the electric car, including battery replacement, would be higher.

So are we making a terrible mistake? Not necessarily.

Most car makers have thought in terms of competing with conventional, full-performance cars. We believe there is an entirely different market, for a deliberately low-performance small vehicle, travelling at about 30 m.p.h. for 30 miles between charges (or up to 100 miles with a more expensive battery option). The trade publication *The Engineer* has suggested that it is a 3-wheeler which can seat only one person. We expect to begin selling in 1986 and I say that the design will be 'surprising'.

If the price is right, Great Britain could be the ideal market. Though petrol-powered 3-wheelers have fallen on hard times lately, an electric version, like all electric vehicles, would pay no car or road tax. Petrol prices in Great Britain have risen, even though oil prices have fallen, because of the weakening of the pound against the dollar and higher excise taxes. And our electric car might be the ideal second car for many families. The number of two-car households has doubled in the past ten years. But most industry observers still predict disaster. We will have to convince them the hard way that this scheme will work – by producing and selling the cars.

Adapted from an article in *The Economist*, June 1983

a) Why has the enthusiasm for electric cars, which developed in the 1970s, slowed down? *(6 marks)*

b) Why did many motor manufacturers concentrate on electric delivery vans and trucks? *(4 marks)*

c) What are the main problems when trying to sell electric vehicles? *(4 marks)*

d) From the Volkswagen examples given, what are their objections to introducing electric vehicles? *(6 marks)*

e) What are the main arguments put forward for going ahead with the new vehicle although many think it a mistake? *(6 marks)*

f) Why is Great Britain thought to be the ideal market for electric vehicles? *(8 marks)*

g) What do you understand by the following expressions:
   i) 'The tide has been out for electric vehicles since 1981.' *(3 marks)*
   ii) '. . . the "drive electric" momentum built up in the oil-hungry 1970s.'? *(3 marks)*

LCC PSC Dec 1984 *(40 marks)*

10 Read the following passage then answer the questions which follow, using your own words as far as possible.

Sheltered housing or grouped dwellings for older people is especially designed accommodation provided specifically for elderly tenants, often with a warden, whose supporting role is usually one of an unobtrusive co-ordinator. A few authorities began to build such schemes after the Second World War, but it was not until 1957 that the Government began to encourage local authorities to develop schemes. Development of schemes has progressed steadily since then. Many private companies and Housing Associations are now providing sheltered accommodation and the overall provision has been encouraged by governments of all political persuasions.

Surprisingly little research has been made into the kinds of people who live in sheltered housing or about the effects of such accommodation on tenants. There seems to be a number of goals implicit in the policies for selection of tenants, particularly the prolongation of life and the prevention of the use of more expensive services. Nevertheless, there is insufficient overall agreement on goals and a lack of available research findings on which to base a clarification of objectives. It has been pointed out several times that there is a close relationship between sheltered housing and residential care, with the implication that the former might replace the latter in the long run. At the present time there appears to be less chance of the old person in special housing moving to more intensive forms of care than there is for people from other community situations. A study in Devon suggested that for most tenants 'grouped (sheltered) dwellings are currently providing a setting within which it is expected that their care requirements may be met until death'.

Clearly there is a growth in the provision of sheltered housing and the emphasis is shifting from residential care for some older people at least. The relevance of the growth of such provision for discussion lies particularly in the need for a more clearly defined role for the wardens of the schemes and training the wardens. A recent report by the body 'Age Concern' suggested that:

'The warden plays a large part in determining the quality of life in grouped schemes, and has a vital contribution to make in their day-to-day running. Therefore it is essential that wardens be given the opportunity to increase their background knowledge and to refine their skills in order to carry out their task more effectively.'

The report goes on to propose a course of training for wardens that would give knowledge of the physiological and sociological ageing processes, of human needs (physiological needs, security, social needs, self-esteem, growth and human potential), of the nature and value of roles and relationships, of interpersonal communication and of services and facilities, home safety and maintenance of buildings and equipment.

The task of the warden has many elements in common with that of the residential worker. The main area of functioning is, of course, concerned with creating an environment with basic components of comfort and safety. The warden will also have a part to play with regard to the tenant group as a whole with the encouragement of friendship, mutual help and a sense of shared experience through group activities. If these functions are to be carried out effectively the warden will need support from a number of directions. A recognition of the warden's need for a separate life requires administrative and practical help for holiday and weekend relief. At least as important is the need for other caring groups in the community to work with the warden in providing the best environment and help with the individual tenant. The administrative split between housing, health and social services has too often led to wardens feeling isolated and unsupported – as well as frequently leaving them carrying inappropriate burdens of nursing and domestic responsibilities.

Adapted from *Residential Work with the Elderly* by C Paul Brearley, published by Routledge and Kegan Paul.

a) What do you understand by the term 'unobtrusive co-ordinator' as used to describe a warden of sheltered housing? *(3 marks)*

b) Why do you think the author finds it 'surprising' that little research has gone into the kinds of people who live in sheltered housing and the effects such accommodation has on tenants? *(4 marks)*

c) The author says that the overall provision of sheltered housing has been encouraged by governments of all political persuasions. Assess what might have been different had this issue become a party political matter. *(7 marks)*

d) What is the suggested relationship between residential care and sheltered housing for the elderly? *(6 marks)*

e) What factors influence the criteria for selection of sheltered housing occupants? *(3 marks)*

f) Why does the 'Age Concern' report stress the need for the appropriate training of wardens and what should this training include? *(6 marks)*

g) What elements are common to the work of a warden in a sheltered environment and a residential care worker, and in what ways are they different? *(8 marks)*

h) What is the effect of the administrative split between different elements of local authority services? *(3 marks)*

LCC PESD June 1987 *(40 marks)*

11 Read the following passage and then in your own words as far as possible answer the questions which follow.

Hotel security

Security in a hotel is unique in that problems are considerably more varied than in any single-purpose institution. A hotel should be considered as a self-contained village or even a small town as it has many of the characteristics of such a community. Depending on the size of the hotel, the security risks to be considered include the added risk dimension that comes with public restaurants, bars, theatres, cinemas, night clubs, casinos, banqueting suites, plus the many and varied problems of a large, often heterogeneous community.

The hotel is one building in which the owner is required by law to take reasonable precautions to secure the personal property of the guests or clients. Under the Hotel Proprietors' Act the owner of the hotel can be held liable for the loss of the client's property if it can be proved that the loss was due to the negligence of the owner or his servants. Ensuring the safety of the clients' personal property and the adequacy of staff training so that the owner cannot be sued for negligence are thus vital aspects of a hotel's security plan.

Unlike most other buildings a hotel must, generally speaking, allow access at all times. Security at the points of admission and egression is not a straightforward matter. This is complicated by the necessarily strict imposition of fire regulations; often doors cannot be secured as this would endanger rapid evacuation of the building. If unauthorised use of exterior doors is not prevented, the result will not only be theft by staff, but also what is known in the industry as 'walk-outs', that is guests who leave the hotel and forget to pay the bill.

Public entrances to hotels are notoriously difficult to control. Ideally, such doors should be in full view of hotel staff. Inaccessible or hidden doors can be viewed by closed-circuit television and the playback facility can help to identify a malefactor after an incident has occurred.

There should also be vigilance at staff entrances. It is an unpalatable fact that staff may be responsible for misdemeanours which are blamed on clients. Temporary, part-time and casually employed staff are often difficult to trace after the termination of their employment and must be considered with some caution. But precautions taken should not be so obtrusive as to offend the majority of honest staff.

The public lobby of a hotel is invariably a hive of activity. Control is difficult and is only possible if there are sufficient staff. Some should be obviously visible as this is a good deterrent, but it is wise to ensure that some staff are less manifestly involved in security. All staff must be security conscious. Too often one can walk into a hotel and see staff engaged in an animated conversation, paying no attention to the activities around them.

Guests' baggage and other property is easy prey for the thief, but it can also if not well organised be easily collected by the wrong party and despatched to a destination other than that of its owner. In recent years bags and cases have been left in lobbies and foyers by terrorist groups whose intentions have been sinister and dangerous.

Room keys are a constant headache to hotel security with an average of 30 per cent of keys missing each year. The reasons for this may be innocent: some people keep them as souvenirs, and some genuinely lose them. However a substantial proportion of hotel thefts has been committed with stolen keys. One answer to this problem is supplied by new technology as electronic locks are now available. With these entry is by key-card; the combination of the lock can be altered each time a room is allocated, thus rendering useless all previous key-cards. Such a system obviates many of the problems of key issue, but the main drawback at the moment is cost, which might be prohibitive for smaller institutions.

Adapted from *The Security Survey* by Denis Hughes and Peter Bowler (Gower Press)

a) Say what you understand by the term *heterogeneous community* and say why this may be found in large hotels.   (*4 marks*)

b) Under the Hotel Proprietors' Act, under what circumstances is it likely that a hotel will *not* be found liable for the loss of a client's property?   (*5 marks*)

c) Describe what you understand by the term *walk-outs*.   (*4 marks*)

d) How can the use of closed-circuit television and video assist hotel security?   (*4 marks*)

e) Why do you think it is said to be an unpalatable fact that hotel staff may engage in criminal activities?   (*4 marks*)

f) What do you understand by the metaphor *a hive of activity*?
   Say how this description is particularly apt when applied to a hotel lobby.   (*6 marks*)

g) How may terrorist groups take advantage of the luggage confusion in a hotel lobby?   (*4 marks*)

h) What are the main advantages of the electronic lock system, and what problems may there be in their introduction?   (*4 marks*)

LCC PESD June 1988 (*35 marks*)

8 Meetings

Come together . . .
The Beatles

An audio-typist once produced a set of minutes for a 'haddock-stirring committee' (an *ad hoc steering committee*) while an exam candidate, asked to give 'Hon Sec' and 'AOB' in full, typed *Honourable Secretary* and *Annual Office Banquet*! A knowledge of the basic terminology and documents relating to meetings is essential for anyone entering the business world.[1]

The notice

Most people are likely to be involved in fairly informal meetings (committee meetings, managers' meetings, meetings of staff associations) for which the notice will be informally expressed. Often it will be a short letter, memo or note stating the type of meeting to be held, and the day, date, time and place of the meeting:

```
MEMO

To:    Mrs Ellen Burgess         Date: 5 November 19..

From: Joan Rothery              Ref:   JR/SC

Social Club

The next committee meeting will be held on Wednesday,
20 November 19.. at 7 pm in Room T35.

If you have any items for the agenda, would you please let me
have them by 10 November?
```

For regular weekly or monthly meetings a separate notice is often dispensed with; the above details are simply given on the agenda by way of confirmation.

The agenda

The agenda is a list of items of business for a meeting. It is often sent out with the notice to save time, postage and effort.

[1] See Appendix 4 for a glossary of terms.

```
┌────────────────────────────────────────────────────────────────┐
│              NOTICE OF ANNUAL GENERAL MEETING                  │
│                                                                │
│  NOTICE IS HEREBY GIVEN that the Annual General Meeting of the │
│  members of the Anytown Building Society will be held in the   │
│  Grand Hotel, Market Place, Anytown on Wednesday, 22 April     │
│  19.. at 4.00 pm for the following purposes:                   │
│                                                                │
│  1  To receive the Directors' Annual Report and Accounts for  │
│     the year ended 31 December 19..                            │
│                                                                │
│  2  To receive the Auditors' Report.                          │
│                                                                │
│  3  To declare the re-election of Directors.                  │
│                                                                │
│  4  To appoint Messrs Maths & Stats, Chartered Accountants, as│
│     Auditors for the ensuing year.                             │
│                                                                │
│  By order of the Board                                        │
│  A Scrivener, Secretary                                        │
└────────────────────────────────────────────────────────────────┘
```

An example of a formal notice – a Building Society AGM

In its simplest form it consists of numbered items in the order in which they are to be dealt with. Additional papers (letters, reports, balance sheets) may accompany the agenda and, if so, their reference number (e.g. Paper 1) should be quoted beside the appropriate heading on the agenda.

The outline of a standard agenda is as follows:

1 Apologies for absence
2 Minutes of previous meeting
3 Matters arising from the minutes
4 Correspondence (if any)
5 ⎫
6 ⎬   Main items
7 ⎭
8 Any other business
9 Date of next meeting

This outline should be adapted for particular meetings, such as the *first* meeting of a committee (when items 2 and 3 are redundant) or an Annual General Meeting where special business is conducted.

Consider the following example where such changes are necessary.

Example

Since the move of the Head Office to new premises a year ago, Mr Christopher Falkener (for whom you work) has become concerned about lack of tidiness in the office and the growing incidence of minor accidents. He has consulted the Company Secretary, who is head of legal affairs, and has decided to call a meeting of his fellow Directors and Senior Managers to discuss the situation in the office.

He is anxious to stimulate, throughout the organisation, an awareness of safety matters and the existing legislation relating to health and safety at work.

Mr Falkener asks you to draft a memorandum for him giving notice of the meeting to be held in two weeks' time, and outlining the agenda for the meeting.

Use the following notes as a basis for the memorandum:

- since move new offices becoming very untidy
- staff should be encouraged to keep things tidily
- disappointing since new premises lighter and more spacious
- untidiness bad for staff; also creates bad impression for visitors
- problems with security: complaints about missing files left lying around

- health and safety hazards
- waste paper bins full of bulky items and paper cups from vending machines, installed for benefit of staff
- several minor accidents
- clerk tripped over cardboard box left deliberately as a joke by someone in Marketing Department (bring up at meeting)
- typist twisted ankle while carrying typewriter against specific instructions of supervisor: she is contemplating suing Comlon (must be brought up at meeting, too)
- Managing Director to open meeting discussing health and safety legislation
- Company Secretary to talk about legal aspects of occupational safety

Write a memorandum with a suitable agenda for the meeting.

LCC PSC June 1986 (*35 marks*)

Before reading the commentary, criticise the agenda below, written by a student, and then draft an answer of your own.

AGENDA

1   Appologies for abscence
2   Minutes of the previous meeting
3   Matters arising from the minutes
4   General untidyness in offices
5   Health and safety legislation – MD
6   Health and safety hazzards
7   Legal aspects of occupational safety – Company Sec
8   Practical jokes
9   AOB
10 Date of next meeting

Commentary

1   Not enough thought has been given to the kind of meeting referred to in the question. It is a 'one-off' *ad hoc* meeting and therefore items 2, 3 and 10 (and usually items 1 and 9) can be omitted.
2   The order of the items could be better: explicit information in the question has been ignored – in particular the statement that the Managing Director will open the meeting.
3   Some of the headings could be improved: 'Practical jokes' is irrelevant to the injured typist who is not mentioned elsewhere.
4   There are four spelling mistakes.

(A suggested agenda is given in Appendix 1.)

The chairman's[1] agenda

This is a more detailed version of the ordinary agenda. In addition to the headings, the secretary adds briefing notes, reminders and other useful information to help the chairman conduct the meeting efficiently. A wide right-hand margin is normally left for the chairman's own notes.

Example

You are secretary to Miss Bettine Rayner, the General Manager of Petroushka Joywear, manufacturers of ladies' suits and separates. Miss Rayner is on her way back from a conference in Rome but at 10 a.m. tomorrow will chair a regular meeting of executives to discuss sales for the past month and other matters. She has asked you to prepare an agenda for the meeting and also a chairman's agenda for her guidance.

Normally three Area Managers attend, i.e. Mr Bland, Mr Manners and Miss Teague, but the latter is in New York and her deputy, Miss Paling, will attend instead. Mr Manners is in York and will be late. Miss Ashton, the Chief Accountant, and Mr Beeston, the Transport Manager, will attend for their items only and must leave by 11.30 at the latest.

Items put forward are recent breakdowns in delivery (by Mr Beeston); failure of the group contract system in Derby (Miss Teague); new premises at Hull (Mr Manners); losses from shoplifting (Miss Ashton). The Chairman is to introduce an item on new plastic window display figures. For this she will have to be able to report on costs and delivery dates. She may not have these details available.

Miss Ashton will supply statistics of the month's sales but these will have to be provided for everyone tomorrow.

Mr Bland, besides wishing to query his omission from the list of those present at the last meeting, held on 6 May, wants to raise an item on shop security under AOB unless it is brought out in the 'shoplifting' item.

1 Prepare the simple agenda for the meeting. *(10 marks)*
2 Prepare the full chairman's agenda. *(10 marks)*

RSA CIB Stage II June 1980

Commentary

1 As this is a regular meeting, the standard items will appear on the agenda. Confirmatory details should also appear as no separate notice is likely to have been issued.
2 A number of factors may affect the running order of the main items – here the early departure of Miss Ashton and Mr Beeston means giving priority to their items while the late arrival of Mr Manners means that his item should be low on the agenda.
3 For the chairman's agenda some invention will be necessary. Care should also be taken with the given information. The structure of the final paragraph often misleads students into putting both the query and the item on shop security under AOB. Why is this incorrect?

Assignment

Sketch out answers of your own before consulting the suggested version of the chairman's agenda that follows.

[1] 'Chairperson' is now also used, but 'Chair' is less widely accepted. As Lady Seear remarked: 'I can't bear being called a "Chair". Whatever I am, I am not a piece of furniture.'

Suggested answer

PETROUSHKA JOYWEAR

The monthly executive meeting will be held on Monday, 6 June 19.. at 10 am in the Board Room.

CHAIRMAN'S AGENDA

		NOTES

1 Apologies for absence

   (Miss Teague is in New York and Miss Paling will deputise; Mr Manners is in York – hopes to come but will be late.

   Miss Ashton and Mr Beeston will attend for their items only and must leave by 11.30 am)

2 Minutes of the meeting held on 6 May 19..

   (Copy attached. Mr Bland to query his omission from the list of those present – this was a typing error.)

3 Matters arising from the minutes

   (Minute 7: the Grand Hotel has confirmed the availability of the Dior Suite for the Autumn Fashion Show on Saturday, 10 October.)

4 Monthly sales figures

   (To be tabled at the meeting.)

5 Losses from shoplifting

   (Miss Ashton to report on recent losses and the need for improved security.)

6 Recent breakdowns in delivery

   (Mr Beeston to report on the spate of breakdowns and the need for regular servicing or replacement of older vehicles.)

7 New plastic window display figures

   (Your report on costs and delivery dates. The figures have now arrived – Paper 1 attached.)

8 Failure of group contract system in Derby

   (Miss Paling to report on the disappointing results and advise that affairs be wound up forthwith.)

9 New premises at Hull

   (Mr Manners to report on his recent
   negotiations for the Prospect Street site.)

10 Any other business

   (Mr Bland may wish to speak on shop security
   unless this is covered in item 5.)

11 Date of next meeting

   (Monday, 7 July)[1]

Anne McBratney
Secretary

IN THE CHAIR

Like the conductor of an orchestra, the chairman is there to conduct
the meeting. S/He should be a good time-keeper and preserve
harmony by ensuring that everyone follows the score and that some
members do not blow their own trumpets at the expense of others.

Main duties

Before the meeting

- plan and prepare for the meeting
- agree a draft agenda
- ensure that members are notified

During the meeting

- ensure that a quorum is present
- ensure that the minutes of the previous meeting are correct and
  sign them
- introduce items of business clearly and in the right order
- promote relevant discussion and sum up at various stages
- maintain control and ensure that the rules are followed
- be responsible for taking votes and declaring results
- ensure that records are kept

After the meeting

- agree a draft of the minutes
- communicate decisions to people concerned
- monitor progress

[1] For less regular meetings the place and time may also be given.

The minutes

Once a meeting has taken place the minutes are prepared as a record of what happened (and so the past tense should be used). If the minutes are sound, someone who was not present at the meeting (such as Miss Teague) would be able to know from reading them exactly what was discussed and what decisions were reached.

The minutes begin with a heading, stating the type of meeting and the date, time and place of the meeting. This is followed by the name of the presiding officer and the names of the others present (or the number present in the case of a large meeting such as an AGM). For example:

```
PETROUSHKA JOYWEAR

Minutes of the monthly executive meeting held on Monday, 6
June 19.. at 10 am in the Board Room.

Present:    Miss B Rayner   General Manager (in the Chair)
            Miss A Ashton   Chief Accountant (for Agenda item 5)
            Mr M Beeston    Transport Manager (for Agenda item 6)
            Mr W Bland      Area Manager - Midlands
            Mr J Manners    Area Manager - North East
                            (from Agenda item 9)
            Miss R Paling   Deputy to Miss J Teague, Area Manager -
                            South
```

The minutes then follow the items as listed on the agenda.

Presentation and length of minutes vary from the verbatim transcript of parliamentary debates in *Hansard* to the briefest possible summary of decisions favoured by some board meetings. Any organisation may have its own particular house style which should, of course, be adopted by its staff. The following examples show some of the methods currently in business use.

Imagine that this discussion of item 9 of the Petroushka Joywear meeting took place:

Miss Rayner: Right, on to item 9. John, would you bring us up to date on how things are going in Hull?

Mr Manners: Yes. As you probably know, I made an offer of £250 000 for the site in Prospect Street. Everything seemed to be going OK when they suddenly upped their asking price to £300 000.

Mr Bland: They'll be lucky!

Miss Rayner: Well, what about Maine Road? Or Welby Close? Didn't we feel they'd do just as well?

Mr Manners: They'd certainly be cheaper at this price. But I feel that all things considered Prospect Street would suit us down to the ground. I must say I regard this as a temporary hiccup – I'm pretty sure they're just trying it on. If we offered them a bit more I think they'd jump at it.

Miss Rayner: How much more?

Mr Manners: Another ten or twenty grand should swing it.

Miss Rayner: That seems reasonable. Let me propose that John increases our offer up to a limit of £270 000.

Mr Bland: I'll second that.

Miss Rayner: Those in favour? Good. (*All assent*) We'll see if that does the trick. Now, any other business . . .

As a *resolution minute* (which records only the resolution that is passed) this might have been recorded:

```
9  NEW PREMISES AT HULL

   It was resolved that Mr Manners should negotiate an
   increased offer up to a limit of £270 000 for the Prospect
   Street site.
```

As a *narrative minute* (which records some of the background details or discussion in addition to the resolution) it might have read:

```
9  NEW PREMISES AT HULL

   Mr Manners reported that he had made an offer of £250 000 for
   the Prospect Street site but that the vendor was asking for
   £300 000. It was suggested that other sites be reconsidered,
   but Mr Manners felt that the proposed site would be ideal
   for their purposes. It was resolved that he should negotiate
   an increased offer up to a limit of £270 000.
```

COME AGAIN?!!!

```
Item 7, Grand Design

           It is clear that Cabinet Committee is agreed that

           the new policy is an excellent plan, in principle.

           But in view of the doubts being expressed, it was

           decided to record that, after careful consideration,

           the considered view of the committee was that while

           they considered the proposal met with broad

           approval in principle, it was felt that some of the

           principles were sufficiently fundamental in

           principle, and some of the considerations so

           complex and finely balanced in practice that in

           principle it was proposed that the sensible and

           prudent practice would be to subject the proposal
```

to more detailed consideration with and across the

relevant departments with a view to preparing and

proposing a more thorough and wide-ranging

proposal, laying stress on the less controversial

elements and giving consideration to the essential

continuity of the new proposal with existing

principles, to be presented for parliamentary

consideration and public discussion on some more

propitious occasion when the climate of opinion is

deemed to be more amenable for consideration of the

approach and the principle of the principal

arguments which the proposal proposes and

propounds for approval.

A Cabinet Committee minute written by Sir Humphrey Appleby

Reproduced from YES PRIME MINISTER, Volume 1, by Jonathan Lynn and Antony Jay, with permission of BBC Enterprises Ltd.

As an *action minute* (which has an action column on the right-hand side of the page to record the names or initials of people who are to carry out some task) it might have appeared:

9   NEW PREMISES AT HULL

Mr Manners reported . . . (as above)
It was resolved that he should
negotiate an increased offer up to a   JM
limit of £270 000.

The more formal the meeting, the more likely it is that the names of the proposer and seconder of motions and the results of voting will also be included. The above minute might then have ended:

Miss Rayner proposed, Mr Bland seconded, and it was
unanimously resolved that Mr Manners should negotiate an
increased offer up to a limit of £270 000.

In less formal meetings, formal motions may only occasionally be included and informal agreement is usually more appropriate. Such decisions will be recorded 'It was agreed that . . .' or, in the case of advisory groups without executive powers, 'It was recommended that . . .'

```
MEMO

To:    The Headmaster, Ward B3
From:  The Staff

We understand that the operation was successful and thought
that you would like to know that at a staff meeting today it
was resolved to wish you a speedy recovery by 31 votes to 9.
```

When minutes are set on exam papers, candidates may be asked to write a single minute based on given information or a short set of minutes often based on a résumé of a meeting. In each case, narrative minutes are usually asked for or expected. Examples of both types of question are given in the exercises.

The most demanding and realistic test is set by the LCC as part of the Private and Executive Secretary's Diploma, the Meetings examination being a component in its own right. Candidates receive a preliminary notice of the theme of the meeting six weeks before the date of the exam. The test itself lasts for approximately $2\frac{1}{4}$ hours: 15 minutes to read an information sheet detailing what the meeting is to be about, who will be present, and what is required of the secretary; 20–25 minutes to watch and take notes from a videotape of the meeting; and 1 hour 40 minutes to type the relevant document – which is not always a set of minutes as the following checklist shows:

Year of exam	Topic	Task
1977	Health and Safety at Work Act 1974	Minutes of a company's Safety Committee meeting
1978	Exporting	Draft notes of a meeting to discuss a company's Export Year
1979	'Travellers-Fare' Centenary Celebrations	Notes of a meeting with representatives of British Rail catering organisation
1980	Seminar: 'Micro-electronics in the 1980s'	Summary of final session for absent employer
1981*	Interview of Director of LCC to celebrate centenary	Summary for preparation of centenary leaflet
1982	AGM of Building Society	Minutes
1983*	Board meeting (including discussion of proposed installation of word processor)	Minutes and notes on installation of word processor
1984*	Product Launch Committee	Draft minutes of narration
1985	Seminar – 'The Changing Face of Training'	Summary for seminar booklet
1986*	Board Meeting – Merchant Bank	Formal minutes
1987	Sheltered-Housing Scheme	Summary as basis of MD's report
1988	Monthly PR Meeting	Minutes of narration (with action list)

*Comlon, the magazine of the LCC Examining Board, has published the script of these exams with additional comments/guideline answers in subsequent issues as follows: 1981 (April 1982; May 1982); 1983 (October 1983; Winter 1984); 1984 (Summer 1984; Winter 1985); 1986 (Autumn 1986; Winter 1987).

This exam is not a test of high-speed shorthand – which may be a positive handicap as it is a temptation to take down as much as possible. Instead it tests the ability to extract the main points and present them in good English in a suitable format. Candidates with no shorthand – who *have* to be selective – pass while others fail.

Thorough preparation is vital and the following suggestions may prove helpful:

1   During the course:
    ● Watch a number of the videotapes mentioned above (which can be hired from the LCC) and carry out the required task.[1]
    ● Involve yourself at work or college in as many different types of meeting as possible.
    ● Attend the AGM of any clubs or societies to which you belong and draft a set of minutes.
    ● Attend local council meetings and take minutes. (The actual minutes are usually posted up on notice boards later.)
    ● Listen regularly to radio talks or TV programmes such as 'Question Time' and write a brief summary of the discussion that takes place over a 20–25 minute period.

2   Before and during the exam:
    ● Use the background notes: plan the heading of the document based on the given information; decide how to identify speakers without using their full names or titles (initials? numbers?); note any unusual spelling of names.
    ● Do some research: if you are told that one of the directors is abroad on a business trip, consult an atlas to check the spelling of places he may be visiting. This will prevent 'howlers' such as 'Chilly', 'Quala Lumpa' and the 'Sewage Canal'!
    ● Choose a suitable display: do not write action minutes if there is nothing to enter in the action column. Headed paragraphs and numbered points are effective in summaries, reports and notes.
    ● Be selective: try to distinguish between the significant and the unimportant *while it is being said*. Some candidates try to reproduce everything – including trivia such as the fact that the meeting ended when the tea-lady arrived!
    ● Do not add any invented details of your own.
    ● Remember that a chairman often repeats points or sums up a discussion. If you miss something important you may get a second chance.
    ● Ensure that you finish: do not waste time on rough drafts but go for the final version at once. As a professional standard of presentation is required, correcting fluid should be used with extreme caution.
    ● Check the English – a common cause of failure is poor spelling, punctuation and grammar.
    ● Check the tense and the expression (colloquialisms such as 'hiccup', 'trying it on' and 'jump at it' should not be used).
    ● Check for omissions:
      – if a draft is required the word 'DRAFT' should appear and double-spacing should be used;
      – all work should be headed;
      – the date should appear in the heading of a set of minutes but at the end of a report;
      – first names only should not be used in minutes;
      – at the end of a set of minutes there should be space for the chairman's signature and date of signature; a reference and date of typing may follow.

[1]Some of the earlier exams are available only on 16 mm film. For further details write to the LCC Examining Board, Marlowe House, Station Road, Sidcup, Kent DA15 7BJ.

Exercises

1 You are secretary to a committee of senior executives who are based in different parts of Britain and Europe. Their next meeting will be held a month from now (actual date left open) in a suitable hotel in Birmingham (as yet unselected). Produce a checklist in a clear and logical sequence of all the arrangements that you would need to make before, during and after this meeting. (A suggested answer is given in Appendix 1.)

2 'It is impossible to lay down a standard method of preparing an agenda paper, as so much depends upon the nature and importance of the meeting concerned.' Discuss this statement using as many practical examples as possible in your answer. What points ought to be borne in mind in most cases?

ICSA Meetings June 1988

3 The notice and agenda of the monthly Sales Meeting must go out today to all in the Sales Department. The meeting is to be held in two weeks' time at 1000 hrs in Room C11. Send the notice in the form of a memorandum to the Sales Department. Items on the agenda include sales figures and the resignation of the Sales Director as well as the usual items.

PEI EFS Advanced (20 marks)

4 Imagine that you are Miss Frances Fulland and that you work for Cartland and Co. Ltd, a large store which has 22 Buyers, each in charge of a department. The store sells fashions, hosiery, toys, china and glassware, household and gardening goods, perfumery, jewellery, lighting and stationery. It also has special displays for periods such as Christmas, Easter and Summer.

You have been working there for about two years but six months ago were promoted from the General Office to be assistant to Mrs Rita Thames, the store's General Manager.

Once a month Mrs Thames chairs a meeting of the Buyers of the Departments. Last week you had to compile the agenda for the meeting to be held at 10.15 a.m. on Thursday, 18 June. You had to collect the information for this task. You knew that standard items would appear on the agenda and remembered that the last meeting had been on Friday, 15 May.

Mrs Thames said that she wanted to announce the Special Birthday Event to be held in October and to invite suggestions for new ideas and displays for it. She also said that she had been told that Mr Slade, Buyer for Glassware, would be late as he was in Manchester that morning.

You received the following items:

a) Mrs Gellatly (Toys) sent this note: 'Frances, don't forget to put my Christmas display on the agenda. If Mr Bell has his way I shan't have room for the soft toys or the bicycles this year! Don't forget now. Jane Gellatly'.

b) A phone call from Arthur Predall (Garden Goods) to say that another local shop, Barden and Sons, was underselling the store in respect of lawnmowers and could something be done about it.

c) A letter from Mr Slade asking that more space be allowed for three weeks for Glassware to enable the Department to make a special display of Bohemian Glass. 'The price is right and the time to cash in is now but I haven't the space to do it. We could make a killing.'

d) A phone call from Mr Bell, Buyer of Carpets, to say that he wanted you to put a formal motion on the agenda to stop Toys spreading all over the top floor at Christmas. 'You know, Frances, something like . . . that the meeting resolves that each Department should keep reasonably to its own area at Christmas and not upset everyone else all around – only you know how to put it better than I do. But I want it done formally so that we have a vote. Fred Carney of Soft Furnishings will second it. We're all fed up with Auntie Jane.'

e) A reminder from Miss Tedson, Chief Accountant, to include the monthly sales figures which she will supply to be put on the table and upon which she will comment.

f) Another note from Mrs Gellatly: 'Frances, please put another item on for me. I am trying to get the Melbourne Puppets to put on a display in Toys for Guy Fawkes' Week. It will mean taking a bit from Carpets but they won't sell any in November. Be a good girl and put it up as urgent. Jane Gellatly'.

g) Call from Mr Predall to say he will be unable to come to the meeting and Mrs Grant, his Underbuyer, will attend in his place.

Write a notice of the meeting, which will be held in the Board Room, including an agenda. Do not write a chairman's agenda.

RSA CIB Stage II June 1981 (20 marks)

5   You are private secretary to Mr Richard Barton, Director for Administration, who, among his numerous duties, acts as chairperson on the Personnel Policy Committee which is convened once a month. The purpose of the monthly meeting is to discuss any pressing personnel problems or the need for possible changes in policy.

The Committee usually meets on the last Friday of every month in the Board Room at Head Office beginning at 1000 hours. You, as Secretary to the Committee, have the duty of helping Mr Barton to prepare the agenda and you produce the minutes of each meeting.

Other members of the Committee are: Mr Tim Wilson, Director for Marketing, Ms Brenda Vincent, Director for Pattern Research and Pattern Design, Mr John Bond, Personnel Manager, and Mr John Alexander, Manager of Office Services.

Following the last meeting held on Friday, 27 May, you are discussing with Mr Barton the agenda for the next meeting to be held on Friday, 24 June. He asks you to include two items on the agenda, namely the proposed new promotion policy and the introduction of job enrichment schemes.

During your discussions with Mr Barton, you made the following notes to assist you in preparing the chairperson's agenda for the next meeting:

minutes of prevous meeting – circulated with notice of next meeting – sent out on 10 June;

promotion – policy in past – always promote internally – vacancies only advertised in *Company* magazine – Mr Barton thinks this has made Comlon introspective;

proposed change of policy – vacancies to be advertised in local and national press as well as *Company* magazine – need for new ideas – new 'blood' – people with experience in other firms – may lead to some dissatisfaction among existing staff;

therefore proposes to introduce job enrichment – need to find ways of increasing job satisfaction – wants suggestions from members – better environment – training – social events – still important if change in promotion policy not agreed;

matter from May meeting – request from a technical college that we accept two management students and two secretarial students for one month's work experience – proposed we should accept them – if agreed – to whom will they be allocated? – college requires their being given serious training and realistic experience with responsibility.

Mr Wilson has notified you he will be on holiday when the next meeting takes place.
    Prepare the chairperson's agenda for Mr Barton to use at the meeting.

LCC PSC June 1988 (35 marks)

6   You work as an assistant to Ms Moira Patterson, Sales Director of NC Software Ltd, a firm which sells computer programs and other software by mail order. It has now become a major supplier of specialised business packages in the UK.

The Sales and Development Committee of NC Software Ltd takes place monthly. The meetings, which are quite informal, are chaired by Ms Patterson, and it is your job to take the minutes and circulate them to members. Ms Patterson expects minutes to be concise.

This month's meeting is now taking place. Present are Ms Patterson, Mr Roy Williams (Company Secretary), Mr David Rodgers (Chief Accountant), Mr William Owen (Managing Director) and Miss Shirley Jenkins (Consultant on Business Matters).

The formalities of the meeting have been covered, and agenda item no. 4 is about to be reached. The discussion proceeds as follows:

Ms Patterson:	Now, item 4, the 'Desk Diary' software package. This is not good news. We dropped a bit of a clanger here, as you all probably know.
Miss Jenkins:	I don't know what happened.
Ms Patterson:	Well, briefly, we got the rights to sell the 'Desk Diary' package, so we put a big advertisement for it in *Business Software* magazine – quoting a price of £29.99.
Mr Rodgers:	And it should have been £49.99. Not much difference, eh?
Ms Patterson:	All right, David. It was our fault – there's no getting away from that.
Mr Owen:	That's not important – but what have we done about it?
Ms Patterson:	Well fortunately we were able to change the advertisement before it was published anywhere else, and *Business Software* put a correction in their next edition. But we now have a problem – what do we do with the orders that enclosed £29.99?
Mr Rodgers:	Surely we send apologetic letters and tell them we made a mistake.
Ms Patterson:	But that wouldn't do our reputation much good, would it? Do you know how much we'd lose if we accepted the orders, David?
Mr Rodgers:	We've had about 50 orders, and selling them at £29.99 we'd lose about £8 on each. But I don't think we have a legal obligation to accept the orders, do we?
Mr Williams:	No – there's no legal reason for us to have to sell at £29.99. But we could be in trouble with the Advertising Standards people if we almost double the price.
Mr Owen:	£400 is not a fortune, you know. I propose that we accept the orders at £29.99. Of course new orders must be at the correct price. Are we all agreed on that? ('Yes' all round)
Ms Patterson:	We must keep faith with our customers. I'll write to all those who've paid £29.99, pointing out how generous we are. I'll stress that the price is now £49.99. We'll send them a full price list in fact.
Mr Rodgers:	And we'll double check our advertisements in future!
Ms Patterson:	Of course. Now can we move on to item 5. This is just a quick one, but I thought I'd better let you know. It's about the American Company, Michigan Programs, that we've dealt with very successfully recently. Well, they've produced a top class accounting program called 'Profit and Loss'.
Miss Jenkins:	I've seen it reviewed in American magazines. It looks excellent.
Ms Patterson:	They've decided to produce a British version. But their new policy is to allow only one sales outlet in each country. Now I want us to be the British supplier. If you agree, I'll write to them immediately.
Mr Owen:	Yes, let's go for it. Maybe it would help if we put a few facts and figures together to support our case – you know, sales figures, our share of the market – that sort of thing.
Ms Patterson:	Good idea. So I take it you agree we should apply? (Nods of assent) Fine. Now on to item 6 . . .

Record items 4 and 5 as they would appear in the minutes. Use an appropriate minute style, but record only items 4 and 5.

RSA CIB Stage II June 1988 (*15 marks*)

7   You work as administrative assistant for the Amethyst Book Club, an organisation that sells specially printed editions of books to customers all over Britain by means of mail order. Its affairs are discussed monthly at the Forward Planning Committee which is attended by senior staff.

A meeting of the Committee is in progress. Several items have been discussed and you are responsible for taking the minutes. Present at the meeting are Ms Elizabeth Sibbald (Managing Director), Mr David Yeates (Chief Editor), Miss Valerie Brooks (Sales and Marketing Director), Mr Dipak Patel (Company Secretary), Mr Paul Gibson (Chief Accountant) and you as Minute Secretary.

The meeting has reached the point when agenda item No. 6 'Children's Books' is to be discussed and continues as follows:

Ms Sibbald:	On to item 6, Children's Books. Now you want to say something about this don't you, David?
Mr Yeates:	Yes – if I may. I've been giving this a bit of thought and I wonder if it's time to put a few children's books into our lists.
Miss Brooks:	But if I can come in here, David; haven't we talked about this before and decided that kids are well catered for elsewhere?
Mr Yeates:	Yes, Valerie, that's right. But if you remember, when we talked about it before it was the idea of a separate children's list that we turned down. I'd like to see us introduce a few books for the younger readers to our normal list.
Mr Gibson:	Of course, quite a few of our books are bought by children. That picture book about the Apollo programme – a lot of kids bought that, or at least got their parents to buy it.
Mr Yeates:	Quite – a lot of Mums and Dads choose books with the kids in mind, so why not stick a few kids' books onto the list? Maybe add two or three a month – call it 'Children's Corner' or something.
Ms Sibbald:	Steady on David! We've not decided to go ahead at all yet, never mind every month.
Miss Brooks:	I still don't like the idea. There are plenty of Children's Book Clubs around, so I would think the market is pretty well tied up.
Mr Gibson:	But surely it's worth a try? We thought the market for cookery books was well catered for (laughter) . . . what? Oh, cookery books, well catered for – sorry for the pun! But we did have best sellers on our hands with the last couple we did.
Mr Patel:	Could I ask you David, through the chair, are you thinking about fiction or non-fiction books?
Mr Yeates:	Well, what do the rest of you think?
Miss Brooks:	If we're going to try it at all, it's got to be a fiction book – we've no chance with non-fiction.
Ms Sibbald:	I think you're right, Val. Look, I think we are agreed in principle but we need to look into it a bit more. Is that right? (Murmurs of 'Yes' all round) Good. Well, David, I suggest you make a list of, say, half a dozen possibles and we'll discuss this again at our next meeting.
Mr Yeates:	I think Jim Dawson's the man to do that – he's our fiction editor. I'll ask him for this list, if I may.
Ms Sibbald:	Yes, and how is Jim? Has he recovered from his accident?
Mr Yeates:	He's not back at work yet – he was badly shaken, and his arm was badly broken. But he seems much better. He's out of hospital and doing stuff for us from home.
Ms Sibbald:	Good. Then let me propose that we get Jim Dawson to produce a list for us and we'll discuss it next time. But all being well, we'll add one work of children's fiction to our monthly list and see how it goes. Everyone happy with that?

(Mumbles of 'Yes')
Anyone against?
(No reply)
Anyone want to say anything else before we move on?
(No reply) Right on to item 7 . . .

Record item 6 as it would appear in the minutes. Use any appropriate minute style but record only item 6.

RSA CIB Stage II June 1985 (15 marks)

8   You are the Secretary of the Streamline Design Ltd Staff Social Club. At a recent meeting you make the following rough notes on the agenda. Write the formal minutes of the meeting.

(10 marks)

AEB EBU Specimen Question Paper

Meeting – S Club Committee room – 1800 – 3/4/88
Present: J. Jones (Chairman), P. Mills, M. Hopkins
S. Baldwin, E Smythe, S. Wood.

1. Apologies – Peter Robinson – wife in hospital

2. Minutes – prev. meeting – OK

3. Matters arising – none

4. Arrangements for social – Scott confirmed booking Red Lion 4 July. Tickets being printed. Mills & Hopkins – volunteered to run raffle.

5. Tennis Tournament – Jones: worried about lack of entrants. Baldwin – diffs with practice. Hopkins – entrance fees too high. Jones – money needed for maintenance. Discuss next meeting.

6. AOB – proposals for change – constitution – next meeting. Members to approve at next AGM.

7. Date/time next meeting – 2 weeks' time – same place/time.

9 Prepare minutes for the following meeting, amplifying the information given:

LANGTON'S SPORTS AND RECREATIONAL SOCIETY

Notice of Meeting

The meeting of the committee will take place in the Dining Room, Langton's Limited, on Wednesday, 8 March 19.. at 2 pm.

AGENDA

1   Apologies for absence

2   Minutes of previous meeting

3   Matters arising from the minutes

4   Correspondence

5   Reports

6   Holiday Abroad

7   National Theatre

8   Christmas Party

9   Competition

Synopsis

Six of the seven members are present. In Matters Arising the Chairman announces the date of opening of the new squash courts. A letter is read from the Social Club of Crescent's Ltd with an invitation to a joint meeting in September which is declined. It is decided to send a letter to Mrs Mills, a founder-member of the society, who is retiring from company service. The Hon. Treasurer circulates his report showing a healthy financial position. The Holiday Abroad organiser says that Malaga has been selected but travel arrangements are not settled. She considers the cheap air fare a better financial deal than the express coach fare. One member asks about rail concession fares. The Chairman wishes the details finalised by the next meeting. The Recreations Secretary mentions the good response to the National Theatre outing in late September, the advance block booking achieving a generous discount. It is decided to hold a Christmas social evening. Some members think it should take the form of a dinner-dance, some a social and one is in favour of a formal dinner. A sub-committee is formed. The Sports Secretary thinks that a team should be entered for the National Sportswomen Competition, explaining that it is a k.o. competition for teams of women representing firms all over the country. After much discussion the committee is unsure and the Sports Secretary says that she will write off for full details. The next meeting will be one month hence. The meeting ends at 4.50 p.m.

RSA DPA June 1978 (*20 marks*)

10 You work as Accounts Supervisor for Shadhalts plc, a group of department stores. It is Thursday, 18 June. At 9.30 a.m. there is a meeting about the Department's induction programme for new accounting personnel to which you and Usha Patel (the Financial Accountant) have been invited. The meeting is held in the office of Mrs Anne Catcliffe (Chief Accountant).

Before she starts to speak she asks you if you'll take the minutes. She then explains that the three of you are going to constitute a task group. Your remit will be to address itself to the devising of an effective induction programme. Although you're familiar with the nature of the problems surrounding the current induction programme, Mrs Catcliffe runs over them for you. Up until now there has been only a group induction scheme which has taken the form of the group's Director of Personnel travelling around the department stores in the group and personally inducting new staff. To economise on his time, employees have been inducted in batches, which has resulted on occasions in 'new' staff being inducted up to eight months after joining the group. The group's Chief Executive is aware of the bad feeling this procedure has generated and the poor reputation for training which Shadhalts currently have. Consequently he has issued a directive instructing all departments in all of the group's stores to devise their own induction programmes. He wants departments to induct new employees on an individual basis immediately they are engaged by stores. Mrs Catcliffe now asks you and Usha for your suggestions.

After much discussion the three of you agree upon a number of elements to be included in the Accounts Department's own induction programme. You all feel a 'mentor' system (whereby a long-serving member of staff will 'look after' new employees until they are settled in) would be a good idea. Communication is something at which you feel the Department doesn't excel. Accordingly, you decide to explain, as fully as possible, matters such as grievance and disciplinary procedures; holidays and sickness benefits; maternity leave; staff benefits (including staff charge cards and staff discounts); staff training; and staff progress. In addition you feel that what any new arrival to the Department needs is a genuinely warm welcome. Finally, it is decided that the production of a staff induction booklet containing all of the items mentioned above would be an efficient way of packaging all this information. To make sure that this booklet starts off on a friendly note, Mrs Catcliffe asks you if you'd draft a personal letter of welcome from you, a longstanding employee, to new arrivals.

Mrs Catcliffe closes the meeting at 10.45 a.m. Write up the minutes as requested.

AAT P June 1987 (20 marks)

11 Prepare minutes for the following meeting, amplifying the information given:

THE WICKBOROUGH COUNTY PLAYERS' ASSOCIATION
Notice of Annual General Meeting

The fourteenth Annual General Meeting of the Wickborough County Players' Association will be held in Room 224, The Guildhall, Castle Street, Wickborough, on Tuesday, 16 June 19.., at 7 pm.

AGENDA

1   Apologies for absence

2   Minutes of previous meeting

3   Matters arising from the minutes

4   Secretary's Report

5   Treasurer's Report

6   Elections: Officers of the Association
                Members of the Committee
                Honorary Auditor

7   Any other business

(Name)
Secretary

Synopsis

Five named office holders and committee members attend, along with 25 ordinary members. Guy Harding (committee) is in hospital. The Secretary pays tribute to the late James Hennessey, OBE, formerly patron of the Association. The year's main stage productions are reviewed: Alan Bennett's *Habeas Corpus*, Robert Bolt's *A Man for All Seasons* and Alan Ayckbourn's *Absent Friends*; two principal players are praised for their performances. The organised trips to Stratford and one other (named) venue are mentioned. Current membership is reviewed and Jean Johnson's special efforts in forming a Youth Section of the Association are noted. The Secretary concludes on a note of optimism.

The Treasurer points to certain items in the Income and Expenditure A/c and Balance Sheet before the members, notably the disturbing rise in costs of props and costumes. Fund-raising efforts are called for. Some stage lighting needs replacing. While *Habeas Corpus* and *Absent Friends* show a profit of £17.26, *A Man for All Seasons* has made a loss of £64.33.

The final financial position is announced. Elections and re-elections take place. Any Other Business includes an enquiry whether money can be had from the local authority; the Secretary will explore possibilities. The Committee and all who have helped them with productions are thanked.

RSA DPA June 1981 (*20 marks*)

12 Assignment: 'Let's Clear the Air!'

Learning outcomes
This assignment enables the student to:
1   Compose memoranda and letters
2   Draft a questionnaire
3   Write a notice, agenda and set of minutes
4   Practise comprehension and explication
5   Compose an article for a staff newsletter
6   Use reference books
7   Consider an appropriate register
8   Design a poster
9   Compose a press release for a local newspaper

Resources
- Reference books for your local area (Task 6)
- A selection of 'No Smoking' posters (Task 7)
- Copies of press releases aimed at local media (Task 10)

Situation
Mayday moved to new premises six months ago. The company now occupies four floors of a five-storey building (the fifth floor remains empty at present) and staff work in large open-plan offices, a radical change from the working environment in their former building.

Mayday has always prided itself on its friendly working atmosphere, but recently the Managing Director, Giles Shepard, and other senior personnel have become aware of growing friction among some members of the staff. Although only a tiny minority are smokers, some employees smoke heavily and a few smoke pipes and cigars. Complaints have been made to Heads of Department about the dangers of 'passive smoking'.

Matters have been brought to a head by two confrontations during the past week. In the Accounts Department Kathleen Davenport, who is going through a divorce, is virtually chain-smoking, to the great annoyance of people around her. One of them, Pete Thorley (an ex-smoker), lost his temper, approached her desk and took her to task in front of the whole office. Immediately the rest of the staff joined in, taking sides and holding an impromptu but heated debate.

The second incident took place in the staff restaurant. Just as Joan Harrison was about to begin eating, Mark Pratt, sitting at the next table, lit up his pipe. Joan rushed over, snatched the pipe out of his mouth and threw it to the floor. Another angry exchange took place. Joan later submitted an official complaint in writing to the Managing Director which had been countersigned by 25 other employees.

Task 1

Mr Shepard decides that urgent action is needed. He asks you (his private secretary) to compose a memorandum and accompanying questionnaire to be sent to every member of staff to determine their feelings on the issue.

As he briefs you, you take the following notes to use as the basis for the memorandum:

- recent tension btn staff; work/morale affected ∴ cannot continue
- *whether* people smoke or not is a personal matter; *where* they smoke is a public concern
- smoking not only irritating: may cause damage to health in longer term
- legal factors may be involved: co. then liable?
- fire risk too
- restrictions may be nec; questionnaire to consult staff before final decision made at senior mgt mtg
- help will be considered for smokers who can't give up at once
- opinions of staff *are* important; deadline for return 30 June
- many benefits of a no-smoking policy
    - reduced risk to health and safety
    - cleaner working environment
    - improved co-operation and efficiency
    - better for customers/visitors

With reference to the questionnaire, he says: 'Find out how many of our staff smoke and how many are affected by smoking. Ask if they would like any restrictions – if so, at what times and in what areas. Ask the smokers if any of them would like help in giving up. You know the kind of thing. Don't forget the deadline. I need the information for a special meeting of senior staff I'm calling for 5 July.'

Task 2

As the questionnaires are returned, you process them.[1] You also help to prepare for the forthcoming meeting which is to be held on Monday, 5 July at 1000 hours in the Board Room. Mr Shepard will speak first, then the Company Secretary will outline the legal position. The Health and Safety Officer will also be present along with the trade union representative and the four Heads of Department. Possible courses of action will be discussed.

Mr Shepard asks you to draft a suitable notice and agenda for the meeting.

Task 3

On Monday, 5 July you attend the meeting in order to take the minutes. You note that the following are present:

Mr Giles Shepard, Managing Director (Chairman)
Mr Antony Blond, Company Secretary
Mrs Patricia Foster, Health and Safety Officer
Mrs Gill Evans   ⎫
Mr Mike Plaskett   ⎬ Heads of Department
Miss Lynn Tabbenor   ⎭
Mr Sid Goodman, Trade Union Representative

---

[1] Copies of the questionnaire could be circulated among other groups and processed on their return.

Draft a concise set of minutes based on the following discussion, recording the main points and the decisions reached.[1]

Mr Shepard:	Before we begin, ladies and gentlemen, I have received an apology from Clive Harris, who's away ill. A pity – I was relying on him to put the smoker's case today!
	As you know, we are here to review our policy on smoking. Quite frankly we have no policy. The question is, should we have one, especially after the events of the last week or so? Do we have a moral obligation or even a statutory duty to protect our employees?
	Before we moved, by good fortune rather than by design, smokers shared the same offices and we had no complaints. But now we're in a different ball-game. Feedback from the questionnaire indicates an overwhelming majority in favour of a total smoking ban.
	Everyone's worried about 'passive smoking'. And they have a point: smokers can choose whether or not to smoke but non-smokers can't choose whether or not to breathe. The problem for management is how to reconcile their conflicting interests.
	But reconcile them we must because employers who have no policy will in future be skating on very thin ice. Am I right, Tony? What is the latest legal position?
Mr Blond:	It's a bit of a grey area at the moment. At Common Law employers are under a duty to take reasonable care to protect their employees' health. Some feel that 'reasonable care' should include a smoking policy. Other duties can also be cited. The Public Health Act 1936 requires employers to keep the atmosphere free of 'noxious effluvia'. Tobacco smoke may well fall within that definition.
	Furthermore, the Health and Safety at Work Act 1974 imposes a duty on an employer to provide and maintain 'a working environment for his employees that is, so far as is reasonably practicable, safe, without risks to health, and adequate as regards facilities and arrangements for the welfare of employees at work'. Providing no-smoking areas for those who ask for them might apply here. Under the same act employees have a duty not to endanger the health and safety of their fellow employees.
	It now seems likely that, given the scientific evidence, a non-smoker could win a case against an employer who had failed to take action to protect his/her health or against any smoker who refused to co-operate with an employer's smoking policy. Breach of the act carries criminal liability. Not surprisingly, employers have decided to act now rather than wait for the courts to decide the issues.
Miss Tabbenor:	Have there been any such cases?
Mr Blond:	Certainly – in America, Australia and Sweden where they were won. But not yet in this country. Here in fact smokers have taken employers to court after smoking bans have been unilaterally imposed to claim breach of contract. Some have even won. It shows how carefully employers must act when introducing a smoking policy. As a first step they should consult their workforce – something we've already done – and then take it from there. But the trend now is for non-smoking to be regarded as the norm in enclosed areas. Essentially, smokers have no *right* to smoke at work.
Mrs Evans:	If we imposed a ban and some smokers ignored it, what would happen then?
Mr Blond:	They could be disciplined in the same way as for any other breach of the health and safety regulations.

[1] As a more realistic exercise, members of the group could simulate the meeting while the others (without books) take the minutes.

Mrs Evans:	And if they still ignored it, could they be dismissed?
Mr Blond:	Yes, if necessary.
Miss Tabbenor:	Would it be legal for us to advertise only for non-smokers in future?
Mr Blond:	Of course – no unlawful discrimination is involved in such a stipulation.
Mr Shepard:	Thank you, Tony. So that's the legal position, ladies and gentlemen. Pat, have you anything to add on the health and safety aspects?
Mrs Foster:	Not much – except to underline what you have both been saying. Smokers are a health hazard – and not only to themselves. More and more employers have recognised that fact and are implementing policies to limit smoking in their workplace – Volvo, BP, IBM and Boots, to name but a few. The tide of opinion has turned against the smoker.

It's hardly surprising when the latest research confirms that the increased lung cancer risk to non-smokers from passive smoking is in the range of 10 to 30 per cent. This means that several hundred of the 40 000 deaths from lung cancer each year might be caused by passive smoking.

But this is a long-term risk. Let's not forget that smoking exacerbates existing complaints and some people's lives are being made a misery *now*. Pete Thorley has a chest problem and Joan Harrison is asthmatic so it's small wonder that they finally blew their tops. At the moment we're doing nothing to protect them and would surely be liable if they took action.

One final point: a couple of weeks ago there was a fire in a waste bin – nothing serious – but it seems to have started from a carelessly discarded cigarette. Had it happened just before we all went home, we might now be back in our old offices!

So from every point of view I think the question is not *should* we introduce a policy but *when* and *how* we do it.

Mr Shepard:	From what we've heard so far I think we're all agreed on that? (Nods of assent) Sid, where does the union stand on this?
Mr Goodman:	In general, we would support the policy. But I don't like the sound of people being sacked for smoking. I'd like to suggest that smokers who want to give up should be given time off to attend withdrawal courses. And some provision should be made for smokers who can't or who don't want to give up.
Mr Shepard:	That's fair enough. We don't want to turn this into a witch-hunt.
Mr Plaskett:	What about that empty store-room on the second floor? Couldn't we make that a smoking room for use during specified times?
Mr Shepard:	I don't see why not. We could get it fire-proofed and have an extractor fan installed. And we can certainly arrange time off for counselling.
Mrs Evans:	What about time off for the non-smokers? Couldn't we arrange an extra half-hour one lunchtime each week for a keep-fit or aerobics class? There's plenty of space on the fifth floor.
Mrs Foster:	That's a good idea. Let's positively emphasise health and fitness. For a start we should get rid of that cigarette vending machine . . .
Miss Tabbenor:	Poor old Clive!
Mrs Foster:	. . . and install a healthy snacks dispenser instead.
Mr Plaskett:	Do we need to give a period of notice of any change in policy?
Mr Blond:	Yes indeed. Otherwise smokers may walk out and then sue us for unfair constructive dismissal. At least twelve weeks is recommended.
Mrs Foster:	It's reckoned to be a good idea if a new policy is introduced to coincide with an annual event such as the Budget or National No-Smoking Day.
Mr Blond:	And it must be widely publicised so that no one can claim that they have never heard of it! The newsletter, stickers and posters can all help to get the message across.

Mr Shepard:	To conclude, let me formally propose that a smoking ban be introduced throughout the building after three months' notice, the only exception being a designated smoking room for use during specified periods. In addition time should be allocated for counselling and fitness activities.
Mrs Foster:	I second that.
Mr Shepard:	All those in favour? Thank you. The motion is carried unanimously. We'll have these no-smoking requirements included in the disciplinary rules and send a copy to all members of staff.
Miss Tabbenor:	I should like to propose that in future the company hires only non-smokers.
Mr Plaskett:	We may miss some good people if we do.
Miss Tabbenor:	I think the risk's worth taking. So much better in the long run.
Mr Shepard:	Will anyone second the motion?
Mrs Evans:	I will.
Mr Shepard:	Those in favour? Those against? The motion is carried *nem con*. Anything else? No? I now declare the meeting to be closed. Thank you all very much – it's been a most useful session. The coffee should arrive at any minute . . .

Task 4

Over coffee, the Company Secretary is asked to clarify several points that came up during the meeting. What answers do you think he gave to the following questions?

a) 'Why should employers "act now rather than wait for the courts to decide the issues"?'

b) i) 'Why is there no unlawful discrimination involved in hiring only non-smokers?'
    ii) 'Can you give an example of what does constitute unlawful discrimination in employment?'

c) 'What is the difference between a moral obligation and a statutory duty?'

d) 'Can you explain the following:
    i)   "to keep the atmosphere free of 'noxious effluvia' "?
    ii) "smoking bans have been unilaterally imposed"?
    iii) "unfair constructive dismissal"?
    iv) "the trend now is for non-smoking to be regarded as the norm in enclosed areas"?'

e) 'Can you list the steps a company should take before implementing a no-smoking policy in order to prevent claims of unfair constructive dismissal by smokers who resign rather than continue to work there?'

Task 5

Mr Shepard asks you to write a lively article for Grapevine, the staff newsletter, giving the results of the questionnaire (you may use graphic display if you wish), stating the company's new policy on smoking (effective from 5 November) and urging employees to participate in the keep-fit sessions which will begin on 1 August.

In the run-up to the ban, the cigarette machine will be removed, ash-trays will be phased out and an exhibition will be mounted in the foyer. This will provide initial counselling and literature, a lung-function test with expert evaluation, videos ('Do You Mind If I Smoke?' and 'Smokers' Luck') and a plastic model – 'Smoking Sue' – which smokes a cigarette and collects the tar deposit in her 'lungs'.

Task 6

Mr Shepard then asks you to make enquiries about the costs of fire-proofing and ventilating the smoking room.

a) Consult appropriate reference books to find the names and addresses of suitable companies in your area.

b) Write a letter of enquiry and request an inspection visit and an estimate.

c) Write to the chosen company/ies and ask for the work to be completed before 5 November.

Task 7

As November approaches, Mr Shepard wants stickers on all doors and in all corridors as reminders. He sends you out to find some. You are shown a wide range and have to consider their register and likely effectiveness in your organisation. Which of the following might you buy – and why?

IN THE INTERESTS OF ALL STAFF WE WOULD INVITE YOU NOT TO SMOKE ON THESE PREMISES	**YES, WE DO MIND IF YOU SMOKE**
SMOKE-FREE ZONE	**SMOKERS OUT!**
THANK YOU FOR NOT SMOKING	**YOU SMOKE, I CHOKE**
PLEASE DO NOT SMOKE	**SMOKE GETS RIGHT UP MY NOSE!**
NO SMOKING	**SMOKERS – ONE WARNING THEN DISMISSAL**

Task 8

Mr Shepard also asks you to design a poster to be fixed on the staff notice-board in each department, drawing attention to the fact that smoking is now prohibited. Try to do this in an original and persuasive manner.

Task 9

The no-smoking policy has been in operation for only a week when Mr Shepard learns that Kathleen Davenport is ignoring it. He asks you to write to her, reminding her of the new restrictions and the possible consequences if she continues to disregard them. A copy of the warning should be sent to Personnel to be included in her file.

Task 10

After two weeks the ban is totally successful. Three moderate smokers have already given up and most of the others claim (with gratitude) that they are smoking much less. Kathleen Davenport and her husband have been reconciled and she has joined one of the withdrawal courses, which are proving popular. Clive Harris often occupies the smoking room on his own. The friendly working atmosphere has returned.

That evening Mr Shepard reads the following letter in the *Bugle*, the local newspaper:

Sir
As the annual blitz on drink driving approaches, it reminds me of another peril to innocent people – smoking at work.

It's bad enough for non-smokers to have to put up with other people's selfish smoking in cinemas, pubs and restaurants without having to suffer it all day long in the workplace too.

Apart from the obvious dangers of 'passive smoking', why should anyone have to spend their working lives in rooms that reek of tobacco smoke? And after King's Cross, no one can be complacent about the fire hazards.

Smoking should be brought under the Health and Safety at Work Act and banned at once. After all, who wants to go down with lung cancer just for the sake of a few nicotine addicts?

Workers of the world unite! You have nothing to lose but your chain-smokers!

Smoked Out
(Name and address supplied)

Similar correspondence follows in subsequent editions and then an editorial.

Mr Shepard asks you to write a brief press release for the *Bugle*, announcing the new policy in force at Mayday and describing how the policy was successfully introduced. He asks you to mention that Mayday's clients and visitors have been very supportive and that the benefits of the policy – lower fire insurance premiums, reduced cleaning and redecoration costs – should more than offset any expense that has been incurred. The exhibition in the foyer is open to the general public until 5 December.

9 *Oral examinations*

Act naturally . . .
The Beatles

LCC panel interviews

A panel interview is a compulsory component of most of the LCC Group Awards. Although candidates may pass all their written and typed papers, they may still not gain the award because they fail (or are referred) in the interview.

The examiners are not their lecturers. Panels for the Diploma exam comprise three members of director and senior executive status, those for the Certificate three members of middle and senior management. One member, who will act as chairman, will introduce the others and lead the interview. Both panels wish to establish whether or not candidates have the personal qualities to justify the award.

Assessment falls into four main areas:

- Personality
- Manner and appearance
- Understanding and appreciation of the role and duties of the Private Secretary/ Administrative Assistant
- Oral fluency and articulation

To help them, the panel will have background information sheets which each candidate completes by hand some weeks before the interview is held. Care should be taken in filling in the sheet as this will help form an initial impression even before the panel see you.

Take a photocopy and use this as your rough draft so that you can see how best to display your personal details in the space available. If you particularly wish the panel to ask you about certain things, you can often 'feed' questions to them. Knowledge of languages (Polish, Dutch, Punjabi), out-of-the-ordinary experience of countries visited (work on a kibbutz) or interesting hobbies (synchronised swimming, showjumping, Tai Chi) will almost certainly provoke questions. Try not to leave blank the section that invites you to add further relevant details. If you were awarded medals for any of your exams, say so. If you have taken part in the Duke of Edinburgh's Award, run a marathon or passed your driving test, tell them. Consider adding details of any sports awards, certificates for music, acting experience, voluntary work, involvement in student newspapers or committees, church activities and courses you have taken (First Aid, computing, Advanced Driving).

Check your rough draft carefully – to list 'Office Procedures' as one of your subjects or put 'Personel Secretary' as the career hoped for may invite the question 'How accurate is your spelling?' When you are satisfied, fill in the original form. Black ink is especially effective, particularly as the form will be photocopied. Remember to keep a copy for yourself.

Some preparation for this component may be built into the course by way of debates on current affairs, discussions of case studies, five-minute talks or, ideally, mock interviews conducted by staff unknown to the candidates. If the latter can be videotaped, so much the better. The replay will amply demonstrate such aspects as oral fluency, personality and body language (posture, fidgeting, eye contact). Good candidates speak up and speak clearly. They look at the questioner initially but, when replying, glance at the other members of the panel as well so that they all feel included in the reply. They smile occasionally. Above all they sell themselves as they would in a job interview by being enthusiastic – especially about the work they intend to do.

Although the pass rate for this component is high (92 per cent for the Diploma and 88 per cent for the Certificate) candidates do fail for a variety of reasons – most of which are avoidable. First of all, some candidates (even at Diploma level) make no effort to dress suitably ('a good impression may not be conveyed if pink hair and distressed clothes are worn' commented one examiner's report). Candidates should dress as for an important job interview.[1]

Secondly, some are defeated by their own nerves – which may make them talk too little or too much. Panels make allowances for initial nervousness as long as it disappears. Practice should help minimise this problem.

Thirdly, poor personality sometimes leads to little effective communication between panel and candidate; answers which are monosyllabic, naive, flippant or arrogant should all be avoided.

Finally, and most surprisingly, some interviewees seem to have no understanding of the role of the secretary/administrative assistant or of how to tackle a simple office problem. The exercises at the end of this chapter should help here.

The interview lasts for about ten minutes. It will seem short and enjoyable if you are well prepared and an eternity if you are not. The panel will try to put each candidate at ease, but at some point may ask questions designed to test the reaction of students under stress. Other questions are likely to be pursued if the student is not forthcoming or appears to be merely pretending ('You say you speak reasonable French. What is the French for . . . ?'). Diploma candidates may be asked about current affairs and should therefore read widely; other candidates (who often freely confess a complete lack of interest in this area) should at least read the headlines to ensure that they have some knowledge of what is happening nationally and internationally.

The following questions will give some idea of the range of topics that might be covered and may be helpful for role-playing sessions:

The course

- Why did you take a secretarial course?
- Why did you take this particular course?
- What did you think of the course?
- Does the course prepare you for all situations in office work?
- Did you find any aspects of the course difficult?
- Do you think the practical side of the course – such as the work experience – is sufficient?
- What sort of equipment did you use on work experience?
- What was the most interesting part of your work experience?
- Would you feel that the course had been a waste of time if you failed the exams?
- Do you intend to further your education after your course ends?

Career

- Do you consider yourself career orientated?
- How are you going to get a job?
- Would you like to work abroad?
- Would you prefer a job with a high salary or one with prospects?
- What kind of hours would you prefer to work?
- What do you hope to achieve during your first year at work?

[1]But do not emulate the job applicants for senior accounting positions mentioned in a recent survey. One would-be executive turned up for his interview in full motorcycle leathers and then refused to remove his crash helmet. Another wore a personal stereo headset, which he occasionally removed so that he could hear the questions being put to him. A third had a ring on every finger, a bracelet and a gold medallion. His interviewer recalled: 'He looked like Del Boy out of *Only Fools and Horses.*'

- Why are so few women promoted to top management positions? Do you think this will change during your working life?
- Would you prefer to work for a man or a woman? Why?
- Most people are looking for a 'challenging' career. What does 'challenging' mean to you?
- What sort of supervisor do you think you will be when you are given greater responsibility?
- What does success mean to you?
- What do you most like/dislike in your present job?
- Would you move out of the area for promotion?
- How has this course helped you in your career aims?
- What do you imagine you will be doing in five years' time?

Qualities

- What are the qualities of a good secretary?
- Do you have these qualities?
- What is your chief weakness?
- What is your best point?
- Do you ever lose your temper?
- Are you able to keep confidential information to yourself? Example?
- Are you a punctual person?
- Do you like meeting people?
- Are you able to work under pressure? Example?
- How adaptable are you? Example?
- Everyone likes to criticise. What do you criticise people for?
- What do people criticise about you?

Office questions

- What reference books do you have in an office?
- How relevant is Information Technology to the future?
- What is meant by the 'paperless office'? Should office staff fear it?
- What is flexitime? Would it appeal to you?
- Do you think that shorthand is still important?
- What piece of new equipment has impressed you?
- If your boss wishes to communicate with a company in Australia, what method of communication would you recommend and why – letter, telephone, telex or fax?
- What kind of work does a chamber of commerce do?

Role of the secretary

- What duties would you expect a private secretary to do?
- How would you feel about doing work of a personal nature for your boss? Do you consider it part of the private secretary's job?
- Why do secretaries need good communication skills?
- What job would you not like to do as a private secretary?
- Would you lie for your boss?
- How would you cope with a visitor if your boss was running late and was not able to see him for a while?
- Most people would say that a secretary's job is boring. Why then do you want this role?
- If a secretary's job is such a good one, why do so few men take it up?
- Do you think that in the future there will be no secretaries in the office?

Hypothetical questions

- If your employer was ill and likely to be away for at least a fortnight, what would you do?
- What would you do if your boss suddenly collapsed in front of you?
- You are asked to show a party of Japanese around your company. What preparations would you make?
- What would you do and talk about at a social function organised by your company?
- Your premium bond comes up and you win £50 000. What would you do with it and why?
- Your boss intends to visit Saudi Arabia on an important business trip. What might you do to help him prepare?
- The receptionist telephones to say that a strange-looking man has been into the building, left a parcel on a seat and disappeared. She is new to the job. What would you do?
- You feel that your boss is over-critical of you and your work. How would you deal with the situation?
- Your employer appears after lunch in good spirits and slightly tipsy. Normally he is formal and polite, but now he begins to make advances to you. How would you handle him?
- If you could choose any career – from pop star to princess – what would you choose?

Current affairs

- What newspapers do you read?
- Tell us of any news item that has interested you in the past week.
- Do you think a secretary should have a knowledge of current affairs? Why?
- What do EEC and CAP stand for?
- Can you name five member states of the Common Market?
- What do you think of equal opportunities?
- What do you think of the cabinet reshuffle/by-election result/resignation of . . . ?
- What do you understand by *glasnost* and *perestroika*?

Interests

- What do you do in your spare time?
- Are you a member of any groups, clubs or societies?
- What was the title of the last book you read?
- What kind of music do you like?
- What is your favourite television programme?
- What was France/Germany/Spain like?
- What does your Saturday job involve?
- How did you get that job – and what have you learned from it?
- Can you drive?
- What have you gained from your hobby?

Final Questions

- Are there any questions you would like to ask us?
- What impression of yourself would you like to leave on this panel?

Talking point

The following excerpts are based on mock interviews with 18-year-old college students. Consider their weak and strong points:

Candidate A

First

Interviewer:	Why did you choose this course?
Candidate:	It was suggested by the Careers Officer at school who said it was a very good course.
Interviewer:	Has it lived up to your expectations?
Candidate:	Yeah. I feel I've covered everything a secretary should know.
Interviewer:	Everyone's looking for an interesting job at the end of their course. What does 'interesting' mean to you?
Candidate:	Not just typing. Hopefully the work will be varied.
Interviewer:	What qualities would you look for in a boss?
Candidate:	(Pause) Oh, dear. I don't really know about that. It's something I haven't really thought about.
Interviewer:	Think about it now.
Candidate:	I think he must be well organised to start with so that I can take a lead off him . . . I think . . . (Long pause) Er . . . I'm stuck on that one.
Interviewer:	We can always come back to it.
Candidate:	OK. Thank you.
Interviewer:	Would you like to meet a lot of people in the course of your work?
Candidate:	Yeah.
Interviewer:	If this were a job interview and I asked you tell me why we should appoint you rather than the other four candidates, what would you say? Don't be modest.
Candidate:	Well, er . . . I've had experience of secretarial work and er . . . I enjoy working with people. (Pause) I think I would be able to help your company.
Interviewer:	What do people criticise you for, would you say?
Candidate:	Er . . . lack of confidence, really, but . . . (Pause)
Interviewer:	Do you think that's a justified criticism?
Candidate:	Think so, yeah, but er . . . confidence can come in time.
Interviewer:	What do you tend to criticise people for?
Candidate:	Er . . . (Long pause) Can't think of anything.

Second

Interviewer:	You say that you enjoy working with people. Where do you meet them? Do you have a weekend job?
Candidate:	No.
Interviewer:	Why not? Do you not have time or do you just not want a job?
Candidate:	Well, I do have the time but I didn't want one really.
Interviewer:	What do you do then with your spare time?
Candidate:	I help me mum a lot, like cooking. Also I like going for walks, walking.
Interviewer:	Do you go on your own or with other people?
Candidate:	With friends.
Interviewer:	How many?
Candidate:	Two or three.
Interviewer:	Do you prefer to be in a group of two or three as opposed to one of twelve?
Candidate:	Yeah.
Interviewer:	And what sorts of interests do you get involved in with them?
Candidate:	Well, we just go out socialising.

Third

Interviewer:	You list reading as one of your hobbies. What kind of books do you read?
Candidate:	At the moment I'm reading *Pride and Prejudice* . . . It's a big book and it's got *Sense and Sensibility* and *Northanger Abbey* as well.

Interviewer:	Do you like Jane Austen?
Candidate:	Yeah. I've seen her films on television.
Interviewer:	What do you like about her type of fiction?
Candidate:	I just find it interesting.
Interviewer:	Yes, but she's not to everyone's taste by any means, is she?
Candidate:	No, it is difficult to understand but if you read it slowly I find it's all right.
Interviewer:	You say you also like watching television. What do you watch?
Candidate:	Serials.
Interviewer:	Such as?
Candidate:	I like things like *Brookside*, *Dynasty*, things like that.
Interviewer:	What particularly attracts you to the soap opera type of programme?
Candidate:	Well, *Brookside* because a lorra the things in it are realistic which may happen in life.
Interviewer:	But that's not true of *Dynasty* – that's escapist for most people. Why the contradiction – the realism of *Brookside* as opposed to the escapism of *Dynasty*?
Candidate:	I think *Dynasty* lets you see how rich people live.
Interviewer:	Would you like to live like that?
Candidate:	Not really.
Interviewer:	Why not?
Candidate:	Too much money, you know, gets you into a lorra trouble.

Candidate B

First

Interviewer:	Why did you wish to become a secretary?
Candidate:	During my last year at school I talked to a lady who is a personal secretary to a managing director and she outlined the duties for me and told me that it was an interesting job and so gave me an insight into what being a private secretary does entail.
Interviewer:	How did she describe the duties?
Candidate:	Well, she told me how she organises travel arrangements, accommodation, typing, being more or less the assistant to the managing director, taking over his role if he's away. Really a lot of it was public relations – meeting a lot of clients and customers – and that does appeal to me.
Interviewer:	You're already getting onto the qualities needed in a person to fulfil this role. Would you like to expand a little on these – the qualities needed to become a top-class secretary?
Candidate:	Well, I think the main one is confidence because when you are at the top a lot of it is communication with customers and potential clients and therefore you have to promote the company's image and you must be able to get on with a lot of different people. And then I think a high standard of work, typing . . . (Pause) Er . . .
Interviewer:	Initiative?
Candidate:	Initiative, yes – you've got to be able to work on your own because your boss won't always be there to say 'Do this, do that'. A lot of it is your own initiative.
Interviewer:	Diplomacy? Tact? Loyalty?
Candidate:	Yes, I think loyalty is another important area. You can't disclose to the outside world what is happening in the company. And tact and diplomacy with other members of staff.

Second

Interviewer:	Do *you* find it easy to keep a secret? If a close friend told you something and asked you not to tell anyone else, would you find it easy or difficult to keep it to yourself?
Candidate:	In some cases I find it quite easy, but if it was an important matter, something that I felt must be told, I might be inclined to do what is for the best. But if my boss told me not to disclose company secrets, obviously I wouldn't disclose information.
Interviewer:	Could you ever foresee a situation where you might have divided loyalties between the company that employs you and your boss? (Pause)

Interviewer:	Suppose, for instance, that you became aware that your boss was taking company money, what would you do? Is your loyalty to your boss or to the company?
Candidate:	Well, first of all I would talk to my boss about it and give him a chance to explain because I might have seen something and misread it. But if he asked me not to tell the company and he was in the wrong, I would have to tell. If it was a minor offence, though, and not to do with money, my loyalty would probably be towards my boss.

Third

Interviewer:	There's a big move now for companies to encourage employees to become shareholders in the firm they work for. What advantages are there in that?
Candidate:	They know all about the company; they are involved in it so they have the right to buy shares.
Interviewer:	How is it going to be an advantage to the company? Why should the management encourage employees to take shares as they did in British Telecom when they gave them preference over other potential shareholders?
Candidate:	Er . . . (Long pause) Do you mind if we come back to that a bit later, please?
Interviewer:	No. Think about it in the meantime.

Second

Interviewer:	Are you a nine-to-five person basically, would you say?
Candidate:	Well, as you know from the form I work part-time in a shop and really that isn't nine-to-five. I don't like to leave anything undone. If the going-off time is five o'clock and something hasn't been done, I like to finish it.
Interviewer:	What about a situation when you are secretary to a chief executive and there's an overseas visitor arriving and you have to cope on behalf of your employer who's not available. But you also have a very important date that night with someone you met for the first time the previous weekend. What would be your priority?
Candidate:	The overseas customer – especially if I had to make travel arrangements or hotel accommodation.
Interviewer:	And you'd trust to luck with the date later on?
Candidate:	Yes.

First

Interviewer:	This Saturday work – you say you're a supervisor in the shop. How did you get this position?
Candidate:	Well, it went on the work I'd done. My boss assessed me and said I had the right qualities.
Interviewer:	And you supervise other assistants?
Candidate:	Yes, six.
Interviewer:	Do you ever have to tell them off?
Candidate:	I do in some cases but there tact comes in because they're the same age as me. But I have to tell them off if the boxes haven't been put away, if they haven't done the right amount of cleaning or if they're not pulling their weight as far as selling is concerned.
Interviewer:	What do you think they say about you, these six girls of your own age? Do you think they say she's a bit of a 'bossy boots'?
Candidate:	Before I took the position I discussed it with all the girls and asked them if they wanted me to be supervisor and they decided they did. I warned them that this would mean telling them what to do. But we work as a team, and I seem to get on well with all the staff so I don't think they hold any grudges against me. I did discuss it with them before I took the position and they all agreed.
Interviewer:	And you don't think they may have changed their minds since?
Candidate:	(Smiling) No, I don't think so.

Third

Interviewer:	Can you now think what advantage it might be to a company to have its employees as shareholders?
Candidate:	(Grimacing) Er . . . (Pause) No, I'm sorry, I can't. My mind's a blank.

Interviewer:	How do you feel that your Saturday work is helping to prepare you for a secretarial career?
Candidate:	There's a lot of customer contact and so I don't find it difficult to talk to strangers. It's given me confidence and I've also got an inclination to work in the Personnel Department.
Interviewer:	Might you investigate the possibility of taking a personnel course and getting a professional qualification?
Candidate:	The college does an evening course but I'm thinking of getting a post as an assistant to a personnel officer and getting on-the-job experience.
Interviewer:	What impression would you like to leave of yourself on this panel?
Candidate:	I hope that you think I'm confident, well-organised, efficient in my work, able to manage circumstances and people, and would make a competent secretary.

Other oral tests

Oral assignments are set for most of the other Business English/Communication examinations (RSA, AEB, City and Guilds, etc.) which vary from one board to another. However, three main areas covered are:

1   telephone technique
2   reception skills
3   communication to or within a group.

Clarity, fluency, accuracy, the ability to organise material and establish a rapport with individuals or a group, are the main criteria for assessment.

```
MESSAGE FORM _____  Dept _____

M _____  of _____

telephoned/called                              URGENT ☐

_____

_____

_____

_____

Please ring Tel. No: _____  Ext _____

   write Address: _____

Date _____  Taken by _____

Time _____  Dept _____  Ext _____
```

Figure 13

Telephone technique

For this assignment candidates are expected to give or receive a variety of messages (such as making travel arrangements for another member of staff or receiving details of a complaint). They sometimes have to complete a message sheet (similar to Figure 13) which may also be marked.

Telephone calls help to create the right image of an organisation and as a mark of their importance 'a good telephone manner' is frequently specified in job advertisements as one of the necessary requirements of a post. Such a manner needs to be practised and acquired for it is indispensable for anyone in the business world.

People with good telephone technique

- greet the caller appropriately by identifying the organisation/department and offering to help
- identify themselves and the person speaking (if necessary) when making an outgoing call
- speak with a 'smile in the voice' and sound helpful and interested
- establish a good working relationship with callers by assessing their likely background knowledge, status and personality and adopting a suitable level of approach
- remain calm, courteous and diplomatic whatever the circumstances
- are able to deflect anger by standard procedure ('May I have your name, please?' 'Is that spelt . . . ?' 'And your address?')
- give or obtain all the necessary details (including the caller's telephone number when follow-up action is likely)
- double-check all details (names, addresses, dates and times) before allowing the caller to ring off
- know how to end calls appropriately, e.g. by thanking the caller or by offering reassurance that a complaint will be investigated promptly
- relay messages that are selective, organised, legible and accurate

Assignment

In the following dialogue the part of the Personal Assistant was taken by students who invented their responses as the calls progressed. Read the dialogue and then carry out the exercises.

Situation

The student is PA to Mrs Pat Makin, Managing Director of Lingua Franca, a company that runs special short courses in foreign languages for business organisations. When Mrs Makin is away from the office (as she is on this occasion) she expects her PA to use her initiative in dealing with any problems that arise. Incoming calls come through direct.

1   Receiving a message

PA:	Good morning. Lingua Franca. May I help you?
Ken Lowe:	Good morning. My name's Ken Lowe. I'm the Personnel Officer of Transworld. I'd like to speak to Mrs Makin, please.
PA:	I'm afraid she's out of the office all day. May I help – I'm her Personal Assistant?
Ken Lowe:	Yes, thank you. You've organised an intensive Spanish course for some of our export staff which began last week. They have an hour and a half each morning from 9 to 10.30. On the whole it's going very well indeed.
PA:	Oh good.
Ken Lowe:	There's just one thing. The lecturer is always about 20 minutes late.
PA:	Oh, I'm sorry about that. Do you have the name of the lecturer?
Ken Lowe:	Yes. Miguel Gonzales. The class calls him 'Speedy'.
PA:	(Laughing) Oh dear.
Ken Lowe:	It's rather inconvenient as you can imagine. He always gives them the full hour and a half, but the late start is holding up other work. I'd like you to do something about it.
PA:	Yes, certainly. I'll have a word with Mrs Makin and we'll sort it out for you. That's Miguel Gonzales arriving late at Transworld for Spanish class. Could I have your address and telephone number, Mr Lowe?

Ken Lowe:	Yes, we're in Nelson House, Trafalgar Row, EC8. My number is 371297, extension 237.
PA:	Thank you.
Ken Lowe:	I was hoping that you could do something straightaway because tomorrow we have a sales conference and most of the class can't stay after 10.30.
PA:	Oh, I see. In that case I'll try to contact the lecturer.
Ken Lowe:	I'll leave it with you then.
PA:	Thank you, Mr Lowe. I'm very sorry you've had the trouble.
Ken Lowe:	Not at all. Goodbye.
PA:	Goodbye.

a) Discuss the student's handling of the call.

b) Before reading the dialogue that follows, consider how you would relay the message when making the call to the lecturer concerned.

c) Role-play the call with another member of the group taking the part of the lecturer (who should offer a stream of excuses, apologise and promise he will be there on time in future).

d) As the PA (and imagining that you will be out of the office the next day when Mrs Makin returns) leave a message for her telling her what you have done.

2 Relaying a message

The following dialogue shows how two students conveyed the message in role-play. Discuss their relative merits.

Student A

Miguel Gonzales:	Hola.
PA:	Good morning. Is that Mr Gonzales?
Miguel Gonzales:	Si.
PA:	Well, actually we've just had a complaint about you.
Miguel Gonzales:	Que?
PA:	About your late arrivals at Transworld –
Miguel Gonzales:	I explain! The first day I got lost because I had never been there. You see, I have to go to company car park –
PA:	Yes, well we did give you the details, didn't we?
Miguel Gonzales:	– and when I got there I couldn't get the car in. Full. I park in street. On Tuesday the traffic –
PA:	Mr Gonzales, I don't think –
Miguel Gonzales:	– was very bad. And on Wednesday –
PA:	Mr Gonzales, these excuses *won't* do. You should start off that much earlier.
Miguel Gonzales:	I give full hour and half, always.
PA:	Yes, but they have important business to do – they *cannot wait* after 10.30. They have got to get back to their business – they *can't* stay! I know that your lecture goes on for the full hour and a half but they must start at 9 o'clock. It is *vitally* important that they start at 9 o'clock!
Miguel Gonzales:	Well, you have told me. I understand now. I am very, very sorry – it will never happen again. You will never have anybody say that I am not there on time – never!
PA:	Well, please make sure it never happens again.
Miguel Gonzales:	No, never.
PA:	Goodbye, then.
Miguel Gonzales:	Adios.

Student B

Miguel Gonzales:	Hola.
PA:	Hello. Is that Señor Gonzales?
Miguel Gonzales:	Si.

PA:	Hello. This is Jacky Clarke. I'm the Personal Assistant to Mrs Makin at Lingua Franca.
Miguel Gonzales:	Oh yes.
PA:	I understand that you've been teaching a Spanish course for us at Transworld.
Miguel Gonzales:	Yes, is right.
PA:	I've just been speaking to Mr Lowe, their Personnel Officer, and he tells me how much they are all enjoying it.
Miguel Gonzales:	Gracias.
PA:	There's just one thing. He rang to check the starting time of the class and I confirmed that it was from 9 until 10.30.
Miguel Gonzales:	Si, one hour and half, 9 to 10.30 every day.
PA:	He was rather concerned because the class seemed a little late in starting –
Miguel Gonzales:	I explain! The first day I got lost because I had not been there before. The one-way system is very difficult.
PA:	Yes, it is confusing, isn't it?
Miguel Gonzales:	And on Tuesday – the traffic! Then the company car park was full. I had to park in the street.
PA:	Yes, the traffic is very bad there – I come through it myself and I always have to start out early. But Mr Lowe did stress how important it was for them to begin on time.
Miguel Gonzales:	I give full hour and half, always.
PA:	Yes, I know you do, Señor Gonzales. But the late start is causing problems as some course members cannot stay after 10.30. Tomorrow especially is going to be very difficult as they have a sales conference to go to. So would you please make sure that you are there for 9 o'clock tomorrow and for the remainder of the course.
Miguel Gonzales:	Well, you have told me. I understand now. I am very, very sorry – it will never happen again. You will never have anybody say that I am not there on time – never!
PA:	Lovely. I know we can rely on you, Señor Gonzales.
Miguel Gonzales:	Never late again.
PA:	Thank you so much. Adios.
Miguel Gonzales:	Adios.

Exercises

1   You work for Cromwells. A caller rings the company and asks you to take a message for a member of staff, Mr Garrick, who is not immediately available. With another member of the group role-play the call and then orally relay the message to Mr Garrick (a third member of the group).

Script for caller
'Good morning. My name is Vic/Vicky Browne of Lawrence and James. Is it possible for me to speak to Mr Garrick, please?

'Well, would you tell him that my client, Mr Pask, wishes to sign the Greenway contract as soon as possible? He will be leaving the country on business at the weekend and will be away for over a month. However, he will be in my office this Friday morning from 10 a.m. until midday. Could Mr Garrick meet us there and bring the contract for signing?

'Would you please ask him to ring my secretary on 739885, extension 42, to confirm these arrangements or suggest an alternative meeting by 4 p.m. tomorrow at the latest? Many thanks.'

2 Mr Garrick asks you to ring Mr/s Browne's secretary to confirm that he will be there on Friday morning (at approximately 10.30 a.m.). With another member of the group role-play the call.

3 As a secretary/administrative assistant, one of your responsibilities is to make telephone calls, some of which are routine, some of which require tact and diplomacy.
   a) Briefly explain how you would prepare for and conduct the following calls.
   b) Role-play the calls with another member of the group, inventing names and other details.
   i)   You are asked to ring a hotel to make a provisional booking for an important meeting of senior executives.
   ii) Ring a job applicant and invite him/her for an interview.
   iii) Ring two job applicants to inform one that s/he has been successful in obtaining the post and the other that s/he has been unsuccessful.
   iv) Your company has been running a national competition for the best display of its products by any of its retailers. First prize is a fortnight's holiday in the Bahamas; second prize, a trip on the Orient Express; third prize, a weekend at the London Hilton with tickets for a show of the winner's choice. All the prizes are for two people. Your employer gives you the names of the winners and asks you to ring them.
   v)   You work for an employment agency.
      ● Ring one of the 'temps' on your books to ask if s/he can start work at very short notice (tomorrow!) at a company where several members of staff have gone down with 'flu.
      ● A company that has employed one of your office staff on a temporary basis has just complained that although her work was satisfactory at first, over the past fortnight it has gone from bad to worse. Now she has not appeared for four days and has not been in touch with them. The company is very unhappy with the situation. Ring the worker on her home number to discover what is happening.
   vi) The school attended by the child of one of your clerk/typists has just rung to tell you that the child has been involved in a road accident and taken to hospital for tests. Your employee is on a word-processing course at a local college and you try to contact her there.

Reception skills

Most of what has been said about telephone technique applies equally here – though receptionists meet callers face to face as well as dealing with disembodied voices at the end of a telephone.

Receptionists are usually the first point of contact a visitor has with a company and a smart personal appearance, ready smile and an efficient manner will go a long way in creating the right impression.

Experienced receptionists know how to
● create a pleasant reception area
● receive visitors and respond helpfully
● maintain security procedures for admitting callers
● entertain visitors if they are early or a delay occurs
● deal with unexpected/angry callers tactfully
● take and relay messages accurately
● keep confidential information secure

Talking point

What in your opinion makes for a 'pleasant' reception area?

Assignment

Role-play the scripts below and then consider how well the receptionist performed and what mistakes she made.

The receptionist is Brenda Morris and the company she works for is William Martin & Co., a company which provides materials to the building industry. All the incidents take place during the lunch-hour when Brenda is alone in the reception area.

1   A smartly dressed man aged about 30 arrives at the desk. The conversation continues as follows:

Brenda: Hello, can I help you?
Man: Well, hello! I don't think we've met before, have we? Have you been here long?
Brenda: No – just six weeks.
Man: I thought I would have remembered someone as attractive as you. Tell me, is your manager in?
Brenda: Mr Martin? No, he's at lunch.
Man: Well, perhaps I could see your Chief Buyer for plumbing materials. It's Mr er, er . . .
Brenda: Mr Cross. No, I'm afraid he's not in either. He's visiting Beatties' plumbing factory.
Man: I see – so you get your plumbing materials from Beatties, do you?
Brenda: Oh yes. Their representative visits us a lot.
Man: Does he? Oh good. You might be able to help me then. Have you got a Beatties' price list? Oh, you have. Thank you. And do you know when the Beatties' man is next visiting you?
Brenda: Well, yes, as a matter of fact I know he's coming on the 5th of next month.
Man: I see. Well, thank you for your help, my dear. You've been most helpful. In fact I'll mention this to Mr Martin when I see him next – he's a friend of mine. In fact, I usually see him in the 'King's Arms' at lunchtime. He might be there now.
Brenda: Not the 'King's Arms', is it? He usually goes to the 'Dog and Ferret' at lunchtime.
Man: Of course, the 'Dog and Ferret'. Well thanks very much again. Bye.

2   The telephone rings. Brenda answers the call and the conversation proceeds as follows:

Brenda: Hello, Martin and Co. Can I help you?
Caller: Put me through to Martin, please. I must speak to him now.
Brenda: I'm very sorry, Mr Martin is at lunch.
Caller: Lunch? When will he be back?
Brenda: Not at all today, I'm afraid. He's out on business this afternoon. Can –
Caller: Well I must speak to someone. We should have had a delivery of window catches last week, but we're still waiting for them.
Brenda: I'm sorry. There's no one here now who deals with that. Can you ring back?
Caller: Ring back? I've rung you twice. You promised faithfully you'd send them this morning. I've got men waiting here who can't get on with the job without the window catches.
Brenda: Well, there's nothing much I can do. I'm just the receptionist.
Caller: My God! All I want is a few flaming catches. You are a supplier, aren't you?
Brenda: There's no point in getting angry. Maybe our delivery van has broken down or something. These things do happen, you know.

Caller:	This is ridiculous. Look, you can tell Martin from me that unless we get our order by 4 o'clock this afternoon you can forget any future business from me. Have you got that?
Brenda:	I've told you – Mr Martin won't be in today.
Caller:	(Expletive deleted) You've got my name, haven't you? (Slams the phone down.)
Brenda:	OK, be like that!

3   A nervous young man of about 16 years enters the reception area. The conversation proceeds as follows:

Young man:	I've come to see Mr Marshall.
Brenda:	Marshall? Sorry, no one here with that name.
Young man:	Oh! (Takes out a letter from his pocket – reads it) No – sorry. It's Martin. Mr Martin.
Brenda:	That's better. Well, he's at lunch.
Young man:	I see. Well, I've an appointment to see him. I'm a bit early.
Brenda:	(Looking at diary) The only appointments he's got today are for the job interviews later. You haven't come for one of those, have you?
Young man:	Yes – the clerk's job.
Brenda:	Well, you're keen enough. The interview's not for another hour! Right, what's your name?
Young man:	George.
Brenda:	(Irritated) No, your surname.
Young man:	That is my surname. I'm Graham George.
Brenda:	(Finds name on list) Ah! Yes! Here we are – Graham Alexander George. Oh, you're after Cliff Harris. He was here on a YTS scheme. Have you been on YTS?
Young man:	No. I thought I would try for a permanent job.
Brenda:	Not much chance of getting one of those these days. Most people here started on YTS. Are you still at school, then?
Young man:	Yes. I'm just waiting for my GCSE results. I think I did quite well.
Brenda:	Mr Martin never passed an exam in his life and look at him – he's nearly a millionaire. Anyway, take a seat. You've got a long wait, I'm afraid.

RSA CIB Stage II Summer 1986

Exercises

In the following situations members of the group should play the parts of receptionist and caller. Alternative details are supplied which can be combined at random.

1   You work for Fullcast Alloys Company Ltd. A visitor will call and ask to leave a message for someone who is not available. Make a copy of the company message pad (Figure 13) for your own use. You may ask any questions which you think necessary, such as the spelling of words, or ask for the repetition of any part of the message about which you are uncertain. The visitor, however, will not spend more than three minutes in giving the message and answering questions. You must later relay the message verbally to the person for whom it was intended.

MESSAGE (not to be seen by receptionist)

Good morning/afternoon.

My name is Henry/Valerie (Mrs)/Susan (Miss)

Coombs	**Smythe**	**Barnet**	**Groome.**

I would like to see Mr Harold

Carroll	**Rowbotham**	**Mahoney**	**Knott**

when I have to call again tomorrow. If it is convenient, I would like to visit at

9.15	**10.30**	**12.45**	**3.30.**

I want to discuss with him some problems that have arisen over faults in parts which have been supplied to us. I also want to discuss

new orders   a visit to your   our future plans   new equipment
factory by some
of our staff

I hope this will not be inconvenient for him. Would he please telephone me to say whether it would be convenient for me to come, and at what time. My number is (give the name of any local town)

328382   555466   772237   811185

and I have my own extension.

If the company name is asked for, supply the following:

J G Jones and Company Ltd.

If an extension is requested, supply the following: 51.

RSA CIB Stage 1 Summer 1981

2   You work for Wilburton and Murchison Ltd. Today you are acting as receptionist at the firm's enquiry desk. Interviews are being held for several job vacancies and the callers are applicants who are attending for interview.

In acting as receptionist you are required to confirm the applicant's name and the post for which s/he is to be interviewed.

It is the firm's practice to refund applicants' expenses incurred in coming for interview, and therefore you should have a copy of the short form (Figure 14) which you should complete on behalf of the applicant and ask him/her to sign. On completion of the form you should ask the applicant to go to Room . . . to wait for his/her interview.

Remember that an applicant for a job may be feeling nervous or ill-at-ease and therefore you should endeavour to reassure him/her.

You will be assessed on the impression you give as a representative of your firm and the courtesy with which you treat the applicant, as well as the accuracy with which you record the details on the form.

WILBURTON & MURCHISON LTD

Attendance form for applicants for interview

Name: (Mr/Mrs/Miss/Ms) . . . .

Post applied for: . . . .

Time of arrival: . . . .

Car registration number: . . . .

      OR

Mode of transport: . . . .

Expenses incurred: . . . .

Signature of applicant: . . . .

Date: . . . .

Figure 14

```
WILBURTON & MURCHISON LTD

List of applicants coming for interview

Post of caretaker:

J Falk
W Henshawe
G Price
B Macbride
V Rose

Post of security officer:

D McBride
J Smith
V Rose
E Singh
J Rees

Post of assistant office manager:

V Kershaw
J Smythe
C O'Leary
P Pendrill
G Willis

Post of clerical assistant:

J Wilson
V Cleary
A Carterson
C Umbrill
K Faussett
```

Script for callers (not to be read by receptionist)

A The receptionist should greet you suitably and enquire for your name; failing this, take the initiative (e.g. by saying 'Is this Wilburton & Murchison?' or 'Is this where the interviews are being held?').

Your name is to be chosen from those on the list above.

Give your surname only: the receptionist should check initial and, in addressing you, use courtesy title, including checking whether you are 'Mrs', 'Miss' or 'Ms' if a woman. (If receptionist asks for first name in full, supply a suitable one to match the initial.)

B The receptionist should check which post you are to be interviewed for.

C The receptionist should explain that s/he has to complete an attendance form so that you can claim your expenses. While the details are being entered on the form, interrupt once or twice with a remark such as:

'What's it like working here?'

'Have you been employed here long?'

'Are there many other candidates for this job?'

'Do you think the interviews will be over soon?'

When asked for details of transport and expenses, use one of the following:

Car registration number:

| XUP 24V | BJS 483T | BOC 967S | XM 7004 | WUC 13X |

P. A. CLOW

or

Mode of transport:

'I came by bus and walked the last part.'

'It's all right; I got a lift with a friend who works here.'

'I took the train from home and then got a taxi the rest of the way.'

(The receptionist should record this detail in an appropriate way.)

Expenses incurred:

| £15.75 | £1.84 | £3.07 | 68 pence | £8.48 |

(The receptionist should ask you to sign form – use assumed name.)

D The receptionist should explain where you are to wait for the interview and direct you there. If not, say 'Where do I go now?' (The specified waiting room should be known to the receptionist and sufficiently close at hand for the directions to be simple.)

E The caller could use one of the following approaches in assuming the manner of a prospective applicant:

    nervous   chatty   jovial   ultra-reserved

RSA CIB Stage 1 Easter 1983

3 As a medical receptionist, you receive the following calls.
  i) How would you handle them in the absence of the doctor?
  ii) Role-play the calls with another member of the group.

  a) A college tutor telephones to say that one of her students (who is on the doctor's panel) is at present sitting an important examination but is obviously unwell. The tutor feels that a medical certificate should be sent to the examining board as soon as possible so that the illness can be taken into account.

  b) Mrs Price-Williams rings to complain that earlier today she arrived on time for her appointment at 10 a.m. and several other people who were already there but whose appointments were later were admitted before her. She then had to wait until 10.35 and feels that this is unfair and that the appointment system is not working properly. She is thinking of changing her doctor.

  c) An anxious parent telephones to say that she is having a children's party and fears that two young boys have eaten laburnum seeds. They have stomach pains. She has no transport and doesn't know if these boys are actually on the doctor's panel as they are children of friends and neighbours. She is beginning to panic.

  d) The secretary of the local Women's Institute rings to ask if the doctor would give a talk on a subject of topical interest at one of their forthcoming meetings.

  e) Mr Akhtar rings. His English is poor but you gather that he has recently returned from a trip abroad (Pakistan?). He is groaning. He tries to tell you something about a dog that bit him.

4 A receptionist is to be appointed in the near future at the company where you work and your employer asks your advice on what to look for in a receptionist, i.e. what qualities are desirable/essential and why. With members of the group taking the roles of employer and employee, discuss the importance of reception duties and the phrasing of the advertisement.

Communication to or within a group

Candidates may be asked to address a group on a prepared topic for about three minutes. For example, they might explain to the group some business skill, product, process or equipment with which they are familiar, preferably connected with local industry. Or they might report to the group the results of a personal investigation or observation based on a visit to an industrial or commercial concern or on a period of work experience.

Such an assignment is usually assessed as follows:
- organisation of material (a logical sequence is preferred)
- expression (good fluent English)
- delivery (natural varieties of tone, clarity, liveliness)
- ability to interest the group (rapport, awareness of non-verbal communication signals, responsiveness to questions)

How to plan an oral presentation
- Choose your topic.
- Write down all the relevant ideas you can; some research may be necessary.
- Organise your material so that it flows logically.
- Consider the suitability of any visual aids and integrate them into the talk.
- Tape-record and time your talk. Adjust if too short/long.
- Assess your pace, tone, clarity and audibility.
- Reduce your talk to a skeleton outline or headings on prompt cards.
- Practise giving the talk from the notes.
- Be prepared to answer questions from the group for a further two minutes.

Note
As the first sentence of a talk is crucial it might be as well to learn it to get the talk off to a good start. The rest of the talk should *not* be learnt and delivered parrot-fashion. This will ensure only that your delivery is poor and your audience asleep.

Alternatively, candidates may be expected to contribute to work-related group discussions, speaking both extempore and from notes. Such an assignment might entail the enactment of part of a meeting or involve students in reporting to a group which may, for example, be investigating the facilities of an organisation or area. Candidates should be able to demonstrate an ability to adopt appropriate roles and to work constructively with others to achieve a stated objective.

Exercises

1. Recommend to the listening group a book you have recently read and enjoyed. Introduce and read a few extracts.
2. Select an item from a newspaper which is likely to be of general interest. Give your opinion on it and then respond to questions and comments from the group.
3. At the beginning of the course each student is given an imaginary £10 000 to buy a parcel of shares in about five different sectors of their own choice. They should select their shares from the financial pages of a newspaper and then periodically report on their progress, indicating to the other members of the group if possible the reasons why their shares are performing well or badly. At the end of the course each member should establish his/her imaginary gains or losses for a final oral report.
4. Prepare and then give an oral presentation of one of the following topics:
   - The use or maintenance of any piece of machinery or equipment.
   - An explanation of an industrial, manufacturing or commercial process, preferably connected with local industry.
   - A detailed exposition of the quality of a certain product and its selling points, preferably manufactured by a local company.
   - A report on a close observation of a working group in an industry, commercial office or a 'service' organisation.
   - A report on the candidate's own experience, future plans and contribution which s/he would like to make in the business world.

(AEB EBU syllabus)

5   Choose one subject from those listed below and prepare a brief talk to be delivered to
    the rest of the group:
    ● Successful advertising methods
    ● The use of charts and diagrams or photographic material in business
    ● Filing systems and other forms of reference
    ● How to get the best out of the word processor
    ● Electronic mail
    ● Teleconferencing
    ● Fax
    ● The effect of recent developments in telecommunications on the office
    ● The Data Protection Act
    ● The role of a Public Relations Department

6   **Problem situations**
    Study each of the following topics for five minutes and then make an oral report on how
    you would deal with the situation:
    a) Assume that you work as personal assistant to Colin Beasley, manager of the Acorn
        Building Society. Last night it was your turn to lock up and as there was only
        approximately £2000 in the safe you decided not to take it to the night safe at the
        bank; it was pouring with rain last night and the bank is some distance away. The
        Society's regulations state that *up* to this amount can be left in the safe overnight but
        for obvious reasons they do not really approve of any cash being left. You arrive at
        the office at 8.45 a.m. today and to your horror there has been a break-in. The safe is
        open, all the cash is missing and there is chaos – the thief has thrown books and
        papers everywhere, broken all the potted plants and left the taps running in your
        washroom; the telephone has been wrenched from the wall and the window
        display – pottery from a local primary school – has been smashed. It is Colin's day off.
        What would you do in these circumstances? What order of priority would you give to
        the various tasks you must now do, and why?
    b) You are personal assistant to Mr Hobbs, manager of a large furniture store. One
        morning, before you have left for the office, you receive a telephone call from Mrs
        Hobbs to say that he has a high temperature, appears to have influenza, and will not
        be in the shop today. She says that he has two firms' representatives due in the
        morning and is expecting deliveries of goods in the afternoon. There are the usual
        problems of orders, banking and preparing staff wages. Assume that there are about
        20 staff of various kinds in the shop. Describe what steps you would take to cover his
        absence and to ensure that the working of the shop ran smoothly.
    c) The company for which you work has just been awarded a lucrative contract with a
        Japanese firm. Six members of their staff are to fly to England for two weeks to visit
        your firm, look at the factory and meet members of staff. You have been asked to
        make preparations for their visit. What information do you think you will need *before*
        their visit, and what will you need to organise apart from their accommodation?
    d) Christine Cordrey is an assistant to Mrs Geraldine Geary, Chief Personnel Manager of
        Universal Computers Ltd, a large firm with branches throughout Great Britain.
            The telephone rings. It is Mrs Geary.

            'Christine, we have trouble. You know that we have planned a conference for
        our Branch Managers the day after tomorrow . . .'
            'The all-day one at which Sir Austen Barcroft of the Confederation of Computer
        Industries is to speak?'
            'Yes. Well, I've just had a message through. There is going to be a rail strike on
        that day. I know that about ten people can get here by car but about 25 would
        have to use rail. So we'll have to cancel. I know it is short notice and we have laid

out some money on it, but do what you can and – oh, yes, try to get an alternative date. I could manage any day in the week after next. Make all the necessary arrangements, please.'

Decide what you would do if you were Christine.

e) One day your principal, the Officer Manager, calls you, his assistant, into his office and has this to say:

'I'm really unhappy about the way our office staff (some 30 people) are daily becoming more slipshod and careless about the way that messages are taken and relayed to others and how documents are mislaid or misfiled! I can never seem to find anything I want and only get to hear about something when it's too late! What can you suggest to put matters right?'

What advice would you give your Office Manager? What steps might be taken to improve matters both in the short and the long term?

RSA CIB Stage II

7 You are a member of an *ad hoc* group formed to arrange a social function (such as a Christmas party) for your department. Select a chairman and then hold the meeting, considering such items as the best day and time, financing, advertising, room decorations, food and drink, music, etc.

8 You are part of a working party investigating the adequacy of either the catering or recreational facilities within your establishment. Decide what aspects need to be covered, how (a survey?) and by whom. Conduct your part of the investigation and then report your findings to the whole group.

9 **Assignment: 'When I'm Calling You'**

Learning outcomes

This assignment enables the student to:

1 Practise telephone technique by handling a variety of calls
2 Take and relay messages, both orally and in writing
3 Schedule appointments using a diary
4 Show initiative and the ability to work under pressure

Resources

- Two telephones with recording equipment
- Copies of the diary extract (Figure 15)
- Telephone message sheets

This assignment is one of the oral examinations set for the RSA's Diploma for Personal Assistants, a test involving a series of incoming and outgoing telephone calls.

Examinees would have been given the background information for up to 10 days beforehand. Immediately before the test they had 10 minutes to read through the additional information (which could also be consulted during the test); at the end they had five minutes to complete any notes, messages, diary entries, etc. They never saw the script, which is also included in this section.

Such a test will provide valuable experience for anyone hoping to make a career in the business world. This one can readily be adapted to a variety of purposes so that students (with or without the script) can practise making and receiving calls, by working through a whole situation or focusing on one particular task, such as how to handle a difficult caller. Ideally the role-playing should be recorded for later discussion and assessment.

Background information

You work for the Silverlining Travel Company as Personal Assistant to the Managing Director, Mr George Baker.

He has been away at a conference in Majorca for several days and is expected back today. He has asked you to make only provisional appointments for him during the

MAY

THURS 3	MON 14
	11 a.m. ~ meeting Stevenson in Advertising Dept.
FRI 4	TUES 15
SAT 5	WED 16
SUN 6 Trip to Majorca.	
MON 7	THURS 17
	11 a.m. meeting G. Harper Classical Tours at 28. Greek Street.
TUES 8	FRI 18
WED 9	SAT 19
	SUN 20
THURS 10	MON 21
FRI 11	TUES 22
	10 a.m. ~ Board meeting.
SAT 12	WED 23
SUN 13	

Figure 15

week after his return and to keep these to a minimum. You will be out all day tomorrow (this was agreed prior to his absence) and you have an appointment outside the office which means that you will have to leave the office five minutes after the completion of the test and will not be back that day. You should therefore endeavour to resolve any outstanding problems before you leave. The policy of the company is that all complaints must be put in writing so that normal arbitration procedure can be followed. All financial matters should be referred to the accountant.

Other employees of the Company whom you may need to contact

Advertising Manager	J. Mercer
Personnel Manager	T. Stevens
Reservations Manager	P. Brookfield
Operations Manager	J. Collins
Planning Manager	S. Horscroft
Accountant	G. Thomas

The test will consist of a series of tasks and you will receive two or three telephone calls at 30 second intervals. You will be expected to make at least one outgoing call arising from information you receive during the test. All incoming external calls will have come through the switchboard operator. It is not possible to transfer calls. You may make outgoing calls at any time after you have received your first call.

You may also need to take messages and make notes or diary entries for your employer.

Before the test begins you will have 10 minutes to study the additional information which may be of use to you during the test.

Note

Your test is timed to begin at 11.30 a.m. on Thursday, 10 May (regardless of the actual time and day on which you are tested). The additional information contains a page of a diary which should be amended as necessary.

Conclusion of the test

After your last call you will be allowed approximately five minutes to complete the written part of the test.

Additional information

```
ITINERARY FOR MR GEORGE BAKER

MANAGING DIRECTOR OF SILVERLINING TRAVEL COMPANY

BUSINESS TRIP TO MAJORCA 6-10 MAY

Sunday, 6 May

0610            Taxi from home to Heathrow Airport (Kendalls)

0930            Report and weigh in luggage

1000            Depart for Palma on Iberian Airways Flight No. IB612
                Terminal 1

1130            Arrive Palma
                Take delivery of hire car (Hertz)

1200            Meet P Garcia at Hotel Bellavista, Calle San Juan, Palma.
                He will provide detailed information about arrangements
                for the rest of the stay.

Thursday, 10 May

1100            Leave hire car at Palma Airport

1130            Report and weigh in luggage

1200            Depart on Flight IB 712 for Heathrow

1330            Arrive Heathrow

1415 (approx)   Taxi home (Kendalls)
```

2 New Buildings,
East Wittering,
Sussex.
23rd April

Dear Sir,

As you said on the telephone I am writing to tell you about our very disappointing holiday in Yugoslavia. I hope these are the details you want. I was staying at the Hotel Park in Dubrovnik, Montenegro from the 7th to the 20th of April on Tour YU/196.

The weather was very bad and it rained nearly all the time. The drains were overflowing and there were puddles everywhere. The rain was so heavy we hardly saw anything on the trip to Kotor and the sun hardly came out at all.

We were very unhappy about the hotel which was very noisy, especially at night, so we found it difficult to sleep. The service we got was very bad indeed. The meals were always late, service was very slow and the bread in the packed lunches was so stale we had to throw it away. Food that was supposed to be hot was always cold by the time we got it and it was always swimming in grease.

When we arrived at the hotel our room was not ready. I think your representative said there had been a double booking. We were given a very small room with no view and no bathroom. Although we tried to get our room changed we had to stay in this boxroom until two days before we left. This is not at all what we expected from your brochure.

I hope this is the information you wanted and that you will be able to sort things out for us. You said on the telephone that there was no need for too much detail but if you would like to know any more please let me know.

Yours sincerely,

John Porter

Our Ref: GB/PA

3 May, 19..

Mr & Mrs J. Porter,
2 New Buildings,
East Wittering,
Sussex.

Dear Mr and Mrs Porter,

TOUR NO. YU/196 – 7 April 19..

I was very sorry to hear of your disappointment with your recent
holiday in Yugoslavia.

I am afraid the rain in Montenegro in April can be rather heavy, but
as you will appreciate we cannot accept responsibility for the
weather.

However, I was most disturbed to learn of the treatment you received
at the Hotel Park. Our representative in the area has looked into the
matter and has confirmed that conditions in the Hotel were far from
satisfactory and we have now taken steps to ensure that the service
given by this Hotel in future will meet our usual exacting standards.

I do realise that nothing can fully compensate you for a less than
perfect holiday, but as some recompense I can offer you the choice of
a cash refund of £150 or a weekend for two in Paris (brochure
enclosed).

Perhaps you would let me know which of these two alternatives you
would prefer.

Yours sincerely,

G. BAKER
Managing Director

enc.

cc. Accountant
    Reservations Manager

2 New Buildings,
East Wittering,
Sussex.
7th May

Dear Mr. Baker,

Thank you very much indeed for your kind letter dated 3rd of May.

We are very grateful to you and would like the £150.

Yours sincerely,

John Porter

Forest Lodge,
Westerham Road,
Keston,
Kent. BR2 6HE

24th April 19..

Managing Director,
Silverlining Travel Company,
49 Eastcastle Street,
LONDON. W1 3AB

Sir,

TOUR NO. YU/196 – 7th APRIL 19..

I have just had the misfortune of spending two weeks in the Hotel Park on the above tour run by your company. As requested on the telephone yesterday, I am now informing you in writing that I am highly dissatisfied with the treatment I received.

My major areas of complaint are as follows:

1 Hotel Noisy – discotheque until early hours nightly
2 Food Appalling – service very slow, meals always late, hot meals always cold when served, very greasy
3 Lunches – although full board paid for hotel refused to provide anything other than packed lunch
4 Packed Lunch – quite inedible consisting largely of stale bread and green tomatoes
5 Accommodation. Contrary to the promises contained in your brochure our room had no bathroom, no balcony and no sea view. The room was dirty and sheets and towels changed only once during our stay.
6 Lifts. Inadequate and out of action for most of our stay. Our room was on the seventh floor.

7   Service. Hotel staff were rude and unco-operative and spoke no
    English. Refused to take luggage to our room on arrival.

I made my feelings quite plain to your representative in situ and she
will be able to verify most of the details given above.

I look forward to a speedy and satisfactory conclusion to this
miserable episode.

Yours faithfully,

J. Carter.

J. Carter

Our ref GB/PA

3 May, 19..

Mr & Mrs J. Carter,
Forest Lodge,
Westerham Road,
Keston,
Kent.
BR2 6HE

Dear Mr and Mrs Carter,

TOUR NO. YU/196 - 7 April 19..

I was very sorry to hear of your disappointment with your recent
holiday in Yugoslavia.

I was most disturbed to learn of the treatment you received at the
Hotel Park. Our representative in the area has looked into the matter
and has confirmed that conditions in the Hotel were far from
satisfactory and we have now taken steps to ensure that the service
given by this Hotel in future will meet our usual exacting standards.

I do realise that nothing can fully compensate you for a less than
perfect holiday, but as some recompense I can offer you the choice of
a cash refund of £150 or a weekend for two in Paris (brochure
enclosed).

Perhaps you would let me know which of these two alternatives you
would prefer.

Yours sincerely,

G. BAKER
Managing Director

enc.

cc. Accountant
    Reservations Manager

```
Our Ref: GB/PA

19th April, 19..

Mr T. Jeffreys,
National Association of Travel Agents,
79 Berwick Street,
LONDON. W1V 3PE

Dear Mr Jeffreys,

Many thanks for your invitation to the Annual Dinner on 14th July.
Gerry Thomas and I are delighted to accept.

I am quite willing to speak after the Dinner and look forward to
seeing you there.

I expect you will let me have more detailed information nearer the
time.

Yours sincerely,

GEORGE BAKER

cc. Accountant
```

DPA Oral Test – Instructions for examiners

Situation 1   Task 1 (Incoming external call)

Marks	Candidate required to	Guidelines for caller/person called
1	Identify herself as *Managing Director's* Personal Assistant/Office	You are Gerald/Gillian Harper of Classical Tours Ltd, 28 Greek Street, London W1 2AA, Tel: 01 398 4642.
1	Say that there has been a misunderstanding or equivalent (not caller has made a mistake)	Begin call by announcing yourself. You are ringing because you expected Mr Baker to arrive for an appointment at 11 a.m. – no sign of him – ringing to check there has been no confusion and he is on his way.
1	Explain that according to Baker's diary appointment is for same day following week	This is inconvenient and you are displeased but not angry – say you have your diary in front of you and have clearly written appointment with George Baker of the Silverlining Travel Co. at 11 am today. It was made a few weeks ago.
1	Consistently express regret	
1	Suggest appointment for following week is kept	Allow candidate to explain and apologise and if she does not suggest scheduled appointment is kept. Say you need to see Baker urgently about Spring allocations and ask what she suggests. You are not willing to see anyone else and must see Baker personally. Say you cannot make the following Thursday because you are going abroad that day and need to have a decision before you go. Say the only time you have available is Monday afternoon and agree to appointment then.
1	Offer alternative appointment	
1	Say this must be provisional and Baker will phone to confirm tomorrow	
1	Conclude call suitably by regretting misunderstanding and thanking caller	

Situation 1 Task 2 (Incoming external call)

Marks	*Candidate required to*	*Guidelines for caller/person called*
		Wait 30 seconds
		You are John/Joan Porter of 2 New Buildings, East Wittering, Sussex.
1	Identify herself	You are a country-yokel type with a slow and ponderous manner and an accent if possible.
1	Say Baker unavailable and offer help or ask what call is about	
1	Establish name of caller at outset	Begin call with 'Can I speak to Mr Baker, please?'
1	Establish letter referred to is one of which she has copy in file – give topic	Say you had a letter a few days ago about your holiday – keep it vague and offer no details until specifically requested by candidate. Date of letter *3rd May*, 19.. Subject: Tour No. YU/196 – 7 April 19..
1	Establish clearly by repeating that caller would like refund of £150	You have been offered refund of £150 or weekend for two in Paris as compensation for unsatisfactory holiday. You have been asked to let the Co. know what you would like to do. (Candidate has copy of this letter.) You have decided to accept the £150. You are ringing to see if they have received your reply (they have). Ramble on extensively about the reasons for your choice – e.g. you want to put the money towards a new colour television, your present one makes a funny buzzing noise, you'd like to watch Wimbledon in colour. You went to Paris with a school trip, didn't like it, water's not safe etc. (or any irrelevancies of your choice). Press for money as soon as possible as you have already ordered the television.
1	Make polite attempt to conclude call and curtail irrelevant chat	
1	Thank caller for ringing	
1	Agree to take action to make sure they get the refund as quickly as possible	

Situation 1 Task 3 (Outgoing internal call)

Marks	*Candidate required to*	*Guidelines for caller/person called*
1	Identify herself	You should receive a call for the Accountant (Gerry Thomas).
1	Establish identity of person she is calling	Answer the call with 'Yes'.
1	Introduce subject of call (arises from call already received)	Receive from the candidate information about the Porters' decision to take the £150 refund. Verify the details she gives you from the carbon copy in your file. Ask candidate for copy of acceptance letter.
1	Verify important details by checking	
1	They want the money as soon as possible	

At conclusion of test

	Provide:	If you receive any more calls from candidate agree that you are who she wishes to contact and co-operate.
A	*Note for Employer*	
1	Harper of Classical Tours had phoned	Accept any information she wishes to give you.
1	Had expected Baker for meeting that day	
1	Wrong diary entry	
1	Appointment made for afternoon of	
1	*date* at *time*	
1	Harper abroad during following week	

1	He should ring to confirm arrangement
B	*Diary Entry*
1	Make new appointment
1	Delete existing appointment

Situation 2   Task 1 (Incoming external call)

Marks	Candidate required to	Guidelines for caller/person called
1	Identify herself as Managing Director's Personal Assistant/Office	You are Joe/Josephine Middleton of Rookery Nook, 67 High Path, York, Tel: 0904 6572 with a regional accent if possible.
1	Explain MD unavailable	You are a very angry dissatisfied customer with an aggressive and rather rude manner. You returned home last night at 4 a.m. instead of the scheduled 10 p.m. from a fortnight in Spain. You stayed at the Hotel Miramer, Fuengirola (Nr. Torremolinos) but these details should be given only when requested.
1	Ask what call is about/offer help	
	Establish:	
1	Name and address of caller	
1	Place/Hotel	Your opening words are 'I want to speak to the Manager'.
1	Dates	Answer rudely e.g. 'I doubt that' in reply to candidate's offer of help. Press to speak to Managing Director. When candidate asks for details of your experience pour out a long saga covering delay at airport – nothing to eat – no pesetas left – home very late – family waiting at airport 6 hours – no information available – holiday disastrous – hotel next to a building site and on a main road – pipes and traffic made a noise all night – opposite a night club – food awful – packed lunches terrible – sea dirty and cold – full of polythene bags, etc. Say you want to come and see the Managing Director tomorrow – you have no other time available.
1	Dissuade client from wanting appointment	
1	Ask client to put complaint in writing	
1	Maintain patient and conciliatory tone	
1	Conclude call suitably with expression of regret/promise that complaint will be investigated	

Situation 2   Task 2 (Incoming external call)

Marks	Candidate required to	Guidelines for caller/person called
1	Identify herself suitably	Wait 30 seconds
1	Establish identity of caller	Begin the call with 'This is Palma Airport'. You are on the staff of Iberian Airways at Palma Airport. If requested give your name as Manuel/Maria Gonzales. Adopt foreign accent if possible. Have *difficulty hearing what the candidate says* – bad line, rain, loudspeaker announcements, etc. Make it difficult for candidate to hear and understand what you have to say. Your message (suitably garbled) is that Baker has asked you to ring and say that he has to call off in Madrid on urgent business and will be arriving at Heathrow a day later than expected at 13.30 p.m. Notify taxi booked to meet him of change.
1	Make a noticeable effort to speak more slowly and clearly than usual	
1	Ask caller to repeat inaudible details politely	
1	Establish essential details by repetition:	
1	Baker in Madrid	
1	Arriving Heathrow	(Candidate has itinerary from which she can check details.)
1	13.30 p.m. tomorrow	
1	Taxi to be notified of change	
1	Thank caller for information	

Situation 2   Task 3 (Outgoing external call)

Marks	Candidate required to:	Guidelines for caller/person called
1	Identify herself including name of organisation	Answer with 'hello'. You should receive a call for Kendall Cars Ltd (you are D. Brown), a firm which hires self-drive vehicles and provides a taxi service. Do not mention the existing arrangement unless candidate does. Confirm you are Kendall Cars and accept information about cancellation of booking – you are not put out about this and make no fuss or difficulties.
1	Identify recipient of call	
1	Mention existing booking for 2.15 p.m. that day (she has to consult itinerary)	
1	Apologise and	Agree to have car available at time requested.
1	cancel existing arrangement	
1	Make new arrangement to have taxi waiting at Heathrow	
1	at a suitable time	
1	Check message understood by repeating or having repeated important details	
1	Conclude call by thanking recipient	

At conclusion of test

Marks		Guidelines for caller/person called
	Provide:	If you receive any more calls from candidate agree that you are who she wishes to contact and co-operate.
	Note for employer (arising from task 1)	Accept any information she wishes to give you.
1	State complaint received	
	Give details:	
1	Name/Address of complainant	
1	Date	
1	Place/Hotel	
	Nature of complaint (summary only)	
1	Delays	
1	State of Hotel	
1	Indicate follow-up action	

Situation 3   Task 1 (Incoming external call)

Marks	Candidate required to	Guidelines for caller/person called
1	Identify herself as Managing Director's Personal Assistant/Office	Open call by asking to speak to Mr Baker.
1	Say Baker is unavailable	You are Lesley Wiles (the firm's Printer) Royal Oak Press, The Hastings, Basildon, Essex).
1	Offer help/ask purpose of meeting	Insist you need to see Baker soon about new brochure. You need to discuss layout etc. You need to show him some draft layouts so refuse any suggestion that the business could be done over the 'phone. Refuse to see anyone else and say you can wait until Baker returns as long as you can see him before the end of next week.
1	After ascertaining it is necessary agree to make a provisional appointment	
1	Suggest date and time next week	Agree to suggested date and time.
1	Check by repeating	

1	Conclude call pleasantly
1	Say the appointment will be confirmed after Baker's return

Situation 3   Task 2 (Incoming external call)

Marks	Candidate required to	Guidelines for caller/person called
1	Identify herself suitably	Wait 30 seconds
1	Establish name and address of caller at outset	Begin by saying 'I want to speak to the boss'.
1	Explain MD unavailable	You are furious but not beyond reason having just spent a most unhappy holiday in Venice at the Hotel Aquadulce. Your name is Joseph/Josephine Standish, 49 Larch Avenue, Kings Lynn, Norfolk, N01 2KJ, Tel. 0962 4935. (Volunteer none of these details until requested to do so by candidate.)
1	Offer help/ask reason for call	
	Elicit:	
1	Hotel/Resort	Tell her at length about your unpleasant experiences – e.g. cockroaches in the bathroom, leaking shower, no hot water in sink, pasta for every meal, you feel as though you have spaghetti coming out of your ears, room not ready on your arrival, double booking, given an Attic room with no view, etc. Aim to be as long-winded as possible to encourage candidate to make an effort to stem the flow.
1	Dates	
1	Express sympathy and regret difficulties and attempt politely to stem flow of complaints	
1	Suggest he puts complaints in writing so that they can be investigated	Conclude by saying you think you had better put it all in writing if candidate does not suggest this. Otherwise agree with her suggestion.

Situation 3   Task 3 (Incoming external call)

Marks	Candidate required to	Guidelines for caller/person called
1	Identify herself suitably	You are T. Jeffreys, Secretary to National Association of Travel Agents, 79 Berwick Street, London, W1V 3PE.
1	Take details and check by repeating:	You are ringing about a change of plan for the Annual Dinner. Fire at the Connisby Hotel. Venue has had to be changed. Now at the Imperial Hotel, 26 Woburn Square, London, W1V 6AJ. Date has now been fixed for a week later (now 21 July). Baker to let him know if it is convenient. Time also put forward by half an hour (now 7.30 p.m.) Mention that the Accountant is also going – pause and if no reply ask the candidate to inform the accountant.
1	New date (21 July) and time	
1	Hotel	
1	Offer to inform Accountant of change	
1	Undertake to let MD know of changes	

Situation 3   Task 4 (Outgoing internal call)

Marks	Candidate required to	Guidelines for caller/person called
1	Announce herself suitably	You should receive a call for the Accountant (Gerry Thomas). Answer with 'Yes'.
1	Identify recipient of call	
1	Explain subject of call clearly	Receive information candidate gives you.
1	Outline changes in arrangements	Confirm you can still attend.
1	Check understood	Thank caller.
1	Ascertain whether he can still go on new date	

At the conclusion of the test

Provide:

A	*Message for Employer*	If you receive any more calls from candidate agree that you are who she wishes to contact and co-operate.
1	National Association of Travel Agents' Annual Dinner	Accept any information she wishes to give you.
1	Change in date, time and venue	
1	Need to confirm able to attend	
B	*Message or correct diary entry*	
1	Meeting with Printer arranged	
1	Need for confirmation	

Situation 4   Task 1 (Incoming external call)

Marks	Candidate required to	Guidelines for caller/person called
1	Identify herself as Managing Director's Personal Assistant/Office	Begin call with 'May I speak to Mr Baker, please?'
1	Establish identity of caller at outset	You are an ex-employee of the Silverlining Travel Company (Name Frances Penn, you were Operations Supervisor for three years and left two years ago). You are applying for an executive position (Operations Manager) with Mediterranean Sunshine Tours, 55 Mount Street, London, and you are ringing your ex-employer to ask him if you may use him as a reference. He gave you permission to do this when you left. Give your name and purpose in ringing when requested to – continue by saying that you know he would like to speak to you if he knew who was calling – hint that you think he is really in the office.
1	Say Baker is unavailable	
1	Explain he is abroad	
	Elicit and check:	
1	Post held in Company	
1	For how long/how long ago	
1	Post applied for	
1	Undertake to give message to employer	Thank her.

Situation 4   Task 2 (Incoming external call)

Marks	Candidate required to	Guidelines for caller/person called
1	Identify herself suitably	Wait 30 seconds
1	Express sympathy	Begin call 'I've had a letter from you people about this disastrous holiday I've just had. It's all very well offering compensation, but nothing can compensate for a ruined holiday.'
1	Verify at outset name of caller and	
1	details sufficient to establish beyond doubt letter referred to	You are a rather rude and aggressive character (ex-services suggested). Your name is John/Joan Carter, address Forest Lodge, Westerham Road, Keston, Kent, BR2 6HE, but do not give these details until specifically requested by candidate.
1	Make polite attempt (at early opportunity) to stem flow of complaints and return to company's offer of compensation	Start cataloguing your complaints to make it difficult for candidate to get a word in – e.g. rotten weather, continuous rain, noisy hotel, food greasy, no cooked lunches, delays in flight, hotel staff didn't speak English, etc.
1	Offer to check whether seats available	
1	Conclude call by saying company will contact him again	State eventually that you have decided on the weekend in Paris – no money could compensate for ruined holiday – but the only weekend you want to go is the weekend of Sat 14 July. (Tour No. is WP 18/3 leaving Friday 13, returning late on Sunday 15 – give these details only if asked and say you have full details of times etc. in your brochure if candidate tries to go into this.)
		Say you would like to know quickly whether places available but you are just about to leave on a long weekend so you do not want to be rung back but would like something put in the post.

Situation 4   Task 3 (Outgoing internal call)

Marks	Candidate required to	Guidelines for caller/person calling
1	State her identity	You should receive a call for the Reservations Manager (Paul/
1	Establish identity of person called	Pauline Brookfield). If you are not called after 30 seconds proceed to Task 4
1	State clearly subject of call including reference to cc of letter and giving name of people concerned (Carter)	Answer with 'Yes'. Check with your file and agree you have cc of letter referred to and accept information offered.
1	Explain they would like to accept weekend in Paris but can only go on the weekend of 13/14/15 July	Say you will check if seats available and report back that they are. Say you will let Carters know the position and send them a booking form.
1	Ask Reservations Manager to contact Carters (in writing) or offer to do so herself	

Situation 4   Task 4 (Incoming internal call)

Marks	Candidate required to	Guidelines for caller/person called
1	Identify herself	Wait 30 seconds
1	Ask for the time	Announce yourself as Lesley Glover, Personnel Department. You
1	Check details by repeating: Friday 18 May	are ringing to give interview date for the appointment of the new Planning Manager. Baker had said he wanted to be on the interviewing panel. Six candidates have been short-listed. Give the
1	Post concerned	date as 'Friday of next week'. Give time only when asked – 2 p.m.
1	Say Baker will confirm on his return	
1	Thank caller for information	

At the conclusion of the test

	Provide:	
A	*Message for employer*	If you receive any more calls from candidate agree that you are who she wishes to contact and co-operate.
1	Concerning a reference	
1	Name of caller and position held	Accept any information she wishes to give you.
1	Job applying for	
B	*Diary Entry*	
1	Interviews for new Planning Manager	
1	Time and date	

Appendix 1

Suggested answers

Chapter 1

Page 3

The Beatles duly received their MBEs today, but the scenes outside Buckingham Palace were hardly as decorous as such occasions usually merit. Driven in a Rolls-Royce, the four Beatles swept through the gates, accompanied only by their manager Brian Epstein.

As they made their way to the Royal Investiture, crowds of teenage girls struggled with hundreds of police, specially imported to control the excitement. As bemused tourists stared, the youngsters screamed, shouted, waved banners, and generally proved that nowhere is immune to Beatlemania.

Inside the Palace, far from the frenzy, the Beatles, like everyone else attending the Investiture, enjoyed the pomp and circumstance of this great occasion.

The Queen was reported to have asked them: 'How long have you been together now?' Quipped Ringo: 'Forty years.'

The Chronicle of the 20th Century – by kind permission of Chronicle Communications Ltd and Longman Group UK Ltd

Page 6

1	ornaments	6	claustrophobia
2	debris	7	wire-netting
3	charisma	8	cynicism
4	success	9	crustacean
5	cheque	10	affidavit

Page 10

The word being defined was 'love'.

Exercise 6, page 16

1	verbatim	13	inventory
2	synonym	14	embargo
3	grapevine	15	pastiche
4	prevalent	16	rota
5	contemporary	17	commercialese
6	manifesto	18	appendix
7	inflammable	19	consensus
8	criterion	20	register
9	delegate	21	provincial
10	itinerary	22	honorary
11	fallacy	23	agenda
12	affidavit	24	ambiguous

Chapter 2

Page 33

```
Comlon Advertising Agency
23 The Strand
London W1
Telephone (071) 569834     Telex 888371


Ref DG/ST


7 December 19..


Miss Susan Sherratt
Flat 2
45 Ruskin Terrace
London SW3


Dear Miss Sherratt

PARLEZ-VOUS FRANÇAIS? SPRECHEN SIE DEUTSCH?

As you may know, in the summer we are planning to open branches in France and
Germany. An exciting opportunity has therefore arisen for some of our
junior staff to transfer for a year or two, and we are now inviting
applications from anyone who may be interested.

The posts will be in Lyons or Stuttgart, and the transfers will take place
as soon as our new branches open in June 19... Furnished accommodation can
be provided in apartments at a subsidised rent which is comparable to rents
in London, and all travelling expenses plus a baggage allowance will be met
by the company.

Applicants should be single, aged under twenty-five, and in good health.
Ideally, they should be able to speak French or German reasonably well or be
prepared to 'brush up' their fluency on an intensive three-week refresher
course at our expense.

This is a chance-in-a-lifetime to see Europe and gain valuable
experience. Those who successfully complete their time there will be
assured of good promotion prospects on their return.

If you are interested, please let me know by 30 January 19.. by ringing my
secretary on extension 92. I look forward to hearing from you.

Yours sincerely

D Graham.

D Graham
Manager
```

Page 35

COMLON INTERNATIONAL PLC
Comlon House
London
WC1 2SA
Telephone 071-932178   Telex 320198

Ref PJ/CH

2 June 19..

Mrs Jennifer Hughes
Secretary, Larkhill Women's Institute
Primrose Cottage
Larkhill
Steepleford
SR1 2LK

Dear Mrs Hughes

PROPOSED VISIT TO FISH-PROCESSING FACTORY - SANDTHORP

Thank you for your letter of 1 June enquiring about a visit to the above
factory.

We should be delighted to arrange a visit for your Women's Institute on
either Wednesday 21 or Wednesday 28 October. Our visiting hours are from
1000 to 1600 and a tour usually takes up to three hours.

On your arrival an introductory talk will be given by our Production
Director, Vernon Lambert, who will describe the whole operation that you
will see on your guided tour - from fresh fish to frozen product. We advise
you to wear warm clothing for the visit as you will spend some time in our
refrigeration plant. Light refreshments will be provided on arrival and
departure, and all visitors will receive discount shopping vouchers and a
recipe book.

The maximum size for groups of visitors is thirty and there are facilities
for the disabled. We regret, however, that we do not allow entry to guide
dogs for reasons of hygiene, nor do we accept visitors under the age of
sixteen.

As we have many requests for such visits, I should be most grateful if you
would let me know as soon as possible the date you would prefer and the
estimated number in your party.

I do hope that you have an enjoyable and informative visit.

Yours sincerely

Phyllis Jack (Mrs)
Customer and Public Relations Director

```
                                            Primrose Cottage
                                            Larkhill
                                            Steepleford
                                            SR1 2LK


                                            12 June 19..

Mrs Phyllis Jack
Customer and Public Relations Director
Comlon International plc
Comlon House
London
WC1 2SA


Dear Mrs Jack

VISIT TO FISH-PROCESSING FACTORY - SANDTHORP

Thank you for your letter of 2 June accepting a visit by the Larkhill
Women's Institute to the above factory.

The more suitable date for us is Wednesday 21 October and we should like to
start the tour at 1300 hours. We expect a party of twenty-five, with one
disabled member in a wheelchair.

We are really looking forward to the visit.

Yours sincerely

(Signature)

Jennifer Hughes (Mrs)
Secretary
```

Exercise 16, page 48

```
DRAFT

Dear Mrs

As you are aware, early in the New Year we shall be opening premises on the
industrial estate serving the 'new town' of Brent Mill, and we have already
approached a number of employees whose engineering skills are vital to the
success of our expansion programme. As one of these, your husband has been
asked to consider a transfer.

We realise, of course, that when it comes to making a decision your
feelings and those of your family are of the utmost importance. It is only
natural for you to feel some reluctance to move, but we are certain that if
you could see the area for yourself you would be reassured and more able to
make an informed decision.
```

On 4 July we are, therefore, organising a free trip to Brent Mill by luxury coach so that the wives of our selected employees may see what a thriving, attractive town it really is. We do hope that you will take this opportunity to accompany us and have a look at the many excellent features the town has to offer.

We shall depart from our main car park in Falkington at 9.50 am and return at approximately 3.45 pm. During the morning we plan to show you the two main residential areas where, incidentally, house prices are on average 12 per cent lower than in Falkington. These areas are well away from the industrial estate; they are served by first-class schools and recreational facilities and are within easy reach of open countryside. The high reputation of St Mark's High School is well known, and the Headmaster, Mr Jolley, has kindly offered to be available to answer your questions and take you on a brief tour of the school.

After a complimentary lunch at the Poacher's Cottage (noted for its cuisine), the party will drive around the town to gain a complete impression, visiting the modern sports complex (which offers a host of activities including ice-skating and swimming), the Grace Hill Arts Centre and the many clubs, cinemas and theatres that provide a lively night life for the town. The final two hours of the afternoon will allow you time to sample the shopping facilities in the recently developed traffic-free precinct.

If you and your husband decide to transfer, we are offering a handsome increase in salary, all removal expenses up to £.... and assistance with any bridging loans that may be required.

If you would like to see what Brent Mill has to offer, would you please return the enclosed card before 20 June? We do hope you will be able to join us.

Yours sincerely

Chapter 3

Page 57

MEMORANDUM

CONFIDENTIAL

To: Mr Colin Jones, Sales Director   Date: 9 March 19..

From: Robyn Spencer, Personnel Officer   Ref: RS/PA 2

REPORT ON CANDIDATES FOR THE POST OF PERSONAL ASSISTANT

The following profiles on Mrs Lesley Anne Lovatt and Miss Jane Wild were prepared after their interviews on 7 March.

Business Experience

For the last four years Mrs Lovatt has been PA to the Managing Director of Acorn, the international publishing group. Previously she had worked for four years as secretary to the senior partner in a firm of solicitors and for two years as a junior secretary in the Legal Studies Department of Sussex University. She is moving to the area as a result of her husband's relocation.

Miss Wild worked for three years as a junior secretary in the Sales Department of Elite Computers before becoming secretary to one of the directors of Globestar, the travel company, where she has worked for the last five years. She has travelled in Europe and North America on behalf of the organisation.

Personal Qualities

Mrs Lovatt (aged 29) has an engaging personality and inspires confidence. Articulate, outgoing, stylish, she confirms the high opinions expressed of her by previous employers who particularly praise her integrity and loyalty.

Miss Wild (aged 26) is ambitious, energetic and enthusiastic; no doubt she thrives on pressure - but she is rather too intense and lacks humour. She is a workaholic and has few outside interests.

Qualifications

(Mrs Lovatt)

'A' Levels in English, French and Law; RSA Diploma for Personal Assistants; Stage III typing; 80 wpm shorthand; reasonable French, limited German.

(Miss Wild)

6 GCSEs (including English, Maths & Spanish); LCC Private Secretary's Certificate; Stage III typing; 100 wpm shorthand; speaks working French and Spanish; familiar with computers/word processors.

Recommendation

Both are well-qualified, experienced candidates. Miss Wild has no commitments which would prevent her from travelling for us if the need arose and she would undoubtedly enjoy the hectic sales environment. However, although Mrs Lovatt has no previous experience in sales, I feel that she has a more balanced, mature attitude and would fit in well with our present sales team.

RS

Exercise 10, page 64

MEMORANDUM

To: Mr Philip Grant   Date: 10 June 19..

From: Joanne Knott   Ref: JK/SC 2

REPORT ON PREPARATIONS FOR STAFF CONFERENCE (17-19 JUNE)

The following arrangements have been made in connection with our forthcoming conference on sheltered accommodation for the elderly:

1.   Venue

   1.1   The Royal Hotel (adjacent to the Docklands area) has been selected.

   1.2   75 single rooms have been booked.

   1.3   Meals/refreshments from dinner on 17 up to and including tea on 19 June have been settled.

   1.4   Conference facilities, including a main lecture room and three committee rooms, have been reserved. Audio-visual aids will be available.

   1.5   After-dinner entertainment has been provided for the two evenings.

2.   Guests

   2.1   A letter of invitation was sent to all employees close to retirement. Of these 70 accepted. (A list of names is enclosed.)

   2.2   Travel/accommodation details have been sent out to all those attending.

   2.3   On arrival at the hotel before dinner on 17 June they will be welcomed by you, Mrs Forbes, Mr Strange and Mr Hastings (from 1830 hours onwards.)

   2.4   Each guest will receive a conference folder containing a name badge, programme, handbook from ACE (Action and Care for the Elderly), details of the surrounding area, questionnaire, writing materials, etc.

   2.5   I have arranged for abstracts of the main talks to be made and sent to all guests and to those who expressed an interest in the conference but are unable to be present.

3.   Main Conference Sessions

   These will take place on 18 and 19 June. Some formal talks will be given but most sessions will have informal discussion in small groups.

4. List of Topics/Speakers

    4.1 18 June

        The Health of the Elderly - Dr J R Parry, a medical practitioner
        Pensions and Related Issues - Mr B Hastings, Comlon Chief Accountant
        Activities for the Elderly - Mr A Moss, Principal, Madeley Adult
                                                Centre

    4.2 19 June

        The Work of ACE   - Dr H Burton-Wood OBE, Chairman of ACE
        Healthy Eating   - Miss D J Wallis, a nutritionist from
                                                 Lockwood Hospital
        Close of Conference   - The Rt Rev David Lamb, Bishop of
                                               Shieldport

    4.3 All guest speakers have been sent programmes, a map showing the
          location and travel details.

5. Visit to Docklands

    Your visit to the Docklands site with Dr Burton-Wood has been arranged
    for 19 June at 1400 hours.

Enc

Chapter 4

Exercise 2, page 103

Telephone Message

For: Mr Gilbert

From: Mrs V S Nijinsky
       Secretary
       International Institute of Contemporary Dance, Music and Art

       Tel: 071 928 371

Date: 13 August 19..   Taken by: Janette Baddeley

Mrs N. asked if we could provide the following for the Oct. conference:

Conference Hall

- a platform with a long table with chairs for 10 people
- a rostrum with a stand for speakers' notes
- a screen, slide projector and means of blacking out the room
- an overhead projector

-a video system
-a sound system for playing cassettes and records

(Mrs N. can bring any of these items if contacted by the beginning of Sept.)

Conference Office

-a photocopier and duplicator (Mrs N. can bring if necessary)
-a telephone

Rooms

-73 double bedrooms (confirmed)
-one of our best singles for Dame Nanette Poliakov
  (evening of 5 Oct. only)

Meals

-buffet lunches

Special Dinner

-a toastmaster (and let her know fee)
-a stand for speakers

NB 22 delegates are vegetarians

Local Information

-maps of Edgeley-on-Sea for her to copy and send to delegates
-details of buses/taxis from station to hotel
-information about the town's facilities

If there are any problems, please contact her by Friday, 7 Sept.

Chapter 5

Exercise 3, page 116

WANT A SUPER JOB? TRY SUPER-TEMP!

Anne Roberts reports on an exciting job opportunity

How often have friends said to you, 'I'm bored staying at home all day. I wish I could get out to work again, but with a husband and children it's impossible!'?

Now it's not, thanks to Super-Temp, a rapidly expanding secretarial agency based at 59 High Street, Sandbach.

If local firms are short-staffed owing to illness, holidays or increased work, Super-Temp simply steps in to help. And for local women with secretarial training and experience, this means a chance to bring their careers back to life.

Last night at their Open Evening, the Manageress of Super-Temp, Mrs Karen White, explained just how the system works:

'Super-Temps', she said, 'can be employed on a full- or part-time basis. We send people in to local firms for anything from half a day to three weeks. All travelling expenses are refunded and full-time staff can earn up to £120 a week.'

For Mrs Jane Green, who has worked for Super-Temp for the last three years, it's the variety of the job that's so attractive.

'You never know where you will be from one week to another,' she told the audience last night. 'This really suits me – you can never get bored with the routine because there is no routine.'

Judging by the response to the talks, the evening was a great success.

'I was really surprised by what Super-Temp has to offer,' said Mrs Julie Spragg of Cheadle. 'I couldn't wait to enrol.'

Another housewife, Mrs Lisa Hill of Abbey Green, told me that this was just the breakthrough she had been waiting for.

'When I married, I finished work as a highly-paid secretary in a large manufacturing firm. Now while my husband goes out to work, I'm just a glorified char. This is the boost I need to establish myself again as a "working woman".'

There you have it, girls! Don't you think it's a great idea? So go for it – contact Mrs White and get yourself a super job!

Chapter 6

Exercise 6, page 138

```
MEMO

To:   Mr Peter Barton                    Date:  6 June 1987

From: Emma Woodhouse                      Ref:   EW/EMY

European Music Year 1988

I enclose the résumé of the article from 'Forum, Council of Europe' that you
requested for inclusion in our conference programme.

Enc
```

EUROPEAN MUSIC YEAR 1988

European Music Year will be the first cultural enterprise in which the Council of Europe and the European Communities have collaborated.

Substantial financial support will fund numerous multinational projects which were suggested by the national committees of many European countries and chosen as the most suitable to further the Year's objectives.

Many other ventures will take place and the final turnover could surpass 60 million dollars.

The Year will cover the whole spectrum of musical activities with one of its main events, 'Music Day', being celebrated throughout Europe on 21 June.

Music Year will give an opportunity to consider the effect of music in various spheres and also feature the wealth of Europe's musical heritage.

Comlon International is proud to help inaugurate European Music Year by hosting this conference for distinguished guests from the music world.

(140 words)

Chapter 8

Page 174

Meeting of Directors and Senior Managers to be held in the Board Room on Monday, 24 June 19.. at 10.30 am.

AGENDA

1   Health and safety legislation – Managing Director

2   Legal aspects of occupational safety – Company Secretary

3   Recent accidents

    3.1   clerk injured as a result of practical joke

    3.2   injured typist – threat of legal action

4   Security and general tidiness

5   Suggestions to increase safety awareness

Exercise 1, page 183

The following answer was written by a student. The list is not exhaustive but does touch on most of the principal arrangements:

Checklist

Matters to attend to BEFORE the meeting

1   Open a file for the meeting and assemble relevant documents.
2   Contact all personnel who need to be present and fix date which ensures maximum attendance.
3   Discover how many will require overnight accommodation.
4   Select suitable hotel in Birmingham, taking into account the convenience of travellers by air, road and rail.
5   Telephone the chosen hotel to confirm availability and facilities.
6   Confirm booking in writing giving exact details of
    – date the meeting room will be required
    – the meeting facilities needed (e.g. visual-aid equipment, smaller rooms for break-off groups)
    – the number of bedrooms required with date(s)
    – format of the meeting in connection with breaks and meals
7   Prepare the agenda/chairman's agenda.
8   Circulate the notice of the meeting, agenda and minutes of previous meeting together with a location map of hotel and travel/accommodation arrangements.
9   Arrange a list of entertainment suggestions for those staying overnight.

Matters to attend to ON DAY of meeting

1 On arrival at hotel check all arrangements with conference manager to ensure that everything is in order.
2 Take file with
   – stationery
   – spare copies of the agenda and previous minutes
   – all relevant papers and correspondence
   – attendance register
3 Be present to welcome executives and make sure they sign the register.
4 Assist the Chairman with minutes of previous meeting, correspondence, etc.
5 Take the minutes.

Matters to attend to AFTER the meeting

1 Prepare draft minutes for the Chairman's approval.
2 Type minutes in final form and send out to all executives, drawing their attention to any action that needs to be taken.
3 Deal with any correspondence arising from the meeting.

Appendix 2

An exam survival kit of 200+ commonly misspelt words.

A
absence
abscess
access(ible)
accommodation
accurate
achieve(ment)
acknowledge
advantageous
advertisement
advice (n)
advise (vb)
agreeable
allotted
amend(ment)
amenity
among
anniversary
apartment
apologies (n)
apologise (vb)
appalling
apparent
appearance
appreciation
appropriate
approximately
argument
article
assess(ment)
assistant
astcrisk
attach

B
bankruptcy
bargain
becoming
beginning
benefited
bloc (group)
brochure
budget (ed)
business

C
calendar
calibre

campaign
cargo(es)
catalogue
category
cheque
coincide
colleague
commemorate
commit(ment)
committee
comparative
competent
competition
competitive
complimentary (free)
computer
concession
connoisseur
conscientious
conscious
contemporary
convenience
copyright
correspondence
correspondent
criticism

D
database
deferred
definite
dependant (n)
dependent (adj)
desirability
desperate
detached
develop(ment)
dining
disappoint(ment)
disastrous
discipline
discreet (prudent)
discrepancy
dissatisfy

E
eighth
embarrass(ment)

emergency
enrolment
environment
equation
equip(ment)
equipped
exaggerate
excellent
exercise
exhibition
existence
expenses
expertise
extension
extremely

F
facilities
facsimile
faithful
fluctuation
fluorescent
forecast
freight
fulfil(ment)

G
gauge
grateful
graffiti
guarantee

H
harass(ment)
headquarters
honorary
humorous
hygiene

I
illegal
immediately
incentive
inconvenience
independence
independent
indispensable

initial
initiative
install
instalment
intellectual
interrupt
irreparable
itinerary

J
journeys

K
knowledge(able)

L
leisure
liaise
liaison
licence (n)
licence }
license } (vb)
lose

M
machinery
maintain
maintenance
menus
microfiche
minutes
miscellaneous
misled
Monsieur
mortgage

N
necessary
negotiable
negotiation
noticeable
nuisance

O
occasion
occurred
occurrence
omit(ted)
omission

P
paid
permissible
persuade
personal(ity)
personnel
plaque
possess

practice (n)
practise (vb)
precede
preference
preferred
preliminary
premises
privilege
proceed
procedure
processor
professional
professor
program (computer)
programme (other)
promissory
prove

Q
quasi
quay
queries
questionnaire
queue

R
receipt
received
recommend(ation)
recurrence
referee
reference
referred
relieved
repetitive
reprimand
requisite
responsibility
restaurant
rhythm
routine

S
salary
satellite
schedule
sense
sentence
separate
sightseeing
signature
similarly
sincerely
skilful
speak
speech
sponsor(ship)

stationary (not moving)
stationery (writing materials)
statistics
statutory
strategy
succeed
success(ful)
summary
superintendent
supersede
supplement
surprise
system

T
tariff
technique
technical
temporary
tenant
tendency
tomorrow
transferred
twelfth
typewriter

U
umbrella
unconscious
underrate
unforeseen
until

V
valuable
vehicle
verbatim
vice versa

W
waive
warehouse
withhold
woollen
wrapping

NB
The following are two words not one:
a lot
all right
as well
at all
in between
in case
in fact
in spite (of)
thank you

Appendix 3

Some basic terms

Acronym a word formed from the initial letters of other words (**ERNIE** = **E**lectronic **R**andom **N**umber **I**ndicator **E**quipment).

Active voice the form of the verb used when the subject performs the action (the manager signed the letter).

Adjective see parts of speech.

Adverb see parts of speech.

Alliteration repetition of the same initial letter, much favoured by copywriters (**n**aughty but **n**ice).

Ambiguity a word or sentence that has more than one possible meaning. (Station notice: 'Ladies' toilet out of order. Use Platform 5'.)

Anecdote a brief story.

Anti-climax (or **bathos**) a ludicrous descent from the impressive to the ordinary or trivial. (Ad: '40s Evening. The original big-band sound provided by our resident duo'.)

Antithesis a contrast of ideas emphasised by choice of words or their arrangement. ('That's one small step for man, one giant leap for mankind' – the first words spoken on the moon by Neil Armstrong.)

Antonym a word of opposite meaning (harmony – discord).

Cliché an expression that has become stale with over-use (a hive of industry).

Collective noun the name of a group of individuals, things or animals (committee, set, herd).

Commercialese see jargon.

Conjunction see parts of speech.

Contradiction in terms a statement that contradicts itself. ('Include me out.' Sam Goldwyn)

Epigram a short, witty saying. ('Work is the curse of the drinking classes.' Oscar Wilde)

Epitaph words inscribed on a tombstone. (An auctioneer chose 'Gone to the Highest Bidder'.)

Euphemism a mild expression used in place of an unpleasant or forthright one, beloved by estate agents ('full of potential' = in desperate need of repair).

Feedback any response from the recipient of a communication.

Gerund a verbal noun ending in -ing (*typing* is a useful skill). NB the possessive adjective is required when the gerund is the object (he did not like *my* consulting an outsider).

Gobbledegook pompous official jargon.

Grapevine the informal way in which information/rumour is passed on within an organisation.

Homophone a word with the same sound as another but different in spelling and meaning (sun/son).

Hyperbole use of exaggeration for emphasis (the papers in my in-tray were stacked a mile high).

Infinitive to + basic verb (to type, to manage, to delegate).

Irony use of language to convey a meaning opposite to that stated. (See, for example, Mark Antony's description of the assassins of Julius Caesar as 'honourable men' as he works to destroy them.)

Jargon   once a language belonging to a special group, trade or profession; now long-winded and cliché-ridden expressions used for their own sake. Common in business (**commercialese**), poor journalism (**journalese**) and government departments (**officialese**).

Journalese   see jargon.

Malapropism   a misuse of words as a result of similarity of sound or spelling (salary will *commiserate* with age and experience).

Metaphor   a compressed form of simile. Instead of saying one thing is like another, we say one thing is another (Death – 'the anaesthetic from which no one comes round'. Larkin: *Aubade*)

Mixed metaphor   where the comparison is confused by mixing two metaphors in one image. ('This situation is now a real hot potato. If I don't do something it could become a banana skin.' James Hacker: *Yes, Prime Minister*)

Mnemonic   an aid to the memory. '**R**ichard **of Y**ork **g**ave **b**attle **i**n **v**ain' gives the colours of the spectrum: red, orange, yellow, green, blue, indigo and violet. The name **U F Biggles PhD** gives the 12 member states of the EEC: UK, France, Belgium, Italy, Greece, Germany, Luxembourg, Eire, Spain, Portugal, Holland and Denmark.

Noise   any interference outside the control of transmitter or receiver.

Non-verbal communication   the ways in which meaning may be conveyed consciously or unconsciously, not by words but by other actions. (A dubious decision at Wimbledon might evoke a plaintive glance from Gabriela Sabatini rather than the verbal histrionics of John McEnroe. In interviews, experienced interviewers will watch for the unconscious signals that 'leak' from candidates – said to be more revealing than the verbal communication.)

Noun   see parts of speech.

Officialese   see jargon.

Onomatopoeia   choice of a particular word whose sound echoes the sense. (To evoke a sense of ice skating, Wordsworth wrote: 'All shod with steel/We *hissed* along the polished ice'.)

Oxymoron   putting together words that seem to contradict each other. (Sir Geoffrey Howe has been described as 'charismatically boring'.)

Palindrome   a word, sentence, etc. that reads the same backwards as forwards (sex at noon taxes).

Paradox   a statement that appears to contradict itself ('I must be cruel only to be kind'. *Hamlet*).

Parts of speech   the classes into which words are divided in grammar. The main ones are as follows:

1   **Noun**   a word that names (things, people, ideas, groups, etc.): **Beatles**.
2   **Verb**   a word that shows what the noun is doing: The Beatles **sang**.
3   **Adjective**   a word that describes the noun: The **popular** Beatles sang.
4   **Adverb**   a word that adds to a verb or an adjective or another adverb: The popular Beatles sang **harmoniously**.
5   **Pronoun**   a word that stands in place of a noun to prevent repetition: **They** sang harmoniously.
6   **Relative pronoun**   a word (who, whom, whose, that, which) that introduces further information about the noun: These were the popular Beatles **who** sang harmoniously.
7   **Preposition**   a word used with nouns or pronouns to show place or position or time or means: The popular Beatles sang harmoniously **in** the theatre.
8   **Conjunction**   a word that connects words, phrases or clauses: The popular Beatles sang harmoniously in the theatre **and** then left for the party.
   NB Words change their part of speech depending on the work they do in a sentence:
   Recording is taking place (noun/gerund)
   The **recording** session lasted all day (adjective)
   They were **recording** in the studio (verb)

Passive voice   the form of the verb used when the subject is the receiver of the action (the letter was signed by the manager).

Past participle   part of the verb usually ending in 'ed' (typed, managed, delegated).

Personification   when an abstract idea, inanimate object or non-human animal is given the qualities or emotions of a human being ('Laughter holding both his sides'. Milton: *L'Allegro*).

Possessive adjectives   my, his, her, our, your, their. These show possession and qualify their nouns (**my** guitar).

Possessive pronouns   mine, his, hers, ours, yours, theirs. These show possession and stand for nouns. (This guitar is **mine**. Where is **yours**?)

Preposition   see parts of speech.

Present participle   part of the verb ending in 'ing' (typing, managing, delegating).

Pronoun   see parts of speech.

Pun   a play upon words (Face the Fax).

Purple passage   when a writer goes 'over the top' in straining to be poetic, eloquent, sonorous, etc. ('The trees explode into bud . . . the brilliant sky hovers uncertainly like a shy bride at the door of her nuptial chamber . . .' Sue Townsend: *The Secret Diary of Adrian Mole, Aged 13¾*.)

Rapport   a harmonious and sympathetic relationship between people.

Receiver   the recipient of a communication.

Register   the language, style and vocabulary appropriate to particular circumstances.

Repartee   a witty retort. (When a woman of Churchill's acquaintance said to him: 'Winston, if I were married to you, I'd put poison in your coffee,' Churchill replied: 'If you were my wife, I'd drink it.')

Rhetorical question   something phrased as a question for dramatic effect to which no answer is required or expected. ('If Winter comes, can Spring be far behind?' Shelley: *Ode to the West Wind*)

Sentence   the expression of a complete idea (she duplicated the memo). Note that a sentence usually has a **subject** (she), a **main verb** (duplicated) and often an **object** (the memo).

Simile   a comparison introduced by 'as' or 'like' (sick as a parrot).

Slang   language not usually accepted in formal speech or writing (grotty).

Split infinitive   occurs when an adverb is placed between the 'to' and the basic verb, often creating an awkward effect. (We are to shortly open a new superstore.)

Synonym   a word of similar meaning (bright – intelligent).

Tautology   stating the same thing a second time (free, with our compliments).

Transmitter   the sender of a communication.

Truism   a self-evident truth; a commonplace or trite statement. ('It's not every day that we have the chance to mark the 85th birthday of Sir John Gielgud.' Radio 3 announcer)

Verb   see parts of speech.

Appendix 4

Terms of meetings

Abstain   when some members vote neither 'for' nor 'against' a motion, i.e. they do not vote at all.

Addendum   an addition to a motion.

***Ad hoc* committee**   one formed for a special purpose and then disbanded.

Adjourn   stop a meeting and resume it at a later date.
Advisory committee   one which makes only recommendations to a main committee.
Agenda   a list of items to be discussed at a meeting.
Amendment   a proposal to alter the terms of an original motion.
Annual general meeting   a statutory meeting held once a year which all shareholders/ members can attend.
Any other business   a standard agenda heading which permits minor points to be raised.
Articles of association   rules governing a company's activities.
Attendance record   a book which each member present signs.
Chairman's agenda   an agenda for use by the chairman giving additional notes about items and providing space for his/her own notes.
Closure   a motion to end the discussion on a matter before a meeting.
Consensus   agreement by general consent with no formal vote taken.
Constitution   rules governing the activities of voluntary organisations.
Convene   call a meeting.
Co-opted   specially appointed to act on a committee by the majority vote of existing members.
Executive committee   one which has the power to put decisions into effect.
Ex officio   when a person attends a meeting not as a regular member but by virtue of his official position.
Extraordinary meeting   a non-routine meeting.
Extraordinary general meeting   a meeting for all members to discuss an urgent matter.
Honorary   unpaid.
In attendance   people invited to attend a meeting as observers or to give advice.
Lie on the table   a motion on which no action will be taken is said to 'lie on the table'.
Matters arising   a standard agenda item whose purpose is to inform members of the latest developments arising from previous business. Substantial items should be listed separately to prevent overloading the agenda.
Minute book   a book containing a signed copy of every set of minutes from the date of the first meeting of a committee.
Minutes of narration   a summary of the discussion and decisions reached.
Minutes of resolution   a record only of the resolutions reached.
Motion   a proposal put before the meeting.
Nem. con. (also *nem. dis.*)   no one disagreeing.
Notice   notification to members of the day, date, time and place of the meeting.
Point of order   a query relating to the rules of procedure.
Proposal   an item submitted for discussion before a meeting.
Proposer   person who puts forward a course of action by formally stating a motion.
Proxy   person authorised to vote on behalf of someone else.
Quorum   the minimum number of people who should be present at a meeting for it to be valid.
Resolution   a motion that has been voted upon and carried. *NB* some people/textbooks do not discriminate between 'motion' and 'resolution'.
Rider   an addition to a resolution.
Seconder   a person who supports the proposer of a motion.
Sine die   indefinitely.
Standing committee   permanent committee carrying out day-to-day business.
Standing orders   rules of an organisation which govern the manner in which its business is conducted.
Sub-committee   a committee appointed by a main committee to carry out work on its behalf and report back.
Substantive motion   a motion altered by an amendment.
Ultra vires   beyond the legal power of a meeting.
Unanimous   all in favour.

Appendix 5

Checklist of good examination technique

1 **Before** the exam:
   - Ensure that you have seen a copy of the syllabus and that you have covered every topic.
   - Practise as much as possible using past examination papers and consulting comments in examiners' reports. Photocopy all material and file for future reference.
   - Arrange a 'mock' exam to ensure that your timing is sound. Your aim must be to finish the paper – or at least to attempt every question.
   - Digest the background notes that some boards send to the candidates some weeks before the exam. If possible put them to practical use to familiarise yourself with names and places. For example, a group could compose its own question, based on the given data and some research, and then answer it.

2 **On the day** of the exam:
   - Aim to arrive about 15 minutes before the start.
   - Bring
     * pens/pencil/eraser/ruler
     * compasses and protractor for diagrams
     * a dictionary and calculator (if allowed)
     * felt-tip pens for logos, letterheads, advertisements
     * a diary (where necessary)
     * correcting materials
     * the background notes (spare copies are not supplied)
     * your candidate number/identification
     * a watch

3 **During** the exam:
   - Read through the instructions carefully, identifying *key* words and noting the instructions.
   - Number/letter your answers correctly.
   - Do not copy out the questions.
   - Judge the length of each answer by reference to the mark allocation.
   - Ensure that you answer the question *as it is set* – not a preferred (easier?) version of your own.
   - Plan your answer in note form, establishing the *order* of the ideas and the *tone*. Write your answer from the notes. Do not spend time in writing a draft and then making a fair copy (except for summaries).
   - Aim for a 'professional' presentation by
     * beginning each answer on a fresh page of the exam booklet
     * writing legibly
     * giving basic production details (author, recipient, date, title)
     * keeping corrections to a minimum (correcting fluid should not be used to blank out whole paragraphs)
     * cancelling rough work with one diagonally ruled line
   - Leave at least 10 minutes at the end in order to check.
   - **Check again!** A common error is to see what you think you have written – not what you actually wrote.
   - Do not be tempted to leave the examination room early.
   Good luck!

Index